SINS OF THE FAMILY

SINS OF THE FAMILY

FELICITY DAVIS

PAN BOOKS

First published as *Guard a Silver Sixpence* in 2011 by Pan Books

This edition published 2016 by Pan Books
an imprint of Pan Macmillan
20 New Wharf Road, London N1 9RR
Associated companies throughout the world
www.panmacmillan.com

ISBN 978-1-5098-3700-7

The picture acknowledgements on p. 325
constitute an extension of this copyright page.

1 3 5 7 9 8 6 4 2

A CIP catalogue record for this book is available from the British Library.

Typeset by Ellipsis Digital Limited, Glasgow
Printed and bound by CPI Group (UK) Ltd, Croydon, CR0 4YY

To five strong women:
Hannah, Emily, Elsie, Marjorie and Felicity.

Author's Note

All the events in this book are true, but I have changed some of the names to protect the privacy of those still living.

CONTENTS

Note to Reader

The whole experience of researching my family history and putting pen to paper has had an enormous impact on who I am as a person, and how I want to live my life. To have answers to those ultimate questions that whirl around in our hearts and minds, especially when moving on from abuse, allows us to develop our sense of worth and also our self-identity. Fortunately for me, *Sins of the Family* gave me the opportunity to unlock those sinister secrets that had been locked away for so long and also to 'file' them away in my own personal history. I am fortunate; I found the answers that I had been searching for and I know that many of my readers would also like to delve into their family history in order to understand what has happened to them.

From the first telling of my story, I have had letters from readers all around the world, either wanting to share their story or just to ask for advice as to where to start. What I would say to anyone who is looking for answers is – go out and find them. My starting point was to gather anecdotal stories from my family and then, as we Yorkshire folk say, hard slog through the many avenues that those clues lead us down. Be prepared for the mixed bag of emotions that you will feel as you meet and greet your long-lost ancestors of the past. I have gone through heartbreak, and still do when I think of the pain that has swept across five generations of my family, but I also feel a greater sense of well-being because I have unlocked the secrets of time. There are risks, and the journey may be dark and painful, but I can tell you here and now, hand on heart, the experience will be life-changing.

My final piece of advice comes from the New Testament reading which I had found on the lectern of the church where my Gran and Granddad got married all those years ago – 'There is a time for everything and a season for every activity under heaven' – words which seemed to give me the permission I was waiting for, to go and seek the truth. So as I close my note to you, my reader, I strongly believe that there is a time for everything and possibly that time for you is now.

I wish you well in your search.

Felicity Davis, 2016

Prologue
DO IT AGAIN

'That's not how you walk across a room,' Gran snapped at me. 'Do it properly!'

Obediently I turned, went back to the living-room door and set off again. Over the rug, past Gran on the sofa, her tiny frame upright, her implacable grey eyes fixed on me. Almost to my bedroom door, and safety.

'Stop! Do it again, and get it right this time!'

Back to the living-room door. I took a deep breath and started walking. I only managed a couple of steps.

'No, no! Do it again.'

I set off again, over the rug, past the sofa. *I hate you, I hate you. You're a bad woman.*

Gran hissed and my heart jumped into my throat. I stopped and glanced sideways at her, her body rigid, the tip of her tongue sticking out between her yellowing false teeth, her lips curled back. My hands were trembling. *Don't hit me.*

'What am I doing wrong, Gran?' I asked pleadingly. 'I just want to get it right – what do I do?'

'Do it again!'

I was about seven years old when this torturous routine started, and it lasted as long as I lived with Gran. Sometimes I would avoid eye contact with her to see if that made a difference; sometimes I'd try a cheery, upfront 'Hello, Gran!' I'd walk briskly, or softly, or I'd stop as I came through the door and look at her and say, 'What shall I do, Gran?'

Nothing made the blindest bit of difference. I'd have my hand on the doorknob ready to make my escape and she would suddenly snap, 'You didn't do that right. Go back and do it again.'

I'd retrace my steps across the room to the door I'd come in by. I'd repeat my walk past her across the room and do it again, and again, and again. It wasn't the worst thing she did to me, but the weary inevitability of this inescapable little drama – which I never understood, but which oppressed me with its misery – typified my childhood. I was trapped in Gran's world, along with my granddad and my unmarried mother, in a little prefab bungalow in Scarborough, completely at her mercy.

'Your gran has had a hard life,' my granddad would often tell me. 'She hardly knew her own mother, you know. She did something terrible and had to go to prison, and your gran never saw her again.'

'What did she do?'

'Oh, it was a long time ago. But she never knew what it was to have a mother. And then she had an accident that damaged her brain.'

I understood that I shouldn't probe into the detail of the story that lay behind these intimations, and the brain injury, like other such excuses, was never mentioned again. Because I loved my granddad, I accepted his underlying message that it was Gran who was the victim rather than me. In any case, most of my energy was focused on getting through endless, miserable days of trying to foresee where the next attack would come from. What unreasonable, unpredictable excuse would Gran come up with next to cause grief and hurt and dish out abuse?

I never felt a grain of love or empathy for Gran and I broke free from her control as soon as I could. But it wasn't until I was fifty and had finally made something of my life that I recognized that I hadn't ever escaped her completely. The scars caused by my fractured childhood had never totally healed, which meant that at a time when I should have been feeling proud of myself and my achievements, I felt hollow and incomplete. I realized that to be totally free, I needed to understand why Gran had behaved the way she did.

So in the summer of 2007, I sat in the library in Barnsley, where various family documents suggested Gran's family had come from, looping reel after reel of tape on to microfiche spools, and telling myself that even if there was some truth in my granddad's story, it was very unlikely that there would be much trace of it in the official records.

History, after all, is for the famous. It's only the descendants of kings and queens, warriors and politicians, the exceptionally bad or the exceptionally beautiful who can walk into a library and hear authentic echoes of long-dead ancestors talking to them across the centuries. Someone like me could only expect to find a name scrawled in a copperplate hand by a clergyman or government official noting a marriage, birth or death, or a census record giving an occupation and address.

My ancestors were no more famous than me, and I began to realize, as I looked through the records and found them living a dozen to a house, that they were a lot less well off. I wondered why on earth I was bothering. I wasn't going to find any hard evidence of their emotional lives, anything that would flesh out their characters and give me the answers I was looking for.

But then the words of my great-great-grandmother, Hannah, leapt out at me from a page of the *Barnsley Chronicle*. She was speaking to a reporter in 1903.

'Eh, mister, I've had a hard life,' she said wearily. 'Of all the trouble I have had, this has been the hardest.'

Tears pricked in my eyes as I read Hannah's story. This I had not expected.

Chapter One

FELICITY

I hated the approach of nightfall. I hated the dark. As tea-time came and went, as the pots were cleared away, my granddad would get ready for his job as a doorman at the local Conservative Club, where he was on duty from early evening until the small hours of the morning, and I'd begin to feel the first flutter of fear rippling through my stomach.

My mother also had somewhere else to go after tea. Every evening without fail she went to see my dad – at least, that's what she said. She never returned until long after my seven o'clock bedtime. I wanted to throw my arms around her as she headed for the door and beg her, 'Don't go, don't leave me alone with Gran.' But I didn't do it because I feared that it would lead to something worse. I knew that Mum, gentle as she was and incapable of doing anything to hurt me physically, would never respond in the way I wanted her to. She would never go against Gran. Begging for help in front of Gran was therefore out of the question, because I would only suffer even more than usual once we were alone again.

As the front door closed behind them, loneliness seemed

to settle over the little prefab like Miss Havisham's shroud. And I was left with the bogeyman, my gran, who could launch an attack on me at any time. By the time I was four, I knew this was how it would be, every single bedtime, and that there was no escape.

Our nightly ritual went like this. Gran would make me stand with my back to her as I changed into my pyjamas. She would be sitting in her favourite place on the dark blue sofa, close to the wall-mounted gas fire. I knew she would hit me, but I never knew exactly when the blow would land. Head down, my hands would fumble with buttons as I undressed and my skin would prickle with a sick anticipation. Maybe if I was quick enough, this time I'd escape.

Bang. My head would be catapulted sideways to connect with the woodchip-papered wall next to the fire. Again, and again, and again. I had no idea why. It was just what she did.

I never had more than a second's notice. Out of the corner of my eye I might just catch a glimpse of her hand coming towards my right ear. Or I'd catch the beginning of the hissing sound she made when something annoyed her. There was never time to avoid the blow, even if it had occurred to me to try.

Sometimes the clouts would carry on while she twisted my hair up in rags, the old-fashioned way of putting curls into a girl's hair. For years, certainly into my first years at infant school, this was another nightly torture that she never missed, yanking and pulling at my scalp to get the locks wound as tightly as possible into the pieces of cloth before they were tied. It always hurt, and the more I cried, the more often my head hit the wall. I learned to lock every muscle into what I hoped was statue-like stillness, the tears running silently down my face. Only when she was finished did I let the gulping sobs go, just a little, but she always ignored them at this point and took me to the cold, lino-floored bedroom that I shared with my mother.

My old-fashioned single bed had a wooden headboard, with springs in the mattress that I could feel through the thin cotton sheet and which left marks on my legs when I got out of bed in the morning. Mum's bigger three-quarter bed was alongside it, even more old-fashioned with a slatted wooden bedhead. It squeaked with every movement she made, often waking me up when she climbed in late after her evenings out.

Now Gran would sit on the end of my bed and lead me in reciting the Lord's Prayer. We never set foot inside a church when I was a child and no one at home ever talked about God, yet this was a ritual that Gran insisted on. She wanted the old version with its incomprehensible 'thys' and 'which arts', and I had to say it loudly, in a certain tone, and get it absolutely right, including the bit about being forgiven my trespasses and not being led into temptation – *especially* that bit – and if I stumbled over the long, strange words, she would stand up and lean over to slap me around the head. 'Do it right. Get it *right*. How *dare* you!' she'd spit as she slapped me over and over again. If I put my arms up to try to defend myself, she hit harder. Whether to put my arms up or not was always a tough choice.

When she stopped, she would look at me, a little

breathless and panting slightly with the effort she'd put into the beating, and then she'd lean down and put her face about six inches from mine and shout: 'Now do it *again*. And do it *right*.'

She was a tiny woman, only just five feet tall, but I remember her on those terrifying evenings towering over me as if she was a giant in her plain square-necked frock, grey cardigan, and thick American tan stockings. Her iron-grey hair was cut into a kind of wiry bob that reminded me of pictures I'd seen in story books of Gulliver on his travels. The difference was that Gran was unmistakeably female, with soft skin and rosy cheeks that seemed untouched by age, and sharp grey eyes that blazed with unreasonable fury when she was on the attack.

By the time I'd finally managed to get through the prayer to her satisfaction, I would be sitting up in bed hunched with my tiny arms clasped around my calves, unable to control the gulping and heaving as I sobbed. Needing to know why. Needing to know how she could do this to me.

'I'll tell my granddad in the morning,' I would declare. My voice might wobble, but the threat was edged with as much bravado as I could shove into it, like a child promising to bring her big brother round to sort out the playground bully. Gran never replied directly. She sat gazing blankly at the faded pink flowers of the wallpaper on the other side of Mum's bed, lost in a world that only she could see. Sometimes she'd rock back and forth, saying prayers under her breath. Sometimes she'd sit quite straight, no sign of movement in her chest. In the harsh glare of the unfrosted bulb hanging from the ceiling I'd see tears sliding silently down her cheeks, sparkling as they caught the light.

Then she'd sing the softest, sweetest lullabies in her high, pure soprano, or the soaring melody of 'Somewhere Over the Rainbow', her favourite song. Not mine though; it made my flesh creep.

This singing, the tears, her pretty face with its beautiful soft skin and round cheeks, pink like a girl's, worked on me. At moments like these I saw her as special. She was different, and I had to let her be different, and I didn't matter.

I never did tell on her. Every time I said it, I knew that it was an empty threat. I knew that I would never be able to tell anyone else, and certainly not the grandfather who I trusted and loved more than any other human being in the world. It would have hurt him, and I didn't want to hurt him. So Gran's physical abuse of me went on for years with the two of us locked into a painful secret world that only we inhabited, where there were no witnesses and no hope of rescue for either of us. I did sometimes ask for help from the God to whom she made me pray each night, but my pleas didn't seem to do any good.

I was born in the February of 1957 at the General Hospital in Scarborough, the daughter of thirty-eight-year-old Marjorie Baines, spinster, and, as declared on my birth certificate, an unknown father. This wasn't true at all. We all knew exactly who he was, but I have to assume that he wasn't named on my birth certificate because he wouldn't have anything to do with registering my birth. A registrar couldn't put a man's name on the certificate without the presence of either a marriage certificate or the man in question. My parents weren't married and, in any case, I think that, as with so much else in my mother's life, it was her parents who sorted out the registration of my birth for her.

It was perhaps no surprise, given the way she was bullied and browbeaten by Gran, that my mother had never managed to find a straightforward romantic relationship for herself or to strike out to make an independent life. She was still living at home with her parents when I was born. That in itself was extraordinary for the times. In the 1950s, unmarried women in their late thirties were still routinely described as spinsters and, really and truly, the word was universally thought of as just another way of saying that a woman was too ugly, dull or stupid to find a husband. It was also automatically assumed that single women, especially older ones, were sexually inactive. They generally were, if only for fear of what their families and neighbours would think of them otherwise.

That obviously wasn't true of Mum. Granddad even told me, when I was older and he was trying to explain to me how things had come to be the way they were in our family, that when she was younger she'd had a reputation for hanging about the quayside in Scarborough where the fishing fleets landed their catches. These boats sailed out of all manner of distant North Sea ports to come to Scarborough, from the Baltic coast right round to Iceland. There were probably many children in Scarborough who had been fathered on the wharves and whose dads had gone back to sea and disappeared for ever. Even where there was a marriage, in the 1950s fathers frequently stepped permanently out of their children's lives if a relationship failed. At the time it was thought to be better for the children that way. Still, single-parent families were a rarity at the time, and as a child I was keenly aware of this. Obviously I was illegitimate, and everyone knew it, because they knew my family, and I was the only one in the neighbourhood, although I have to say that none of my friends from the streets round about were ever nasty to me about it, and nothing was ever said in the playground. Maybe they, and particularly their parents, pitied me so much that it placed me beyond teasing.

We lived at number 45 Quarry Mount, in a row of half a dozen prefabricated bungalows that had been put up on waste land at the foot of a disused quarry just off the A64 on the southern outskirts of Scarborough. In front of the prefabs were four streets of old brick terraced houses that had probably been built to house people who worked at the old town gasworks and the lemonade factory nearby. The bungalows were a kind of flat-pack house constructed from ready-made wood or concrete panels rather than bricks. Thousands of these bungalows were built all over Britain just after the Second World War in response to the urgent need for homes for those returning from war service who wanted to get back to normal life, to settle down and start their own families. Much housing had been flattened by wartime air raids and whole districts were being declared unfit for habitation. Unsurprisingly, people were no longer willing to put up with living conditions in some of the jerry-built terraces that had been thrown up at the end of the nineteenth century with no bathrooms, no indoor toilets and, in some cases, still had no running water, even in 1939.

Prefabs like ours were supposed to be a temporary solution, bridging the gap while a country bankrupted by war got back on its feet, but ours was still standing in the late 1980s. Actually they weren't bad houses at all. The rooms were a reasonable size and I don't recall ours ever being particularly cold. Even though there were four of us in it, it was just about big enough. Most importantly, it had a loo and bathroom at a time when to have such facilities behind your own front door was still considered great good fortune. Not, it has to be said, that we got much benefit from the bath. This was something else that Gran thought was filthy, and we weren't allowed to have baths. Instead we had to have stand-up washes at the sink.

I never felt completely safe at home. I had some sanctuary at the pre-nursery school, Childhaven, where my mother left me from the age of two so that she could go out to work, washing dishes at Bland's Cliff Café. I loved to snuggle down into my nursery bed for an afternoon sleep, safe and secure in the knowledge that I didn't have to be on my guard for what might happen in the night. As I got older and started school, I began to have a glimmer of an idea that this way of going on probably wasn't normal, and that it certainly wasn't fair. I met my first best friend at Hinderwell County Primary; Sylvia. Strangely enough, although I was living a completely dysfunctional life, I made some solid friends at school who had no idea what my life was really like. Much the same pattern would continue throughout the rest of my life.

When I was younger, I'd always hoped that Mum would take us away from Gran's, and find us a place of our own.

'Look, Mum, look what I got on the market today.'

Granddad used to take me down to the weekly market sometimes on a Saturday. There was a comic stall where I could swap my old comics, my *Beano* and *Dandy*, for different ones for a penny, rather than paying much more for just one new comic – a bargain, and a huge treat, because I already loved reading. I was not anxious to show Mum my new *Beano*, however. Granddad usually gave me a thrupenny bit to spend as well, and I never spent it on sweets or anything so childish. I had learned obsession from a pro. So I saved the bits of pocket money that Granddad and Mum gave me, and every now and again I would take my hoard with me on these Saturday morning outings.

No eight-year-old ever fingered tea towels as lovingly and carefully as I did. No other child ever insisted, despite her Granddad's gentle pleas for her to buy herself a toy or sweets or a pair of gloves, on buying a set of matching green coffee mugs. 'Mum, look, aren't these mugs lovely? Shirley's mum has a set like this.'

This was a scene that was played out many times in our cramped little bedroom where there was just room for our two beds and the dressing table on which Mum's dozens of pots of cream, lipsticks and make-up were arranged. Whatever other aspects of life Mum couldn't get a handle on, she never left the bedroom without being perfectly made-up and nicely dressed. She was tiny, about five feet two inches tall, and as slender as the clothes prop we used to hold up the washing line in the back garden. I never recall her hair being any colour other than grey, but although it was thick and wavy, it was much softer than Gran's, like a dark silver cloud around her head. It suited her, cloudy hair to go with her head-in-the-clouds mind. When I came back from my morning at the market with Granddad, she'd be all dressed up as if she had somewhere to go, although she probably didn't, and I would get her to come into the bedroom with me to see what I had to put in the bottom section of the built-in cupboards that we used as our wardrobe.

On this morning, she sat softly down on the end of her bed in her usual way with her hands folded meekly into her lap, looking like a young woman at a dance hoping that she wasn't going to be left without a partner. She watched obligingly as I unscrewed the brown paper bags that the green mugs were wrapped in and set them out in a row. She said nothing. She stared at the mugs as if they were little green men.

'For our place, Mum, for when we get a council flat. Shirley says that her aunt has got a new council flat on the Eastfield estate. We might get one. Have you called the council?'

Mum looked at me, baffled. Then she half smiled and followed it with a little laugh as if she didn't understand the joke but wanted to be polite.

'Have you called the council?'

'Yes, yes.' She was smiling, laughing a bit, nodding her

head and looking just a bit bewildered – or perhaps even sheepish, a bit ashamed – as I put the mugs with the other household bits and pieces I was hoarding to furnish our own home with in the bottom of the wardrobe. No girl ever started her bottom drawer so early.

The new home never materialized, of course.

During my childhood, my absent father was not quite absent enough. He had not vanished off the face of the earth when I was born as other absent fathers did, and I often wished that he had. Instead, Mum slipped away every evening to spend time at his flat, and I had to visit him every Sunday without fail.

My father, Major – Major was his Christian name, not his rank – lived on the Edgehill estate, about twenty minutes' walk away from our house. Our prefab bungalow had been tacked on to the back end of a series of Victorian terraced streets just after the war at about the same time Edgehill had been built by the council. I'm not sure why it gained such a terrible reputation so quickly, but certainly, by the time I was five in 1962, it was regarded as the worst estate anywhere in the Scarborough area, a notorious breeding ground for what we would now call social deprivation and all the problems of unemployment, crime and anti-social behaviour that went with it.

Dad seemed to me to be twice as old as any of the other dads I knew, but in fact he was forty-two years old when I was born, not much older than my mother. He lived in a row of cheaply built council flats at the back end of the estate, two-storey buildings made of brick and plywood panels, and thin walls through which you could hear the neighbours if they coughed. Dad had one of the top floor flats. He was a window cleaner, doing it the old way, somehow riding a dusty black sit-up-and-beg bike with a bucket and wash leathers swinging from the handlebars, and his left arm hooked through a pair of ladders so that he could balance them on his shoulders as he rode along. It was a squeeze getting up to his flat because he couldn't leave his bike or the ladders outside – they would have been stolen in a moment – so they had to live on the narrow staircase.

To me as a child, he never looked quite right. His face was quite handsome: his dark eyes and nose and mouth were all where they should be and were nicely shaped, and he had a lot of wavy dark hair and healthy, tanned-looking skin – I suppose because he was working outside much of the year. But his clothes were scruffy. He looked, to be honest, a bit trampy. He wore baggy cord trousers that were far too big for him round the waist, and he tied a belt round them. Not through the loops, but just below the waistband, pulled tight, so that the tops of the trousers made a kind of frill above the belt. Even when I was quite young, I was embarrassed about this, perhaps because Granddad was always nicely dressed, no matter whether he was about to go to work as a doorman at the Conservative Club, or going to do some odd job in the house or garden. Even if he had old clothes on, they fitted him, and he'd have a nice sleeveless pullover to put over the top of them. Granddad was good-looking, too, with thick waves of silver hair. The difference was that Granddad's face had a kindness in it that would have made the ugliest man look lovely, and my father's face didn't. There was no welcoming twinkle in the eyes; never any sign, in fact, that made me feel as if he liked me.

I don't think Dad paid much attention to himself or his home at all. All the walls in the flat were either a grubby pale pink or pale green, and the woodwork everywhere, round the doors and windows, was dull and grey. I don't think it had been touched since the builders had left in the late 1940s. His home was filthy and depressing, and the dirt made me as miserable as Gran's overwhelming obsession with tidiness and cleanliness.

But at least at Dad's my toys were safe. I kept some dolls there, a Spirograph set, a few sticker books, because Gran would probably have thrown them away during one of her rages about mess and dirt if they'd been left at the prefab. My passion was reading, but I also loved to draw, and Dad's garden was good for that. Whilst it housed his tiny allotment, he had a fantastic nature reserve where I would sit for hours drawing pretty butterflies and untamed weeds.

I also loved my dolls. Gran had appeared to take great pleasure in throwing all of my dolls away apart from my 'Tiny Tears', which of course, to my great delight, could wee and cry. She couldn't get hold of this prized possession because the doll stayed 'sleeping' in Dad's cupboard. Where also, incidentally, I found a trove of treasure from what I can only presume was his past life. I used to dress up in the glossy black top hat whilst twirling the silver-topped cane which I found tucked away under years of dust. I also loved winding up his elaborate HMV horned record player and dancing along to a stack of old 78-inch records that I had found.

Dad had originally been brought up in Leeds and came from quite a well-off family – hence the gramophone and, astonishing in a small, grubby council flat, a huge picture of Jerusalem burning in an ornate gold frame that wouldn't have disgraced the council art gallery.

I knew what was going on in the picture because the one thing I did that made Dad smile was to stand in front of it, transfixed by the flaming yellows, oranges and reds bursting from the dark silhouette of an obviously foreign city with its peculiar towers and roofline. He'd almost always ask, 'What is it, Jackie?'

I would answer 'Jerusalem Burning', like a little parrot, wanting to please him. I had no idea what the words meant, and I didn't know the story. This, for some reason, amused him, and his lips, always set in a grim line, would soften. The painting was real – a real oil painting in a real gilded wooden frame alive with curly bits, not something printed and framed in plastic from Woolworths – and it had no business being there. The older I got, the stranger it looked on the grubby pale-pink-washed wall. It was about four feet by three and dwarfed the mantelpiece of the little coal fire beneath it. It clearly belonged to a previous life that could never have been guessed at from the way he looked and the way he lived during my childhood.

Gradually, I became dimly aware that there were other members of my father's family that I had never met. I had actual half brothers and a half sister who lived somewhere else, although I can't recall any conversation so direct. It didn't really make sense to me anyway, so I didn't believe it. How could there be other children? I would know them if there were. If they were real, they would visit, like I did. Therefore they didn't really exist.

When we arrived one Sunday for our visit, a tall boy was sitting in one of the chairs by the coal fire. He stood up when Mum and I came in, and he shook Mum's hand. He was impossibly mature, maybe sixteen, a good ten years older than me. He wore long trousers and a short-sleeved white cotton school shirt and a school tie, and his thick dark hair was cut short at the sides and back and had a floppy fringe. It was the hair that made me stare, as it was cut in much the same way and parted in the same place as Dad's, with the same distinctive wave in it where the hair-line and parting met on the forehead.

'This is your cousin Richard,' said Dad.

We looked at each other. What does it mean? I asked myself.

'Hello, Jackie, how are you, I've heard all about you,' said the boy awkwardly, as if he was reading out loud from a book. He had a strange, flat accent too, like Dad's.

I wanted very badly to tell him that I was Felicity, that he had it wrong, but I was too shy and overawed to reply to anything he said to me all afternoon. Wordlessly, I showed him my stash of toys, as instructed by my father, and he pretended to be interested but, really, after a few goes of 'that's nice' as I demonstrated what my baby doll could do, there wasn't much more common ground to investigate together.

A little later we were allowed to put some records on

Dad's old wind-up gramophone, so that passed a bit of time. Otherwise the two of us spent an uneasy couple of hours wondering what on earth we were supposed to do with each other, separated by a great chasm of age and gender. I could see that this Richard boy was no better at getting on with Dad than I was, although it was also obvious that Dad was more interested in him, more pleased by him, than he was by me. He smiled at him, something he never did at me. Even though I had no strong feelings for my father, I felt intensely jealous at those moments of closeness that passed between them. I had always wanted a brother or a sister. And I believed that my dad could have brought us all together. But he never did.

Family obviously did exist, so I now had to assume that the other brothers and sister that I had heard of did too. Very, very slowly, as I understood more about the world in general, and as snippets of information about Dad's former life were dropped here and there for me to pick up and piece together, I began to realize that there was at least one very good reason why my parents weren't married. Dad already had a wife.

Piecing together what may have happened, I suspect Dad's wife suffered from some kind of mental illness. On finally meeting Andrew, my half brother, at my father's funeral some years later, the jigsaw pieces were finally pieced together. 'She had a mental illness, but she was in her fifties when she died,' Andrew told me. 'When she got ill, we were all very young. I don't remember her very well. She just vanished. Then Dad vanished.'

Dad was unable to keep his family together, that much

was clear, although Andrew didn't really know why and knew nothing that would explain why our father had moved from the Lake District, where he'd lived with his wife and three children, and come to Scarborough. I also couldn't understand why it wasn't possible for us to have a home together, so that Mum and I could get away from Gran, when he lived so close by. It wasn't done at the time for unmarried couples to live together, of course, but on the other hand, it also wasn't done for unmarried couples who had produced a child to spend every single Sunday together as if they were a family, and then go their separate ways at the end of the day.

Also confusing was the question of my name. Not, as you might expect, my surname, but my first name because, for my father, Felicity didn't exist. He called me Jackie.

'Jackie, come to the table and get your egg and chips,' he'd say in his strange, flat accent that wasn't like the soft, lilting north-east coast accents that I heard around me.

Jackie had been his choice of name when I was born. Even here, however, it seemed that Gran had taken control and got her way. Jackie wasn't a good enough name, in her opinion. Too much like a boy. Too modern. Too common.

'Your gran thought Felicity was a better name. But Jackie is nice too, isn't it?' said Mum in her vague way on the one occasion I can recall asking her what on earth it was all about.

'But Granddad told me I was special, because Felicity Alice Baines spells F.A.B. just like Lady Penelope's Rolls Royce. I'm not Jackie and never will be. Will you tell him?'

'Leave it love. We don't want to upset your dad,' she said in her usual non-confrontational, dismissive way.

'Please, Mum, tell him I hate that name. I'm *Felicity*.'

Mum was so thoroughly under her own mother's thumb, even at the age of thirty-eight, that it was Gran's choice of name that had gone on my birth certificate. How she squared the existence of my official name with Dad, I don't know. I do wonder whether she even got around to telling him that his daughter had another name that everyone except him used.

I never knew whether Felicity or Jackie was the real me, and was not even entirely sure which one I wanted to be. Worse still was the feeling that all these grown-ups had no idea who I was, and didn't much care. I was invisible and, with my father particularly, I had no identity.

'Come and get your dinner, Jackie,' he'd say, looking at me but not seeing me. If I ignored him, he'd just shrug, and turn his back on me and head back to the kitchen to get his and Mum's dinner. He always fried us chips and eggs in lard for our Sunday dinner on his greasy stove, and I have to admit that while it might not have been the healthiest meal, it was very good. It was quite a sacrifice to pretend I hadn't seen it or didn't want it.

'Jackie's dinner's getting cold, Marjorie,' he'd say over his shoulder in a careless tone of voice that suggested he'd already stopped caring whether I ate it, hot or cold. 'See if you can get her to sit down to it.'

He was always like that – calm and quite cold. Nothing he said and no expression in his face betraying any flicker of emotion. There was just one incident when the mask slipped, when I was dimly aware that Mum had been winding him up. This was one of Mum's quirks. She very rarely betrayed any sign of being angry at other people, largely because most of everyday life, including insults, seemed to go right over her head. Sometimes, however, a comment or an incident would get through. She never had enough nerve to stand up for herself directly, however, so she went all round the houses to get her own back. She'd pick on something quite unassociated with the real cause of her hurt, and be spiteful. Little digs, niggly comments, childish insults.

It was whilst I was sitting listening to one of Dad's favourite Mario Lanza records that I became aware of Mum and Dad shouting at the kitchen door. I have no idea what Dad had done to hurt Mum's feelings, but I heard her say in her most spiteful voice: 'You're a useless window cleaner, everyone says so.'

Dad suddenly raised his hand and slapped her hard on the face. Mum ducked her head as if she expected more, but Dad turned his back on us both and disappeared into the kitchen. My tummy was suddenly full of wild, jumping fright and alarm. Whatever else might not be right in this house, I had come to depend on knowing that this kind of thing did not happen here. In that sense, at least, Dad's flat was some kind of refuge from Gran's violence.

I was wary for quite a few Sundays after that, but nothing like it ever happened again, and although I never felt the slightest sense of connection with my father, as the years went by I did come to value our Sunday visits for the pleasure of going to the sweetshop on the way there, where Mum always made sure I got a weekly treat of a bag of sherbert lemons or rhubarb and custard boiled sweets, and for the Sunday afternoon peace of Dad's home.

And Dad was responsible for bringing some joy into my life when I was about eight. Granddad had given me a puppy, Sooty, when I was about four, but he had recently disappeared. I'm not sure why, but I do know I was devastated, crying for days over the loss. During my visits to Dad, I'd see a dog wandering collarless around his estate – a friendly border collie/labrador cross with long golden hair. I must have mentioned him to Dad, because one day he appeared at Quarry Mount with this dog, leading him by a rope tied round his neck. I think he must have just taken him. I can't imagine how it happened, but Gran let me keep him. I called him Silver, and I loved him.

I accepted almost all of my peculiar family circumstances: the mad grandmother; the distant, weak mother who didn't seem able to protect me from her; the peculiar, solitary, aged father who didn't want to make a home with us and who had once had a completely different life in some other part of Britain; I grew accustomed even to the constant discomfort of being surrounded by children who had proper mums and dads, brothers and sisters they could play with, and cuddly grandmothers. But I never came to terms with Gran's wanton cruelty.

Granddad and I would always have a chat before tea, him on one of the dining chairs at the oak gate-leg table in the corner of the living room, and me at his knees on the 'peggy stool', the little three-legged stool that I'd been using since I was a toddler. Usually he would ask me about my day, and when I told him what I'd done at school, he'd take something I'd said that reminded him of a story he knew, particularly stories from his childhood. He'd talk about the squeaking of chalk on old-fashioned school slates that made his teeth go on edge, or the different ball games they played in the west Yorkshire village where he'd grown up, and the tricks he'd played on his teachers, like finding out where they lived and putting treacle on the front doorknob. But on one particular evening, when I was about ten, talk turned to more serious matters.

'I'm sorry, lass, for what we've done to you,' he said to me. I was scared. What was he going to say next?

'What do you mean, Granddad?' He must have heard the panic in my voice.

'You've suffered in this house. No child should have to put up with what you do. But I love her, Felicity. What do I do?' Was he looking to me for answers? 'I wanted to have you adopted when you were born, but your gran wouldn't hear of it. I shouldn't have listened to her.' Silent tears slid down his cheeks.

I gasped with shock and hurt. 'Don't send me away. Ever. Promise, Granddad'.

'I won't, love. Not now. But I should have. You would have had a much better life, one that you deserve, with a proper family, a normal mum and dad.'

'It's OK, Granddad. I love you and would never want to leave you. I'd rather put up with Gran than go away.' I looked up into his face. I knew he couldn't resist my smile.

'Tell me a story about the war. That one about losing your eye in the trenches.'

He laughed and we were back where I wanted us to be, in our make-believe world of action and heroes. Yet it was peculiar to realize that while Granddad was the one who made me feel loved, he'd wanted to give me up, that Gran was the one who had insisted I stayed with the family, and yet treated me as if she hated the sight of me.

As the years passed, I became openly scornful of my mother's weakness. It was almost half a century later, as it became clear that she hadn't long to live, that I realized how bitter I still was about her failure to save me. I knew that somewhere in the dustiest, darkest corners of my mind, I was still blaming her for everything that had ever gone wrong in my life.

This realization brought me face to face with the astonishing idea that maybe Gran and I shared something very fundamental. It was obvious even to me, although I had never been able to feel any love or empathy for Gran, that a dreadful bitterness had poisoned her personality. Her behaviour couldn't be fully explained away as madness or cruelty for its own sake; there were surely unknown experiences in her life that had played a part in making her so vicious.

Lurking at the back of my mind was that untold story of Granddad's, the one about Gran's mother going to prison when she was little. I found myself wondering, for the first time, whether Gran had also blamed *her* mother for the troubled life she'd had, just as I blamed mine.

Until that moment, I would have sworn blind that I had

absolutely nothing in common with my grandmother, born Elsie Swann, granddaughter of Hannah and John Hinchcliffe.

Chapter Two

BARNBY FURNACE

Hannah experienced happier times before she moved to Barnsley. She and her husband, John Hinchcliffe, chose to settle in a little cottage close to a busy waggonway in a hamlet called Barnby Furnace, just a few miles away from Barnsley, in what was then the West Riding of Yorkshire. The Waggonway was one of the earliest railroads in the world, and Hannah and John's windows must have been at wheel level to the enormous coal wagons rolling smoothly along the rails to the new canal a couple of miles up the lane, changing history as they went.

My great-great-grandmother Hannah had been born in about 1822 just a stroll away from Barnby, which was already a bustling little community. Hannah's father was a weaver who worked from home and, as the eldest child, Hannah would have helped out with preparing the wool for spinning, threading the loom, and loading yarn on to hand shuttles. Weaving was a well-paid and respectable trade, and Hannah was literate so clearly had some schooling. But John Hinchcliffe, the husband Hannah eventually chose, was not a weaver. My great-great-grandfather John

Hinchcliffe was, I discovered, something of a pioneer, being among the first men to declare themselves members of the very new trade of 'collier'. Born in about 1813, he reached the age when he had to decide how he was going to earn a living in the late 1820s, just as the Georgian era was drawing to a close. He rejected his own father's trade of stonemasonry and chose instead one that had been recognized as an occupation for the blink of an eye, compared with the ancient craft of his father or that of Hannah's weaving family. John was very particular about describing himself as a 'collier' all his life, even long after he had retired – he was not just any old miner, in other words, but specifically one who brought up coal.

I like to think that the young John first went to Barnby Furnace because his father needed to go to the quarry there for stone, and when he saw the strong-armed, black-faced colliers disappearing below ground it captured his fancy. But who knows? Maybe there was only room for one son in the family business. Maybe it just didn't appeal to him. Perhaps the colliers were better paid than stonemasons too – there was certainly more scope for increasing your earnings, if you were fit and strong, as colliers were paid by the weight of the coal they produced. Whatever the reason, John chose mining and remained single until he was twenty-eight. He was nine or ten years older than Hannah, who was eighteen when they wed.

I'd always thought that, two or three hundred years ago, working-class people generally married at a very young age. In fact the average age of a new husband in the early 1800s in northern England was around twenty-six. By the time

John asked William Thorpe for Hannah's hand in marriage, he would have been considered just the right kind of age to be thinking of settling down.

Were Hannah's parents doubtful about the age difference between her and John, or were they in fact reassured by it, since they could see that he had an appetite for regular work? I suppose he must have been well known locally as a sober and respectable man who wouldn't drink the housekeeping. While there is no living memory of them left in my family, all the evidence of John and Hannah's life suggests that the two of them pulled together and kept a roof over their family's head even in the most difficult circumstances.

The Hinchcliffes paid their rent and kept most of their children alive. To me, this seems as much of an achievement in those days as climbing Everest. Years and years of census returns tell the same story – through almost fifty years of marriage, they stayed together in the same house while their neighbours flitted from home to home and other people's children dropped like flies.

To a girl like Hannah, colliers must have seemed rather glamorous men, rather like the boyfriend I had in the 1970s who had a job none of us had really heard of. At the time I wasn't convinced that you could look after computers, call yourself an IT specialist, and still claim to have a proper job, but I was quite taken with the futuristic nature of his work. Maybe Hannah was attracted to John for much the same reason.

Never mind that John Hinchcliffe came home from his work black from head to foot – at least he had a guaranteed amount of cash to put into the family kitty each week. I like to think that he was a good catch for Hannah. I hope that, young as she was, her parents were happy when she married him. As she walked through the garden gate with her new husband after the wedding breakfast provided by her parents, cheered on by her younger brothers and sisters, and strolled across the dale to the little lane leading down to Barnby Furnace and beyond it to the cottages at Higham Common where they first set up home, Hannah could have had no inkling of the radical changes she would witness, the transformation of the everyday lives of ordinary people that was already underway, or the many hardships and tragedies that this new way of life would pull her own family into.

When they had been married for about ten years, one of the coveted Barnby Furnace cottages became vacant. All along the Waggonway, this row of stone colliers' cottages had been built by the company that leased the rights to the mine, furnace and quarry from the local landowners. A short description of these houses written by a nineteenth-century visitor to Barnby noted that each house had 'a good amount of garden, that the tenants and their families might have some respectable employment for their leisure hours'. Not to mention, of course, somewhere to grow food and, like Hannah and John's parents, keep a pig and some hens.

Hannah's new home at number 14 in the row of cottages sat below the Waggonway embankment and her garden stretched out behind it, backing on to the green fields rolling away towards the Pennines where sheep still grazed among the muck and spoil coming out of the mine, furnace and quarry. The fast-flowing beck offered plenty of water for household tasks such as washing and cleaning and Barnby also had a clean well for drinking water.

John and Hannah's first-born, Henry, was born within a year of their marriage. Then came Charles, and a year later, William. Then came five daughters, Elizabeth, Ellen, Annie, Frances and Emily. John was able to afford the penny-a-week fee to send them to one of the local board schools – primary education which was partly funded by the state and partly by parental contributions. Just two weeks before the 1861 census was carried out, Hannah gave birth to a fourth boy, named John after his father.

By 1861, as they celebrated their twentieth wedding anniversary, they had nine strong, healthy children. By that time the three eldest were working as colliers alongside their father. John had probably begun his career at some point in the late 1820s when women and children as young as eight were still bringing up the coal for their menfolk, but by the time he and Hannah married there were strict rules that no females or boys under the age of ten could go down a deep shaft pit. By 1860, a little after the Hinchcliffe boys were of an age to start work, the legal age limit had been raised to eleven.

Life was clearly good and they had managed to raise a large brood without suffering the terrible losses that were afflicting the working classes in the cramped, insanitary conditions of the great industrial cities. It does seem likely that Hannah and John lost one or two infants between Frances and Emily – there was a four-year age gap between them – but otherwise the balance they had managed to strike between the new means of earning a living offered by the brave new industrial age and the country life of their childhood seemed to work well. Barnby Furnace was surrounded by fields and woods and the Hinchcliffe children had the freedom of all of it during their leisure hours. Even when the boys left school at about the age of eleven or twelve to start working down the mine with their father, Barnby Furnace was still a pretty good place to be when work was done.

John and Hannah were to have one more surviving child, Clara, in 1865, and her birth provides the evidence of a change in the family's fortunes. Her birth certificate gives her birthplace as Barnsley, and her parents' address as 21 Havelock Street, Racecommon Road. The coal seam stretched from Barnby into the south-western edge of Barnsley, which was now rapidly transforming itself from an agricultural market town to a powerhouse of heavy industry.

There is only a stump of Havelock Street left today, a pub on one corner and a shop on the other to show that it was once a prosperous working-class area that could support solid local businesses. What a modern eye imagines, looking at the grubby dark red bricks of the old yard walls and trying to reconstruct Hannah's Havelock Street in the mind, are long, dreary rows of tiny houses that kennelled several generations of working people into social deprivation, stretching off into the hinterland of Racecommon Road.

Yet perhaps it wasn't quite like that. As a child of the

post-war twentieth century, I cannot imagine why John and Hannah wanted to leave their house in the fields to bring their brood up among all the perils of disease and dysfunction inherent in a mid-nineteenth-century industrial town. But when they moved in, the houses in Havelock Street were brand spanking new, and probably offered John and Hannah a room of their own for the first time in their married lives, with a door to it and a bed in it, one they didn't have to make up each night in the living area after dividing the children between the two upstairs rooms of their miner's cottage, and one they didn't have to share with all the little ones.

They probably regarded the communal privies in the back lane connected to a new mains sewer system as a marvellous mod-con, and the scullery in the back yard with its copper for heating water, and the pump in the back lane to fill it from, was more evidence that they had finally 'made it'. It would have been wonderful to leave behind the buckets and the ice-cold beck water of their youth, the heating of water a kettle at a time on the cooking range, and to have one room set aside for recreation with a fireplace of its own that had no other function beyond warming the people in it.

John had little further to walk to work from Havelock Street than he'd had at Higham Common or Barnby, and he now had more choice about where he worked. Whichever way he headed out of town, it was no more than ten minutes to three or four collieries, either at the end of the Silkstone seam to the south-west, or on the edge of the great South Yorkshire coalfield stretching south-east down the Dearne Valley. Half the men in Havelock Street were colliers, and it was absolutely commonplace to see men walking out of town in their working clothes, carrying their safety lamps, and trudging back up the hill at the end of a shift, faces burnished with the midnight glitter of coal dust.

The homecoming men would walk straight round to the back-yard washhouse where wives like Hannah would have hot water ready in the copper, with enamel bowls and jugs of cold on the stone counter alongside it. John, with Henry, Charles, and William, could go into the little lean-to building and wash themselves in privacy before setting foot in the kitchen.

As soon as they stepped through the back door, Hannah or one of the older girls would be waiting to hand them a mug of hot, sweet tea and a filling snack, maybe a potato cake or a piece of suet dumpling. Once they were rested, a hot dinner would appear on the table. The working men and boys would be fed first and best, as was the custom, and the little ones either had their food earlier or waited their turn, depending on what shift John and the boys were working.

I'm sure John and Hannah thought themselves very lucky in all sorts of ways – lucky to have this new house, lucky to have produced three strong boys so early in their marriage who could now earn a man's wage and help pay the rent, and lucky to have some help rearing the tail-end of their big family.

But moving to Barnsley turned out not to have been the best of decisions. Contagious disease was rife in the close quarters of the town, and they hadn't been in their new home for two years when fourteen-year-old Ellen died of what was described on her death certificate as 'infectious fever'. The grief in the little house in Havelock Street must have been dreadful, particularly for Elizabeth and Annie who were closest to her in age, and who now had to live with the sense of a yawning gap between them where their sister should have been.

As it turned out, Ellen's tragic death was just the beginning of their hardships.

The sound dreaded in the villages clustered around the Oaks Colliery was heard at lunchtime on 12 December 1866 – muffled, almost like a thunderclap miles off in the distant Pennine hills. The flash of lightning that went with it wasn't seen by anyone above ground, but was felt underfoot. The very earth beneath their houses shuddered as all the air in the mine galleries hundreds of yards below expanded in an instant with lethal force and layers of rock grudgingly shifted.

A mine owner would only pay for coal brought to the surface and so, in the 1860s, miners worked in pairs as collier and hurrier – the hurrier being the one who hauled the hewn coal to a designated collection point. How the colliers got the coal to the collection points did not interest the mining company – a miner's earnings were calculated by the weight of his coal regardless of how much work it had taken to get it to the scales. Where the seam was thin and the roof was low, and it was impossible to get a wheeled vehicle close to the face, a strong collier needed a strong hurrier to maximize their joint earning power, and this is what Hannah's two eldest boys, Henry and Charles, were doing together in the far reaches of the Oaks pit on 12 December 1866.

By now, Henry was twenty-four and had been working down the pit for over ten years, having started out doing the hurrier's job for his father at Barnby. Charles was twenty-two and would have started his training there too at the age of eleven or twelve. By the early 1860s, when the Hinchcliffes moved to Barnsley, the three of them would have been working as a team, the boys taking it in turns to hew and to haul for each other and their father.

Charles and Henry together would have made a good team, able to earn the best possible price for their labour. It was lucky that the Hinchcliffes had two sons like Henry and Charles living at home and working in the family trade because, by 1866, John Hinchcliffe was not a well man. He was fifty-three, and after three or four decades of working down the mines he was having trouble breathing. There were no pensions or social benefits, so although he was close to the end of his most productive mining years, he needed to carry on working as long as he could, before he and Hannah had to rely on their children to support them.

It was already well understood in districts like Barnsley that miners were more prone to bronchitis, pneumonia and tuberculosis than those in other occupations, but it would be another fifty years before anyone thought about compensating them for the respiratory diseases that were an inevitable result of the work they did. In the meantime, it was accepted that men like John ruined their health providing the vital fuel for the great furnace of Britain's industrial revolution. Hannah and her family knew well enough that when John Hinchcliffe hawked up pitch-black phlegm thicker than tar from his lungs, it signalled the beginning of the end of his ability to be his family's primary breadwinner. The few records I could find for that period showed that he now rarely worked a full week down the pit. William, nineteen in 1866, was now his hurrier, leaving Henry and Charles to be the powerhouse of the Hinchcliffe mining dynasty.

Why didn't John and William go down the pit on 12 December? Almost certainly because it was a Wednesday, and therefore 'making-up' day. It was the one shift when miners did not have to produce a specific quota of coal to keep their place in the pit, so they could use it to make up any shortfall on their quota over the previous week. If they could 'make-up' and meet their quota, there was a bonus to be earned. Naturally, with Christmas less than two weeks away, it was a very large shift of 340 men and boys who turned up for work that morning, all hoping to get the best possible price for the work they'd done that week.

However, for a miner of John's age, the effort required for coal-face work, especially in a pit like the Oaks with poor ventilation, made it almost impossible to meet the quotas, and since they wouldn't meet them even with the making-up shift, John and William might well have decided they were better off taking a rest day.

Another Henry Hinchcliffe, one of many cousins living in the district, had thrown in his job at the Oaks Colliery the previous April because it was so risky. He was a 'shot-lighter', firing small explosive charges set up in sequence on a coal or rock face to loosen it in a controlled explosion, making it mineable for the colliers with their hand tools. Henry's decisions were life and death to them, particularly when making sure that it was safe to put a naked flame to the detonating cord. Crucially he had to check whether any nearby dead spaces had filled with a deadly, explosive mixture of methane and oxygen.

To do his job properly, Henry would have had to know the mine intimately, and to know where the explosive gases were most likely to collect. On the witness stand during the investigation into the events of 12 December, it took him almost five minutes to list all the places where lethal levels of methane were known to collect in the Oaks Colliery. Listening to him, many declared it was no wonder he'd taken himself off to another, safer pit.

Pretty much all the men, not just the senior technicians like Henry Hinchcliffe, knew that the Oaks mine was alive with colourless, odourless methane gas. This was largely because almost exactly twenty years before, in 1847, an explosion in the same mine had killed seventy-three men and boys – the youngest ten years old. It was well known that it was not a safe pit. Many of the colliers there had, like Henry, tried to get out but had not been lucky enough to find other jobs. The men at the Oaks went to work every day not knowing with any certainty that they would come home; that very morning one middle-aged collier in nearby Hoyle Mill had told his wife as he set out to work: 'If thou hears a blow-up, thou may know we are all dead men.'

His wife told a visitor a week later: 'He was that poorly from the heat of the pit that he wouldn't have gone out if he'd not had a promise of help. I was just taking up the dinner when I felt it beneath my feet, a long rumbling like there was a storm on the tops, but I knew it wasn't high up, it was deep underground. I knew then. I knew, just as he said.'

Hannah, at home with her little ones on the south-western side of Barnsley – six-year-old Emily, five-year-old John, and Clara, barely twelve months old – did not know straightaway. They were too far away to feel the explosion, but the boom had been heard in the east of Barnsley and the news travelled fast. If it had not been heard, the smoke would have been seen within moments. Outside, someone shouted: 'There's been a blow-up down at Oaks – tha can see smoke from here.'

John, sitting by the range fire to keep his weak chest warm, sprang to his feet. Breath or no breath, he was out of the door and across Racecommon Road at the end of Havelock Street like a rabbit startled out of cover, so that he could inspect the skyline towards the Oaks for himself. He came back a matter of seconds later to tell Hannah: 'I'm off to the pithead. There's a great cloud as black as night hanging over the pit.'

He sent Emily, young as she was, to find William, who had gone down into the town on an errand, instructing her to tell him to get to the colliery as fast as he could. 'And if thou don't find him in an hour, come back to thy mother,' he ordered, guessing that in fact William would hear the news himself on Market Hill.

Within minutes the crowds began to gather. There were many who lived no more than ten minutes' walk away. It took half that time, of course, for their families to get there that day.

The cage in number one down-cast shaft, the means by which men went down and coal came up, had been at the bottom of the shaft. When the air finally cleared, it was possible to see that the winding cable was hanging limp with nothing on the end of it. The cage in number two shaft had been ripped to pieces too, but there was something to salvage and men were already trying to get a makeshift replacement together so that rescue parties could get down into the mine. Pieces of wood from the pithead structures had been catapulted out by the explosion and driven into the ground in the fields round about.

It is to the credit of one of the mine owners, Thomas Dymond, that he was with the first rescue party that went down the 900-foot deep number two shaft in the hastily re-rigged cage to find out whether there were any survivors. Smoke and dust were still rising from the shaft, and they found the air below foul with dust and more gas. Twenty men were brought up barely alive, most of them horribly burned. Only six of them were still alive when the sun went down that winter Wednesday afternoon.

William Hinchcliffe was, of course, among the volunteers for the rescue parties that were now going down in swiftly revolving shifts. By the evening, another sixty bodies had been recovered. Counting the twenty brought out alive, if barely, that left around 280 men and boys still unaccounted for, lying somewhere in the shattered mine workings.

When the first rescue parties finally managed to get to

some of the areas where men had been working when the blast came, what they saw was like the very worst imaginings of hell. They found men whose clothes had been blown right off them, and others whose clothing had ignited on them, charring their features and making them almost unrecognizable. And there was a horrible amount of evidence to show that not all the workers had died at the instant of the explosion.

'We came upon groups of dead men, some clasped in each other's arms, others clinging to stronger men who seemed to have been helping them in their struggle to gain the bottom of the shaft. Many were seated by the wayside in the attitudes they assumed when they could go no further,' reported one of the rescuers.

And still the rescue parties went down and came up, went down and came up, all that day and all through the night until daybreak on Thursday morning, and always there was a fresh supply of volunteers waiting at the pithead to relieve the last exhausted group. No group of men could stay down long because the foul air, a mixture of smoke and all manner of chemical reactions triggered by the heat, had now filled every corner of the mine.

Colliers rode and walked from miles around to get to the Oaks, through the twilight and into the dead of night, as news of what had happened travelled across the district. Other mine owners sent over their specialist engineers to offer advice, but the ordinary colliers who arrived came under their own steam and went down without any promise of pay. Many, like William and Henry, did it because they had family down there, but also because they knew that the men in the mine would have done the same for them. If they could not save lives, they could at least recover the mortal remains of the victims for their loved ones.

On Thursday, at nine in the morning, a new group of rescuers went down. The last group had come up in a bit of a hurry, telling those at the pithead that they 'had detected a change in the air', and that they feared another explosion was imminent. Once they were at the top, however, it was felt that perhaps they had been a little hasty. Crowds were still gathered about the pithead and spoil heaps hoping for more news, and many were still hoping against hope that more survivors would be found.

Mr Tewart, the mine steward who had been in the first rescue party that had gone down within thirty minutes of the disaster on the previous afternoon, agreed to take a new party down to see what more could be done. A group of twenty-five men went down with Tewart and mining engineer Parkin Jeffcock, most of them volunteer colliers from the Oaks itself, some, like Henry Hinchcliffe, from other collieries, offering to do what they could to help.

In Henry's case, not only did he know the pit almost as well as his own village, but his twenty-four-year-old brother John was down there, along with his cousins Charles and Henry. He had promised his own mother, and his Uncle John, to do all he could to find them, dead or alive. He had been down the day before, working well into the night with the rescue parties, and was now taking a much-needed break.

Then, just after 9 a.m., 'The air was rent with an appalling sound – a dull, long, continued boom, and there was belched forth from the shaft a volume of smoke and cloud of dust and soot which was spread over a wide area,' wrote the newspaper reporter who was standing with some of the families when this second explosion, even worse than the first, ripped through the mine.

An obscenely huge plume of smoke now rose into the air out of one of the two down-shafts. This time the cage was blown right out of the shaft and flung clean over the winding wheel and there it now hung, its gruesomely twisted remains swinging gently back and forth like a scavenged skeleton on a turnpike gibbet.

There were masses of women and children among the crowd, yet there were no screams or hysterics. There was only a stunned silence as these hardy, hard-pressed people worked out for themselves what this must mean. An emotional chill filled the air as they accepted that this explosion had blown away not only their last shreds of hope, but also the lives of the twenty-seven selfless men who had gone down there only minutes before.

About half an hour later, Thomas Dawson from Hoyle Mill declared he was ready to go down again if he could find a volunteer to go with him. Many, even those who still wanted to believe that their men and boys might be alive, shook their heads and said it was madness. There were hurried discussions about how this could be done with the cage gone, but while they were talking there was a third awful explosion below them and everyone around the pit-head platform jumped back. It was now absolutely clear that a huge fire was raging below.

Thursday night saw most of the watchers set off home

without hope. John and William trudged through Stairfoot and up the hill into Barnsley knowing they had nothing to tell Hannah – and no body to prepare for burial.

There was just one truly miraculous survival. At 5 a.m. on Friday, when there were just a handful of men around the pithead, a moan was heard from the bottom of the shafts. Then the pithead bell, connected by a wire pull to the shaft bottom almost 300 yards below, suddenly rang. A very large bucket, a metal container that could hold about two tons of coal, was attached to a chain and lowered down the shaft, carrying two men. The tarry smoke from the fires below clawed at their throats, and it must have been a long and uncomfortable descent, but they got to the bottom. There they found Sam Brown, one of the volunteer colliers from another pit who had gone down with one of the earliest search parties on the first afternoon after the disaster and got separated from his group. He had somehow survived the second and third explosions in a distant part of the mine.

His arrival at the pithead brought the total number of survivors from the disaster to precisely seven.

All hope of finding anyone else alive was officially given up later that Friday morning, when it was accepted that there was no hope for the 286 souls still down there and everyone understood that to have any chance of putting out the fires raging below, the two down-shafts which were feeding them with oxygen would have to be shuttered off and blocked up.

The work to seal the down-shafts was finished on Saturday.

'There is hardly one family in this area that is not mourning the loss of a loved one,' the *Barnsley Chronicle* reported bleakly.

John and Hannah, William and his teenage sisters Elizabeth and Annie sat in the kitchen in Havelock Street that Saturday evening, the house feeling as empty as a cavern despite the number of people in it. Now and then one of the girls would start to weep again, but quietly, knowing that there wasn't a heart in the house that wasn't breaking. They grieved for William in particular, because he had shared a bedroom and, indeed, a bed with his big brothers every night of his twenty years and he was now to sleep alone until he married – if he married. The largest share of the responsibility for keeping the family solvent would now fall to him.

Hannah, who had been too busy all her life to be able to sit still, even stricken with grief as she now was, busied herself with inspecting and refurbishing where necessary the best clothes every member of her diminished family possessed. All of them would go to the funerals of those whose bodies had been recovered, of course they would. This was going to be the nearest they would get to saying goodbye to Henry and Charles.

Three years later, in 1869, when it was finally thought safe to open the mine again and resume the search for bodies, Hannah waited anxiously for news of her sons, but none came. The remains of twenty-six-year-old John, their cousin and Henry's brother, were found that year. The search was officially brought to an end in 1871. The bodies of Charles and Henry were never recovered. To this day they lie somewhere beneath the damp green fields of the Dearne valley.

At least they are not alone. They have each other; and they share their last resting place with the remains of too many other colliery workers in too many other mines all along the great coalfield of the Barnsley Bed.

Chapter Three

GRAN

'They're trying to poison me,' Gran screeched from the doorstep. 'You're all trying to kill me. I know what you're up to!'

Poison, I thought. Hmm, an interesting idea.

'Elsie, love, come inside,' Granddad said patiently. He took her arm but she tore it away.

'Murderers! Help! They're going to murder me!'

She turned and dashed into the kitchen, grabbing pots and throwing them around the place like missiles while we cowered in the hall. There was a brief lull, then suddenly she was standing at the back door singing 'Over the Rainbow' with all the considerable power of her lungs, as if she were Judy Garland herself. A doctor came and gave her an injection while Gran screamed that she was being poisoned again, and then she quietened down and let herself be taken into the back bedroom by Granddad.

The next morning she was bad again, shouting abuse at all and sundry, inside the house and out. Then an odd kind of ambulance drove up, more old-fashioned than the ones with sirens, and painted green instead of the usual white.

It parked in the street outside. Two men in white overalls came into the house and took her arms, one on either side of her.

It was as if Santa himself had walked into the house. She's going, I thought. She really is being taken away. I had happy visions of having Granddad to myself, of Mum being around a bit more because she wouldn't be scared, of all of us not having to tiptoe around each other. Then, as Gran was taken out through the front door, she started to cry and then to wail. This was quite different from the mad and belligerent accusations that she'd been broadcasting for the last couple of days. This was terror and misery, like an animal that knows it's about to be put to sleep.

The sound she was making tore even at my heart, and when I looked at my dear Granddad's face, I saw that he was close to tears. He couldn't stand it. He went out to the ambulance, and I watched through the front window as he put his hand on one of the men's shoulders. The man stepped aside and Granddad held Gran gently by the arm while he had a short conversation with both men. Then he bent towards Gran's face and said something to her, and the two of them turned and came back up the path to the bungalow.

My heart sank. I could hear Granddad telling her not to worry, that she was safe, and that he would never send her away again. The ambulance men watched for a moment before driving away. He put Gran to bed, and from then on the doctor came with his injections most days. Until she decided to return to her post on the sofa by the gas fire and refused them.

Everything went back to the way it was.

To say that I felt alone is an understatement. I was the only child in a household of three adults, and I was locked into Gran's brutal routine. More than that, I was never the focus of anyone's attention. That privilege belonged to Gran, whose many bizarre obsessions with the right way to do things were ruthlessly applied to all three of us. She overshadowed every waking minute we spent in the house, not least because her rules changed so frequently.

She was the lawmaker, the jury and the judge, presiding over us from her spot in front of the fire. It was lit from morning until night when Gran was in residence. On the rare occasions that she left the bungalow, she decreed that it was to be left switched off, and she would feel it when she came back to see whether we had obeyed her. When Granddad was there, it was OK – we knew that he would tell her not to be so ridiculous. But if it was just Mum and me, we wouldn't dare put it back on, no matter how cold it was.

Even the house itself seemed to be held in the iron grip of Gran's will, frozen in the 1950s like a museum piece, because she wouldn't allow any change. While my friends' houses were getting jollier and bright oranges and greens and sophisticated browns in geometric patterns took hold, the prefab remained unrelentingly beige, with every window swathed in white nets which were taken down three times a year and scrubbed in the kitchen sink by Gran, or by Mum if Gran ordered her to do it, using an old-fashioned metal washboard, a piece of green soap and a scrubbing brush. Time and again Granddad offered to get her a twin-tub washing machine, but she snarled at the idea because it wasn't 'right' and carried on washing everything, even bedding, by hand.

Friends were getting fitted kitchens; ours remained as primitive as something in one of the black-and-white Ealing movies that Gran loved – just a big square stone sink with a curtain below it to screen off the pipes and cleaning stuff, a few cupboards and shelves, and an old dresser painted hospital green with a pull-out enamel work surface. I knew people who were getting fitted carpets; we were stuck with lino from end to end of the house and fringed rugs.

'Filthy things, fitted carpets. Bugs live in them. Fleas,' Gran spat when I mentioned the new swirly brown carpet that Shirley's parents had in their living room.

The bedroom walls had floral wallpaper that looked like the children's rooms in my 1930s Enid Blyton books, and the rest of the house, including the passageway and the front hall, was papered in woodchip.

Every spring Gran would turn our lives upside down and drive us all crackers by insisting on repainting the inside of the house from front to back, but always in dingy shades of off-white so that it still felt cold and cheerless. It would have been impossible to tell the difference if it hadn't been for the paint fumes that made our heads ache and lingered in every room for months. Granddad loathed the smell and he would cut up onions and put them on plates round the house because he'd heard that they soaked up the fumes. Gran hated him doing this, but it was one issue on which he stood up to her.

'No human being can live with these fumes, Elsie,' Granddad would say, sounding just about as cross as I can ever recall, and even then sounding ridiculously gentle. Amazingly, she listened when he wagged his finger and told her, 'Leave the onions, or there'll be trouble.'

On this, at least, she would let him have his way.

It was typical of Gran to think up tasks of this kind that would occupy her for weeks and cause immense disruption to the rest of us. She clearly loved that part of it, especially the annoyance it caused Granddad – but a project like this also meant that she didn't have time to do anything as risky as leave the house. She sent Granddad out to get the paint. Every now and again, however, she would take it into her head that she could face going into town herself, usually after making a bitter announcement about how Granddad or Mum had failed to do the shopping properly.

'I'll do it myself,' she'd say grimly, stepping out through the front door, walking down the path and stepping on to the pavement. Then she would turn round, come back in through the gate and go back to the front door. Then she would set off again. And she'd do the same thing again and again.

It was as if she couldn't get it quite right, yet was utterly determined to do it perfectly, no matter how long it took. It could take her all of half an hour to actually set off along the pavement towards the end of the road, and even then she might spend another half-hour retracing her steps up and down the pavement before she finally disappeared towards the shops.

I would watch from the window, my skin crawling with

the embarrassment of it, knowing there was a good chance that friends were out there playing or watching from their own windows and having a laugh with their parents as Gran moved from pavement to tree to lamppost, backwards, forwards and sideways, like a mad overgrown crab in a camel-coloured raincoat. To watch it all from behind a pane of glass was odd enough, but outside, from some distance away, she could also be heard hissing like a snake. She always made this maddening sound when she was in her 'got to get this routine right' mode.

There were days when she just couldn't do it to her satisfaction and would come back into the house forty-five minutes after she'd left, having got no further than next door's garden gate. She would take off her coat and hat and hang them up and carry on as if the last three-quarters of an hour had never happened, betraying no sign that she was conscious of how strange her behaviour was. She would return to her position on the sofa closest to the fire, where she had command of every route through the house, and make herself feel better by exercising her power. If the world outside wouldn't obey her rules, we always did. From this spot, she could tell us, without having to move, what we could and couldn't do, and how we could and couldn't do it.

Most days my only ambition was to get directly from the front of the house to my bedroom without triggering any interest, but if Gran was at her post it was virtually impossible. First came her insistence I walk the 'right' way across the room. This became more frequent once I was too old to be put to bed, and she needed a new way to control me.

Then, when I was about eight years old she came up with a new variation on this theme. By now I was tall enough to reach the light switch, and as dusk fell she told me to put the living room lights on. I got up from the table in the corner where I was looking at one of my books and walked over to the switch by the door. I pushed it down.

'Switch them off!' Gran barked.

Already heading back to my seat, I was startled and took a hasty couple of steps backwards to get to the switch again, flicking it into the off position as swiftly as I could.

'Now switch the lights on again, and do it properly.'

I flicked the switch again.

'That's not right. Do it again.'

Off, on. Off, on. Off, on, off, on, off.

'I don't know what you mean, Gran.'

'You'll stand there until you do it properly,' she yelled.

I stood by the door for what seemed like hours. It was perhaps no more than twenty minutes, but time lost all meaning as I desperately tried to get it right, whatever that meant. Did it mean jabbing at it, flicking it, rolling it smoothly from on to off? It was a wonder all the fuses in the house didn't blow, and it must have looked completely barmy to anyone outside the house watching the lights going on and off incessantly. Throughout the process, Gran alternately barked orders at me and smiled smugly.

This became her regular form of torture, and for me it flavoured the dark early evenings of winter with a dreadful sense of hopelessness. I dreaded October when the clocks went back and it was suddenly dark at half past four.

'For God's sake, that's enough,' my grandfather finally

burst out one evening when I was about eleven, and I'd already been standing by the light switch for half an hour. 'You'll electrocute her. Let it go, Elsie!'

It was startling to hear him go against her like this, because it was so uncommon. He tried not to interfere because nine times out of ten his interference would only make Gran more savage with me, or with Mum if she happened to be the one in the firing line. But very occasionally even Granddad, a man who seemed to have the patience of a saint, couldn't keep quiet. When he did rebuke her, Gran seemed to cower, to shrink in front of my eyes. She had some kind of respect for him and was clearly not happy if she thought he was angry with her. It made me wonder why he didn't do it more often.

But these strange, unsettling and wearying events punctuated the days, and I see now that Granddad was just as bound up in the grim daily struggle of coping with Gran's behaviour as Mum and I were. We were all so focused on finding ways to avoid or appease her that much of the time we barely noticed each other. If it was attention that Gran was after, she got it in spades – it was like living with someone who was perpetually threatening to pull the pin out of a hand grenade. When there was peace, it was fragile; it seemed Gran was just waiting for the chance to shatter it. Evidence of the slightest misdemeanour brought swift and brutal punishment.

Watching her corner my mother, a grown woman who was as gentle as a lamb, and beat her again and again over the head while Mum cowered behind her raised arms and tried to protect herself, was such a normal event that I couldn't recall a time when it had shocked me. Mum seemed resigned to this kind of brutality. She rarely made a sound while she was being attacked, and never fought back. She just waited for it to be over, at which point she'd get on with whatever Gran had ordered her to do. Gran was a couple of inches shorter than her, but she was a solid piece of work and it took nothing to knock Mum over. Mum always seemed so fragile.

Once, as Gran was barking at her to get the plates out for dinner, she was shoved and belted so hard – presumably because she hadn't got them out in the 'right' way – that she fell to the floor and all the plates crashed around her.

This was one of those rare incidents when Granddad stepped in. 'Leave her alone, Elsie,' he ordered as Gran stood over Mum and the plates. She was screeching at her, but I didn't hear. Even though I was used to this sort of violence, I was so frightened that it seemed like I was watching the television with the sound turned off. When Granddad's voice cut through, it was so unexpected that it made me jump. Gran stopped instantly and turned to look at him as if she hoped her glance might strike him dead; but she didn't say anything. She just hissed as she moved slowly away from Mum, backing towards her spot on the sofa, while Granddad helped Mum with the plates.

At about this time we acquired our only modern innovation. Gran bought our first TV. It was no surprise to me at all when I was told that only she was allowed to watch it. I didn't even bother to get excited about it, because I knew she would rarely leave the house. I hardly saw any of the programmes of the 1960s. And it added a new hazard to the already dangerous transit across the living room, because if she thought Mum or I were trying to sneak a look at the screen, she would leap out of her chair and clout the culprit hard round the head – a backhander, Granddad called it. Mum was singled out as the worst offender. She was never able to get the hang of the special, non-peeping way of walking past the telly that Gran demanded.

It wasn't just the three of us who circled her warily. The neighbours gave the two-bedroomed bungalow a very wide berth. My grandparents had been forced to move often in the years before I was born because even the most tolerant neighbours could only stand so much. Wherever she lived, she would frequently go out on to her doorstep and shout obscenities at the top of her voice, always without any provocation. 'Mrs So-and-so's no better than she bloody should be,' she'd scream, naming some poor woman who lived in the street, or who was perhaps that moment walking by. Gran didn't care, and was oblivious to whether children were about or whether angry husbands might hear her.

'She's a bloody prostitute – she does it for money, there's always men climbing in and out of that bloody kitchen window. It's disgusting, she should be locked up, she should be tarred and feathered. Decent people shouldn't have to put up with it,' she'd screech.

She was obsessed with what she perceived as the lack of morals and lack of shame around her. She'd call the husbands bastards and drug dealers, the children vandals and thieves. It was understandable that the decent people she lived among, all ordinary working-class families, felt they shouldn't have to put up with her.

There may be British streets where this kind of thing would hardly turn heads nowadays, but back in the 1950s and 1960s the things my Gran said were outrageous and shocking, especially for the people in our community who set great store by being 'decent' and found it impossible to dismiss her poisonous abuse with a smile or a shrug. Folk took it very personally indeed. Since this was an era when council estates were generally well managed, complaints about a tenant causing offence to her neighbours were taken seriously by the local housing officer. For quite a few years Gran, Granddad and Mum were forced out of council houses and into rented ones and then back again as the eviction notices arrived. Granddad and Mum both had to go out to work to pay the rent, and once they were out nothing could stop Gran putting on her regular doorstep performances. It wasn't until Quarry Mount that the constant moves stopped.

What made our house particularly suitable for a family afflicted with someone like Gran was that it stood at the end of a cul-de-sac. This meant that there were few passers-by and only a handful of neighbours who, fortunately for us, were willing to put up with her public tantrums. The front of the bungalow looked down onto the back yards of the nearest terraced street, but it was far enough away for Gran's annoyance value to be minimal.

The local children, however, found her a rich source of entertainment and this gave me another reason for dreading the dark winter evenings. As my friends got older and word spread about how easy it was to wind my Gran up, gangs of kids would come under cover of darkness and bang on the windows, shouting insults and laughing together.

'You're a witch, you're a witch, you're a witch-witch-witch,' they sang, squealing with delighted fear when she took the bait and flung open the door.

'You little buggers, you're all criminals – I'm calling the police and they'll lock you up for ever. They'll throw away the key when they get you, you little sods.'

From the darkness of the street corners down in the terraces, the kids would shout back: 'You're mad, you are, crazy woman. Crazy, cray-zee, cray-zee. Come on, then, the mad woman, come and chase us.'

She'd go down the path in her slippers and stand silently with her legs apart, hands on her hips, just staring into the darkness. There'd be more explosions of laughter when she suddenly lifted her fist and shook it, shouting: 'Bugger off, or I'll get the law on you, I will. I will!'

All I could do was listen and hope it would stop soon. Some of the kids were probably my own friends from school, and I writhed with embarrassment, but I could see it from their point of view. Gran was just too tempting for them. I felt less forgiving towards the boys from the housing estate across the way who were really foul-mouthed, and who hung around outside for what seemed like hours. They were tougher, more threatening, and Gran's reaction was frightening because of the stamina she had for the fight. Whether she was unaware of their menace, or whether she refused to bow to it, I don't know, but she would stand there for as long as they cared to stay, for hours if necessary, screaming back as they goaded her with foul language. I was forced to go to bed at 7 p.m. on the dot every evening, even after I'd started senior school, so I could do nothing except bury my head under my pillow.

Winter brought wonderful relief in this respect – bitter winds and rain, lots of it. Rain meant the local kids wouldn't put themselves to the trouble of getting soaked just for the sake of an hour's fun at my Gran's expense. To this day nothing makes me feel safer or more comforted than lying in bed on a wild night listening to plenty of rainwater splattering on the window and gurgling down the drainpipes.

Our nearest neighbour was, thankfully, a piece of waste-land, a former wartime allotment that no one wanted any more. This meant that there was no one Gran could annoy on the other side of the house, and I could lose myself in there when the weather was fine and I was allowed out to play on my own. It was overgrown with weeds, nettles, stooping misshapen trees, wild strawberries and wild flowers in early summer, and led up to even more wilder-ness behind the house where the cliff of an old stone quarry rose behind us. Its sheer walls were upholstered in bram-bles, moss and saplings.

This became a welcome refuge. In the middle of the tangled undergrowth I made myself a nest, a secret world I could escape to where no one could find me – not Gran and not the local kids who knew about her. She had put barbed wire round the old allotment, but towards the back I had burrowed a secret entrance through which I could crawl without getting caught on the barbs. I took my precious Heidi books there whenever the weather was good enough for me to lie in the open and read. If I could get into the kitchen without being seen, perhaps while Gran was engrossed in one of her strange cleaning routines, I would steal myself a picnic of sliced bread, a bit of cheese, a biscuit, maybe an apple if I thought I could get away with it. When I got a bit older I made a proper den of sorts and fantasized about living there one day, away from them all. In bad weather, I could retreat to an outhouse where the coal was kept before the gas fire was fitted. My Granddad put hooks in the roof of it so that he could hang a swing in there for me, which meant I had somewhere to play even when it was tipping down with rain. The biggest blessing was that it was a way of getting out of the house when the weather was bad.

At weekends, if the weather was good, I would plead with Granddad to come out into the small back garden and play catch with me. I had a less than innocent motive for this. We would take Silver with us, and as the ball was thrown between us it would drive him crackers and make him bark like mad. This had the deeply satisfying effect of annoying Gran. The louder he barked, the crosser she got, and it was a small but satisfying piece of revenge to be able to say sweetly, 'What, Gran? He's just a dog, he can't help it.'

Oddly enough, Gran had an outdoor refuge too. In the old allotment, she was at her most normal. She was a gifted gardener and Granddad had dug part of it over for her so that she could grow vegetables and flowers. Her temper might have been erratic and unpredictable, but her vegetables could depend on her to keep them regularly weeded and watered. She produced fantastic crops of home-grown potatoes, carrots, onions, green beans and sprouts, and she had a cold frame for lettuces and strawberries. For someone so destructive, she had incredibly green fingers. I learned absolutely nothing from her about gardening, however, because I would sooner have banged my head against the wall than go anywhere near her when she was working there. In any case, there were better things to do, because while she was there, the rest of us could have a go at watching the telly. There was no such thing as daytime children's telly back then, but over the weekend there'd be sports programmes that Granddad loved. I was always his lookout, watching for her to come back so that we could switch it off and scatter before she caught us.

My grandmother was ill. I knew that. Even when I was little and didn't understand much about the world beyond my own front door, I knew that other children were looked after by grandmothers who didn't behave the way she did. I knew that the way she behaved couldn't be properly explained by saying that she was a horrible person. She clearly wasn't nice, but it was obvious to me, even when I was small, that there was something wrong inside her head.

Even the sight of a silver coin could set her off. Every now and again Granddad's sister would send him a copy of the *Wakefield Telegraph* because she knew he liked to read about what was going on back in his old home town. It came rolled up in brown paper and Granddad would let me tear the wrapping off and unroll it. My job was to find the silver shilling or sixpence that she always taped to the front of it for me before she packed it up.

The first time I found a silver sixpence, I was consumed by excitement at this wonderful treat, when I heard hissing. Turning, I saw Gran staring at the coin, transfixed. Granddad quickly slipped it into his pocket. 'It's all right, Elsie,' he said soothingly.

After that, Granddad made sure I only opened the paper when Gran was busy in the kitchen, out of sight. It was just another thing on the list of rules I never questioned.

My gran could have been a wonderful grandmother. She was truly gifted in areas normally associated with nurturing, like her expertise in the allotment, and in the kitchen. It seemed strange to me that she could produce the most amazing pies and stews, soups and roasts – really good food, beautifully cooked – yet would deliver it to the oak table with a grunt or an insult, and then disappear back into the kitchen where she frequently ate standing up on her own, rather than sitting with us.

Generally Granddad or Mum did the shopping and Gran took charge of the housework and the cooking, running it like a military operation, hardly necessary in a house where there were only ever four mouths to feed because no one ever came to visit. Everything in the kitchen was done in silence, and none of us dared to go near her when she was cooking. I saw her throw packets, crockery, even pans full of hot food over Mum and Granddad if they rashly crossed into her territory when she was at work.

After the telly had arrived, she would make her

wholesome soups and stews and then sit in her place in front of it eating her own food, mostly crisps and sweets which she kept stuffed behind cushions and down by the sofa arms. She was quite unable to enjoy these amazing culinary pleasures herself, or to enjoy any praise or thanks we might have given her.

When I was about ten or eleven, Granddad gradually took over the cooking and she withdrew more and more, going out even less, eating her crisps, watching her telly.

And then she disappeared for a week. Granddad told me that she had gone to London, which I accepted at the time. Now I wonder how she would have managed in London on her own. Perhaps she went to hospital, perhaps she went to her family, although we never had any contact with them. I'll never know the answer.

Although she was becoming gradually less active, she was still barking orders, clouting us as we passed and insulting us daily. But as I got older, I found that when I was eating something that Granddad had cooked – often something from the frying pan, but at least delivered with a smile – I was increasingly left to my own devices at the oak dinner table, fork in hand, with a book propped up in front of me as I ate. What a relief that was.

Chapter Four

THE AFTERMATH OF THE OAKS EXPLOSION

The Oaks explosion was England's most deadly mining disaster of all time. The British public had become accustomed to the idea that every few years or so a bunch of miners might die in an underground explosion, but this single tragedy left almost 700 dependants – widows, children, and elderly parents – without any means of support. The scale of the slaughter drew the attention of the whole country. No one could assume that the Poor Law Union workhouses would mop up the totally destitute, or that the rest would get by. Even the largest workhouses held only 400 men, women and children. Barnsley's could hold a maximum of 300 and was not short of customers already. Something out of the ordinary had to be done.

Queen Victoria let it be known that she had become the first donor to the Oaks Explosion Relief Fund. She gave £200, as she had to the families of miners nine years earlier who had died in the Wombwell explosion, which killed 189 men and boys. The response to the Oaks disaster surpassed all expectations. A total of £48,747 (and a spare three shillings) was collected – equivalent to about £2m in today's money. It was such an extraordinary sum that at a meeting of the committee set up to administer the fund, one member felt obliged to say, 'We must ensure that we do not, by the offering of assistance to the bereaved, raise them above their proper station in life, pitiable though their situation may be.' In other words, people like Hannah and John should be helped, but not so much that they got carried away with the notion that this was a gravy train.

There was a lot of muttering about how the Oaks families had it made, as if the explosion had been a cunning get-rich-quick scheme. But in Havelock Street, the Hinchcliffes were in real trouble. Elizabeth and Annie, now eighteen and fourteen, were long out of school and had both found jobs in a local linen mill as weavers – this was acceptable work for an unmarried girl. But being under twenty-one, they were not earning adult wages, even though their shifts of eight to ten hours a day, six days a week, were just as long as the older women's. On top of that, women, of course, were not paid anything like as much as men. It wasn't uncommon for a woman to be paid half or two-thirds of a man's wage for the same work. Unemployment was high at the time and the prevailing view in society was the women shouldn't take jobs from men, who had their families to support. Giving them a man's wages would encourage them to go out to work. It was a useful double standard for employers, who were keen to employ girls and women since they were cheaper than men. And it ignored the reality, especially in mining communities after such disasters, that women were having to support families where the menfolk had been killed or disabled in their workplaces.

Every year more and more women were applying to the Barnsley Poor Law Union for charitable relief because they had been deserted by their husbands and had no family nearby to help them. The number rose from around thirty a year in the 1850s to nearer 500 in the mid-1860s. The dislocation visited on working families by the industrial way of life was really beginning to bite, and the situation was worsened by the fact that the world was also entering the first phase of one of the longest global economic depressions ever recorded. All but forgotten now, this period between the 1860s and the 1890s was referred to by everyone as 'The Great Depression' until, of course, another Great Depression arrived in the 1920s. Unemployment was rising and wages were falling. The deaths of Henry and Charles could not have come at a worse time.

Between the two of them, Elizabeth and Annie were bringing in about half a grown man's wage. Even a full man's wage wasn't enough to cover the rent on Havelock Street – around twenty shillings a month – and feed the people in it. This was why the older boys' wages had been crucial to the family finances, particularly since John's frailty meant that he and William couldn't be relied on to bring in a full week's money. The next child down, Frances, was only nine, so it would be a year or two before she could legally go out to work. Below her there were three more hungry children, six-year-old Emily, five-year-old John and baby Clara, barely a year old. The best that could be said about the situation was that Hannah was now forty-four, and hopefully near the end of her child-bearing years.

But even if William and John had been able to command a good wage, the very real problem for them in the weeks after the disaster was where on earth to find work at all. The biggest employer in the colliery business for many miles around had just gone out of business. Other mines in the area had few vacancies, as those who had tried to leave the Oaks had discovered.

'My husband and my son had left the pit three weeks before,' one stony-faced woman in Hoyle Mill told a visitor as her young daughters wept silently at the back of their kitchen. 'My son had gone back to the Oaks only two days before the explosion because he could find no other work. He sacrificed his life to gain bread for this family.'

The young man had been twenty-two years old, and his two most precious possessions, his fiddle and watch, were still hanging on the kitchen wall.

In the days after the explosion there were still around sixty colliers from the Oaks workforce who had no work to go to, and who were chasing any vacancies at other pits as hard as they could. What work there was was given to miners more experienced than William and more hale than John.

The Relief Fund was going to save the Hinchcliffes from eviction, and from being split up in the dreaded workhouse, where husbands were sent to one side and wives to another, while young children were removed from their parents altogether. Everyone feared the workhouses because mortality rates were so high, particularly in the children's dormitories. The food ration was often barely adequate, and in the workhouses run by harsh managers who observed the official guidelines about the daily allowance of food too literally, inmates who stayed too long slowly starved to death.

There was more than enough money in the relief fund to go round, but there were some aspects of its administration that, to our twenty-first-century eyes, almost defy belief. There was, for instance, no official record of the dead. There was a belated bout of head-scratching in the national government as they realized that there was no legal requirement for an employer to keep a record of who went in and out of their premises. Now that businesses were employing people in their hundreds, it had become important to do something about this, if only so that rescuers knew when to stop putting their lives in danger because they knew that everyone was out of a disaster area. There were records of some kind, of course, if only in the wages accounts. But in the case of Henry and Charles, these would have recorded only the presence of Henry as the wage-earner, since the collier paid his hurrier out of his own wages.

I was stunned to discover that the only reason we know now how many men died in the Oaks disaster is because men from the South Yorkshire Miners' Association, an organization that was then just six years old, went round the district after the disaster knocking on doors day after day, asking everyone they met if they knew of anyone who had gone to work at 5 a.m. on that fateful day and not come back. They took careful notes and slowly compiled a definitive list of those who were missing. There was more than one home to which the Association's callers were directed, where they found an elderly man or woman sitting with the shutters closed and blinds down, not eating, not lighting their fires, having given up all hope. The Association was deeply disliked by the mine owners, who suspected it of being a hotbed of subversion, but without it there's no knowing how many people would have starved to death rather than ask for charity at the workhouse.

Then there were the so-called 'Oaks Bibles', which were handed out in March the following year. Hannah and John were given one, as was every family who had lost family members in the explosion. Great care was being taken to make sure that fund beneficiaries were 'deserving', yet it was considered a valid use of the money to order 700 Bibles with a hardback cover on which was printed, in gold: 'In memory of The Awful Explosion at the Oaks Colliery, Dec 12th 1866'. They were given to parents, widows, to each bereaved child, and had bookplates inside the front cover declaring that they were a gift from the Oaks Colliery Relief Fund because their son, husband or father had lost their lives. When I asked in the area whether any families still had them, handed down the generations, no one actually spat on the ground, but it was clear that by and large, even though the disaster was well beyond living memory, no one thought much of them.

'I think they were quietly got rid of by many people,' one descendant told me. 'You used to see them in flea markets quite often fifty years or so ago with the labels ripped out. Outsiders bought them, souvenir hunters, the children and grandchildren of mining folk who had moved away from the district. Why would anyone living here want a reminder of something like that in their house?'

There was a lot of talk about how the Oaks disaster demonstrated the need for everyone to get on good terms with God, just in case they too were unexpectedly catapulted into the arms of their Maker. There was also much advice offered about how much better the bereaved would be able to cope if they humbly accepted that what had happened was divine will, however mysterious and unfathomable.

'God has ordained that, according to natural laws, gas will ignite,' wrote one particularly silly preacher in a sermon which was hardly likely to bring a bereaved nonbeliever round to his way of thinking. I have a strong faith myself, but I found much of this nonsense quite hard to take. This kind of talk must have rankled with the bereaved families who were looking not only at empty chairs by hearths but also into empty pantries.

The Bishop of Ripon was impressive, though. Although he was based sixty miles away in the north of the county, his diocese covered Barnsley and he came to visit the families himself and attended the first mass funeral on Sunday 16 December. His description of the ceremony, at which I am certain all the Hinchcliffes were present, is very moving.

'The sorrow seemed too deep for loud lamentation,' he said. 'The scene on the Sunday afternoon at the cemetery, when twenty-six of the bodies which had been recovered were buried, was deeply affecting. Thousands were present but there was no noise or confusion; every countenance betokened either seriousness or sorrow.'

The Bishop added, as an afterthought: 'Tracts [religious pamphlets] were distributed amongst the crowd and were, generally speaking, received thankfully.' Which suggests to me that a good many people refused the tracts, or made their views known even more forcefully, and I admire the Bishop's honesty at a time when the world and his middle-class brother seemed dead set on portraying the Oaks families as having accepted their fate with almost inhuman fortitude.

The tragedy brought out the well-meaning in their droves, particularly the wives of clergymen and their comfortably off friends, who toured the districts offering their own peculiar brand of comfort. This was usually a pamphlet printed with a self-denying psalm and an invitation to kneel down and pray right there and then, in their cold kitchens. It rarely included anything which could be eaten or worn or might keep a body warm.

One woman wrote an account of her tour of bereaved Oaks families and had a little booklet printed to distribute to her friends. A copy of it survives in the archives at Barnsley library. She described herself only as 'Mrs AMG', not wanting to court common publicity, and told how she had set out with her friend Mrs H on 21 December, exactly seven days after the pit had been sealed up. They went to a small row of houses on the side of the hill near Ardsley and were told that there were only two houses where families were not in mourning.

I'm amazed that Mrs AMG wasn't told where to get off as she walked about the place, accosting women who were washing dead men's clothes – almost certainly to pawn them – and pregnant widows, asking them to accept the will of God humbly and to sing a psalm or two with them. But I believe that, like the Bishop, she was an honest woman, and her account is one of the few that describes in detail what individuals were having to cope with. She had the most heartbreaking personal tragedies to record – for instance a widow with a small baby who wouldn't wash her kitchen floor because there was still one of her dead husband's footprints on it, and another woman who had lost seven relatives, including her husband and two brothers.

'It will finish me,' said a retired, disabled old collier whose three sons had not come home. He had, he said, been working in the mines since he was ten and had been underground through four gas explosions, and it was like being caught in the heart of a thunderstorm, surrounded by flashes of lightning and deafening thunderclaps.

A blind woman who had lost her first husband ten years earlier in another explosion had lost her fourteen-year-old son, her second husband and her brother. Her son, she said, had only recently dreamed of being in the pit and dying.

'It is so dreadful at night,' one woman told Mrs AMG. 'That is when we have to close the windows and doors, as we always do at the end of the day's work, ours and the men's. We always shut up the houses then, just at the time when the men should come home. It feels as if we are leaving them out in the cold. It is more than we can bear.'

I am grateful to Mrs AMG, busybody though we might accuse her of being nowadays. She was certainly brave, and she clearly listened to the people she spoke to. Like the

Bishop, she was honest about the people who told her flatly that they didn't want her pamphlets and would not kneel down with her to pray, because they expected no comfort from God after the fate that had been visited on them.

Her biggest achievement, in my eyes, is that she noticed more than the poverty of the miners' families. She recorded the emotional losses that no amount of charity could ever make good. To me, the most poignant story she tells is of the woman left alone with four small children who told her: 'My husband was such a kind man. Often, when he came home at night, I would take his black face in my hands and say to him – 'Oh, my happy, happy home!' No one could have wished for a better husband or a better friend.'

Soul mates had been lost, not just breadwinners.

The Oaks tragedy brutally cut the Hinchcliffe children off from the conventional path towards marriage and children of their own. All but two of them had to wait until they were thirty or older before they could think of leaving their parents, and one never married at all. Elizabeth Hinchcliffe, the oldest of John and Hannah's girls, was eighteen when her brothers died. Young people, particularly young men, were beginning to marry somewhat younger in the second half of the nineteenth century than their parents' generation had, and the Bishop of Ripon reported meeting a young woman of Elizabeth's age whose fiancé had been killed at the Oaks six days before they were due to marry.

It is entirely possible that Elizabeth also had a sweetheart who she lost along with her brothers. The Hinchcliffes were a fine-looking family, judging by the picture that still exists of her little brother. Despite the considerable hardship he'd experienced by then, he has regular features, good skin, an open and pleasing face and striking, gentle eyes that have reappeared in other members of our family down the generations. Yet for both Elizabeth and fourteen-year-old Annie, the simple numerical odds of finding a suitable husband had suddenly decreased sharply, given that a generation of their community's young men and teenage boys had been all but wiped out. The chances of twenty-year-old William finding a bride in the immediate future were also diminished, because there was now enormous pressure on him to devote himself to helping his parents raise his younger brothers and sisters and do what he could to keep the family solvent.

So at a time when John and Hannah might have been able to look forward to the imminent arrival of their first grandchildren, the whole family had to pull in its horns and find a way to get through the next decade, at least until the younger girls and John had reached an age when they could go out to work.

Thankfully the family did get assistance from the fund, but not on the scale that a widow would have done, even though Henry and Charles had been the family's key breadwinners. They had died unmarried and without children of their own, and they had siblings of working age, however meagre their earning power might be. As officialdom saw it, that limited the Hinchcliffes' eligibility for help.

William had to wait until little Frances, ten years his junior, had joined Elizabeth and Annie in the linen mill before he could marry. Because there was no younger family partner to go down the pit with, he carried on mining with his father for the decade after his brothers' deaths. Goodness only knows how that must have felt for the men themselves and for Hannah and the rest of the children watching them set off each morning. They must have lived each day with the fear that it would happen again; it's hard to believe that they chose to return to the pits, but what choice did they have?

There is some evidence to suggest that William managed to change trades underground, moving from hurrying and hewing to working with the construction teams who had to shore up the workings to make the roofs and walls of the galleries safe, learning the rudiments of structural engineering which could be applied just as well up top as underground. When he at last married Sarah Ann in 1875, they moved out of Barnsley and back to the scenes of his childhood, to the place where the Hinchcliffes had their deepest roots, in Cawthorne. I found records of him living there apparently happily at the age of forty with his wife and their two little girls, the elder just six years old and named for her grandmother Hannah. And there, at last, he is working safely above ground as a 'builder and contractor'.

Imagine the great sense of relief everyone who was close to him must have felt about this change of career. It was not an era when a man could easily switch jobs in the middle of his working life, and it suggests that William was a man with a great deal of determination and persistence. It's also possible that Sarah Ann was already pregnant with little Hannah when they married. Although I couldn't find her birth certificate, census records suggest that she might have been born within about seven or eight months of the wedding day. That would certainly have been the unanswerable rebuttal of any objections his parents might have had about him leaving home at last.

His father John finally gave up the struggle to earn a crust with his collier's pick the year after William's marriage. John was by then sixty-three, and even if he had been a healthy man, underground work would have been beyond him at that age. It amazes me that he managed to carry on so long. It's intriguing to see that on the 1881 census return for his family in Havelock Street, he insists on describing himself as 'coal miner' with no mention of being retired, even though it would have been more than five years since he had last been winched down a mine shaft. We have the word of Hannah herself for this when she declares some years later that John had not been able to earn a penny for the last twelve years of his life.

John had his pride and never admitted to the authorities that he could no longer contribute to the family finances. Reading down the list of the occupants of number 21 in 1881, it becomes obvious why he was so keen not to lose face before the world: there are five wage earners in the house, and four of them are his daughters, including Clara, the last of his children, who is now sixteen and has joined Elizabeth, Annie and Emily at the linen mill. Without the girls, either William could not have married, or John and Hannah would have ended their days in the workhouse. Only Frances had escaped at that point, marrying her young man at Christmas three years before when she was twenty-two.

The last of the four Hinchcliffe boys, John Clifford, was twenty years old by this time and, tellingly, his chosen occupation had absolutely nothing to do with mine work. It didn't even involve being outside in the open air. The family had somehow managed to get the boy into what was the very new job of shop assistant. His official title was 'draper', which meant that he worked on the haberdashery and cloth counter of the Co-operative Society department store in the centre of Barnsley. Hardly out of petticoats at the time of the Oaks disaster, it can be imagined that Hannah and her daughters probably spoiled little John. He married ten years later, just after his thirtieth birthday, and the marriage did not go well. Within a few years he was back home with his mother.

Of the two older girls, Elizabeth was the one who got lucky. She found her Mr Right at the age of thirty-five, a time of life when most women would have given up all hope of making a home of their own. Her escape was probably bad news for little sister Clara. She and Annie were the only wage earners left in the house throughout much of the 1890s. But Clara did get married in 1897 at the age of thirty-one.

Emily was long gone by then. Determined not to suffer the fate of almost all her other sisters, she had set her sights early on finding a boy to marry. Of all the children, she was the one who came closest to marrying before she was out of her teens, as her mother had done. She was also careful not to pick a collier. The other big trade in these parts was glass-blowing. The furnaces were fuelled by the local coal and the silica sand melted in them was brought in on the canal barges. Glass-blowers were highly skilled and well paid because no reliable means had yet been found of mass-producing bottles by machine, and there was now a huge demand for them as 'takeaway' containers since people were less willing to go to their local shops with their own jugs and bowls. So a glass-blower was good marriage material, but still her father probably said to her, 'He's not proved himself a man,' when she told him she wanted to marry Bill Swann. John, after all, had been at work for almost twenty years before he had married her mother, having demonstrated beyond all doubt that he could be trusted to get up to his work and bring home his wages. Bill Swann, who hadn't started work until he was twelve or thirteen, and was now only just twenty-one and newly qualified in his trade, was an unknown quantity.

Emily had her way, however. The couple went off to Ardsley, on the moor edge above the eastern side of Barnsley, and Emily was released from the drudgery of the linen mill and the burden of supporting her parents. She was to discover quite quickly that she would have been better off putting up with her lot and waiting a little longer, or following her mother's example in choosing an older, more sober man.

Now it was only Annie left behind, becoming in effect her mother's old age pension.

There is a poignant footnote to Annie's life. Like all the Hinchcliffes, given a fair wind and a bit of luck, she had staying power. She died in the 1930s at the age of eighty-three, a spinster who had worked in the linen mills without a break for more than fifty years. She had retired in the year that Hannah died, 1905, and that is the year in which she is listed as being added to the beneficiaries of the Oaks Disaster Relief Fund. Forty years on, there was still enough income in the fund to pay an allowance to the last few remaining relatives. The administrators accepted that her prospects of marriage and independence had been blighted by her brothers' deaths, and it's good to know that at the point when she was finally released from responsibility for her mother, a bit of good fortune came her way. Without the fund, which paid her a monthly allowance until the day she died, she would have been forced to declare herself a pauper and go to the Barnsley Poor Law Union to beg for help, and that would have been a bitter pill to swallow after she'd spent the best years of her life keeping her family out of the workhouse.

The Hinchcliffe family was missing a generation, thanks to the Oaks disaster, and it is not fanciful to think that the family history would have played itself out very differently if Henry and Charles had survived. Henry, Charles, Elizabeth, Annie – they should have been the parents of Hannah's and John's first grandchildren, and those children should have started arriving in the 1860s. Instead the first grandchild was a girl born to Frances in 1880, with Emily's Eleanor a few years later.

Just over a year after Eleanor's arrival, Emily had the second of her eleven children. It came as no surprise, when I was finally able to look at his full birth certificate, to see that he was christened Charles Henry. If Emily hoped to give him as good a life as her brothers had had in their short lives, her hope was in vain.

Chapter Five

FIGHTING BACK

'You're a filthy prostitute! Don't think you can get away from me!'

Gran managed to land a stinging blow on the back of my head as I made a dash for the door, but we both registered that she'd had to reach up high to get the usual vicious swipe to connect. I was thirteen, and I had grown.

I knew the blow was coming. But I also knew what I was going to do when it did. I danced out from under her hand, so she'd think she'd cowed me with the blow, and then stood up again, skipping backwards down the passage, flicking V-signs at her as I went.

'Fuck you, it's only a stupid telly,' I shouted, using a word I'd first heard from her, not my friends, when she stood out on the doorstep delivering her rants against the good character of the neighbours.

Then I shot out through the door into the street before she could catch her breath.

Both of us, I think, were aghast at my blatant rudeness. Running down the road I laughed like a maniac, feeling like a freedom fighter who had just blown up an enemy jeep, and not caring a bit about having to go home later and face the music. She'd lost, I'd won, and it wasn't the first time, either. Things were never going to be the same again.

My grandmother was barely five feet tall. Born in another century into abject poverty, probably never well nourished at any point in her early life, she was never going to be tall. It was probably something of a miracle that she had survived at all. But it hadn't occurred to either of us that one day I would overtake her. I may not have been a very happy girl but I was certainly a well nourished and very healthy one. Not long after my eleventh birthday I was able to look her straight in the eyes. By my thirteenth, just as adolescent attitude and hormones were kicking in, I was taller than her. Not that this would have mattered if I'd respected her. But fear is no substitute for respect, and the worm began to turn.

Gran was very surprised by this turn of events. She'd had it her own way with my mother for such a long time – even though Mum was herself a good couple of inches taller than Gran – that she had just assumed that history would repeat itself.

I was determined that it wouldn't.

Very suddenly, I was much stronger than her, but there was more to it than that. I was a product of a time when there were daily references at school and in the street to the idea that even children had rights. This was quite beyond the experience of both my gran and my mother. Fighting back against the injustice handed out by grown-ups was not as unthinkable for me as it had been for my mother. It was just a question of me finding the courage to attempt it, and I seemed to have been born with a fiery indignation against any kind of injustice.

The day arrived when, on impulse, I decided not to walk like a soldier past Gran and her precious telly, but instead to flail my arms around as I went past so that she couldn't see the screen properly. That was it, the first act of deliberate provocation – and I felt defiant rather than scared. I timed it nicely so that I could get out of the room just as she lunged at me, and into my bedroom just before she reached me.

I wasn't able to hold the door shut against her, however, and I knew I wouldn't have enough time to get across the room, open the window and climb out before she was upon me. So, heart pounding in my chest, I opted for opening the door fast and dashing past her, pretty sure she'd only be able to whack me once.

'You can't catch me,' I shouted, knowing that she didn't have a chance. It was my time now and I was going to enjoy every last minute of the chase.

'Felicity Alice, come back here now! You'll never get away from me.'

'Oh yes I will, you old witch,' I taunted. And I ran. I was laughing euphorically as I scrambled through the window, the casement catch scratching my bum.

It could fairly be said that in many ways I was my grandmother's granddaughter. Certainly my features owed more to her neatly arranged face than they did to either my father or my mother, whose soft, almost vacant appearance and nature echoed my beloved granddad much more. I had not only the glowing dark red hair of Gran's youth but also her volatility, her willingness to rise to an argument. Whether she had taught me that or I'd inherited it from her I'll never know, but it made for an explosive mix once I reached adolescence and combined it with teenage cheek.

It had taken some time to arrive at this intoxicating position. All through primary school, and even into the first couple of years of secondary school, I had remained very firmly in my place. The almost ritual banging of my head against the wall at bedtime gradually petered out, but it was replaced with the routine clout round the head that was her reaction to any transgression.

There were still many barmy rules, for which the punishment was a shower of slaps and blows round the head and shoulders, and the two that I now felt really got in the way of my life were no television and no baths. All my friends watched telly and talked about the programmes at school, and like most children I wanted to be the same as everyone else, so I felt the lack in this dimension of my life keenly, although I don't suppose it did me much harm. The 'no baths' business was much weirder. Gran, who cleaned the house daily, top to bottom, would not allow anyone other than herself to have a bath because, 'it was a filthy thing to do'. I think she meant that having to share the bath with the rest of us was filthy for her – another aspect of her obsessive ideas about cleanliness.

So we had to have stand-up washes in front of the sink. It was always freezing in the winter – there was no heater and no question of having a wall heater or radiator put in. I'd stand there, shivering and miserable, desperate, as all teenagers are, to feel fresh and clean, and all the while standing next to a perfectly good bath. On the rare Saturday mornings when Gran could conquer her agoraphobia sufficiently to get out of the house to go shopping, Granddad would immediately run a steaming hot bath and I would be first to get in. Sinking into the warm water was bliss, but these baths were always fraught with anxiety in case this turned out to be one of the days when her demons got the better of her and she returned before even getting to the bus stop.

Yet there were a few bizarre moments when it seemed as though Gran might be trying to make some kind of peace with me. On my eleventh birthday she arranged a strange party for me – I was allowed to invite Sylvia in from across the road. I had never before had such a thing as a party. We didn't even do Christmas, because she wouldn't have a tree in the house and couldn't tolerate decorations messing up the place.

The spread she put on for my party was wonderful: a trifle, pastries, a cake, a delicious meat pie. I sat on the edge of my seat all the way through it, wondering if this could really be happening, and whether Gran was about to go into crazy orbit and spoil it all. Sylvia's eyes were out on stalks at the food, but she also kept one eye on the door because she knew that Gran could be a bit odd. How could she not, given that she lived a few houses down across the road. Meanwhile Gran sat on the sofa in her usual position of power, legs crossed at her ankles, hands together, palm in palm, her strange smile on her face, and watched us. It was both surreal and nerve-wracking, like being at the Mad Hatter's tea party.

Then on my thirteenth birthday she gave me a present – a toothbrush, soap and a flannel. I had never had any kind of present from her before, ever. I got presents from Mum, who bought them through the year from her catalogue and stored them in a little leather suitcase that she kept on top of the wardrobe, and from Granddad, whose gifts were either edible – chocolate or a selection box – or a small and portable toy, like a nice ball, since anything I was given had to be taken to Dad's immediately, otherwise Gran would certainly have destroyed it during her next tantrum. Here, however, was a parcel from her, and it seemed that she had suddenly decided that it was time I paid attention to my personal hygiene. It made no difference to the no-baths rule, of course, and it didn't seem to register with her that Mum, for all her other failings, had taught me how to wash, clean my teeth and brush my hair. I was too fazed by the novelty to be as scornful as I might otherwise have been, but later, encouraged by Mum to use the new toothbrush instead of my old one, I decided Gran really was several sandwiches short of a picnic.

The mismatch between Gran's world and reality was becoming ever more obvious to me as I matured and had the opportunity to peep into other people's lives. Sylvia's mum, was always willing to let me into their house whenever I knocked on the door, even if Sylvia wasn't in, and there were many, many times when I just didn't want to go back to my own house. Often I stayed at Sylvia's until the last possible moment, until her mum gently pushed me out of the door and told me to go home.

'Don't worry, you can come back tomorrow,' were her parting words to me, always. She seemed to understand, and I loved her for that.

Things had begun to seem not as bad as they had been when I was younger. Perhaps nothing had actually changed, but I was less and less willing to give houseroom in my mind to Gran's mad rules and routines. Increasingly I stopped seeing the rules as mountains that had to be climbed and began to think of them only as tedious orders that I would put up with if I wanted a quiet life, and that I would ignore if I had the energy for a fight. After my first act of open rebellion, I started to see her silly rules as an easy means of getting my own back on her.

Having created so many must-nots, Gran had given me a whole war chest of weapons that a bolshy teenager could turn against her. I now hated her with an intensity that could sometimes feel like physical possession, and it was the most wonderful release to stand at the light switch and flick it on and off – when she didn't want me to – and say innocently, 'Am I doing it right, Gran? Am I doing it right now?', always ready to leap out of reach and get away down the passage before she could get to me. And when she went to the front door to rant, I'd stand behind her yelling at the top of my much younger voice: 'Shut up, you stupid old woman' and drowning her out. If I felt a little sad that I was lowering myself to her level, it was trumped by the more satisfying feeling of triumph that I was taking at least a little revenge.

There was always a chase, the threat of a beating, and I became cunning enough to make sure the bedroom window was open before I began to wind her up. Sometimes, however, my baiting of her was a spontaneous flare-up of fury that I couldn't bite down in a calculating way, and then I had to get into the bedroom and wedge the chair under the knob fast to keep her out.

A day came when I really snapped. I was fed up of holding the door shut against her while she stood outside raging, 'You little slut, you're no better than those druggie prostitutes across the road. You open that bloody door! I'll give you what for! You can't get away from me. You'll never be too big for a bloody good hiding!'

Won't I indeed, I thought. Right. Let her do her worst. Let her see how far it gets here and now. I pulled the chair away and flung open the door – much to her surprise – and flung it back hard against the wall.

'Come on then, do it. Come on, what are you waiting for, you old bag!'

I got hold of the door again and slammed it back against the wall. Then I kicked the door as hard as I could, and again and again. The whole wall shook – all the walls in the prefab were pretty thin, certainly not solid bricks and mortar. As I went off on my own monumental tantrum, well up to her standard, I screamed each time I kicked the door, while the knob on the other side made a great cracking dent in the plaster and plywood.

For the first time I was being the violent, out-of-control one, and I was aware that Gran, who had first watched in speechless astonishment as I played her at her own game, had now begun to cry. I stopped, turned to face her and shouted right in her face: 'Now bugger off!' and slammed the door shut. Then I let myself out through the bedroom window.

The next time I was slamming the door back and forth and Gran had stopped yelling at me and was crying, Granddad took a stand. Unfortunately not against Gran. I was so busy screaming, 'Why aren't you hitting me? Go on, you old witch!' that I was stunned into silence when Granddad slapped me hard across the face.

'That's enough!' he said sternly.

I crumpled into hurt tears. My beloved Granddad had never hit me before. He led Gran away and then came back to my room, where I was curled up on the bed, sobbing.

'I love you, Felicity,' he said wearily, 'but you're out of control. You're going too far.'

After all the years I'd suffered Gran's bullying, a part of me felt that what I had done was fair. Deep down I knew it wasn't that simple. I felt awful. His words didn't make any lasting difference, though. It was too late for that.

My mother and father did not escape my fury. Soon after my thirteenth birthday, I flatly refused to carry on with the weekly visits to my dad. It simply struck me one particularly sunny Sunday, when all my friends were out in the streets playing, that I had better things to do than to hang around in an old man's dingy flat. Especially an old man I didn't like and who didn't seem to know my real name.

Mum wasn't happy about it, but by that time I had

decided she was pathetic and I didn't care what she thought. I had stopped moping about hoping that she would rescue us from Gran, and I knew it wasn't difficult to get away with not doing what she wanted. She had no power. She wasn't a worthy opponent. I still occasionally felt sorry for her, especially when Gran had her in a corner. It was painful, really, seeing one grown-up so afraid of another and so incapable of standing up for herself, but I pushed those feelings right down when Gran turned on her, just wishing it to be over as quickly as possible.

'Slut, put the dishes away, I told you! Why haven't you done it?' she screamed at my mother one evening after tea. Mum had gone off to the bedroom to get herself ready to go to Dad's while Granddad and I did the pots. Gran jumped on her as she walked back into the living room, pinned her against the built-in cupboard in the corner next to the fire and bashed her around the head, making a terrible mess of Mum's freshly combed and hair-sprayed hair.

I hung back in the opposite corner of the room. It was early summer and I had been hoping to sneak out myself before Gran could order me to get to bed, and maybe meet up with some friends in the street and hang around for a couple of hours before it got dark.

I heard Granddad's voice behind me say 'El-sie!' on a slow rising note, as if she was a small child thinking of doing something naughty being warned off by a watchful parent, instead of a pensioner beating the hell out of her grown-up daughter.

I felt a moment of shame that I hadn't spoken up for Mum myself. I could have pulled Gran off her, and Gran wouldn't have been able to stop me. But somehow this was against the rules of engagement, and although I was rebellious in all manner of ways, I never did cross the invisible line to battle with Gran physically. It would have been very easy for me to turn the tables and bash her, but I just couldn't do it.

I began to notice how hard it was for any of us to look each other in the eye after Gran had given Mum a hiding. Granddad had a kind of exasperated, guilty, helpless look about him, as if he was damned if he did and damned if he didn't. I sometimes saw him bury his head in his hands as Gran flared up at one or the other of us, as if he was weary beyond endurance at having to deal with this day in and day out. Why don't you *do* something, I'd think, frustrated by his passivity. Mum would hang her head and keep her eyes on the ground, like a puppy that feels responsible for the kicking it's been given.

Mum adopted this stance when I told her I wasn't going to Dad's any more but, with plenty of practice under my belt, I simply decided not to see that she was hurt.

'You don't really care about me or him,' I snarled at her one Sunday morning when she pestered me to walk over to Edgehill with her. 'You just don't want to have to tell him I'm not coming.'

I said it just to be nasty, but, judging by the way she flinched, this was pretty close to the truth. She couldn't handle confrontation, even over something as minor as this.

After that, I only went over to my dad's when I had no friends to play with or the weather was so bad that it was the only way of getting out of the prefab and away from Gran. It wasn't often. I made a conscious decision to stop fretting over how I was supposed to feel about the man who called me Jackie, and consigned him to the distant outskirts of my life. If he minded, he didn't show it. Occasionally I saw him in the distance on his bike with his ladders, and I was careful to make sure he didn't see me. Once I heard a voice calling 'Jackie! Jackie!' as I walked along Seamer Road on my way home from school, having just got off the bus from town. My teenage dignity was outraged. I couldn't believe he was doing this to me in public. Naturally, I ignored him.

'I want you to come and see me, Jackie,' he called. His voice was odd, weak. 'I'm ill, I need to see you.'

This did make me look round, and I saw that since I'd last seen him some months before, something had happened to him – he seemed to have shrunk and he looked old. He had always looked too old to me, but now he looked even older. I was so ashamed. It was four o'clock in the afternoon and up and down Seamer Road there were loads of teenagers I knew, and I could feel them all looking at me, wondering what was going on.

'I don't care!' I shouted at him, hoping to shut him up before he could reveal in public that he was my father, and turned my back on him. I walked fast to get away from him as quickly as possible. What do I owe him? I asked myself breathlessly as I stalked down the road, trying to ignore my panicky heartbeat. What kind of father has he ever been to me? When has he ever looked after me? I didn't look back.

*

The battle between Gran and me became steadily more verbal. Mum usually took refuge in the bedroom and sat on her bed. Granddad sat at the oak dining table near the kitchen, hiding behind his newspaper while the storm raged and Gran and I traded abuse.

Once I was fourteen, I discovered the miracle of the Saturday job and enjoyed an independent income for the first time. I waitressed and chamber-maided during the tourist season in one of the many hotels in our seaside town, and I worked at John Rowntree's, the rather posh Scarborough grocer's founded by a cousin of the famous York chocolate-making family. With money in my pocket, I discovered fashion and make-up, and started going out with my friends more and more. It was only a matter of time before I discovered boys. Gran's judgement of the new me was predictable. As she increasingly directed her slanderous tirades about immorality at me as well as the neighbours, it didn't seem unreasonable to go and find out what it was that made the opposite sex so very dangerous.

The boy who helped me with this investigation was called Dave, and I found him one early summer's afternoon a few months after my fourteenth birthday as I walked down the valley, which was how we all referred to Valley Road, which ran down into the centre of the town alongside the Victorian pleasure gardens of Valley Park. I was with my friend Elaine from school when I saw this boy across the road. He was tall, with longish blond hair and a lazy, lop-sided grin that made my insides do a hop and a skip. He was with a couple of other boys of about the same age, all about sixteen. They looked impossibly grown-up and manly.

'The blond one is *gorgeous*,' I said to Elaine.

'He lives in the street next to mine,' said Elaine. 'Let's go and say hello.'

We had no trouble doing things like this. Elaine and I and two other friends were The Popular Girls in our year, the ones who were right up there – if the qualifications for being top of the heap involved being good at make-up, having the most fashionable clothes, being pretty, and going out to clubs and pubs. If working hard and concentrating in lessons had been the measurement, then we would certainly have been at the bottom of the pile, but getting good marks wasn't the kind of achievement we rated highly. I had failed my 11-plus, despite having always been at the top of my classes throughout primary school. Now, at the comprehensive school, where little was expected of any of us, I had come to the conclusion that education was the most boring way imaginable of marking time until you grew up and could run your own life.

I discovered years later, when I was a teacher myself, that in those days it was not uncommon for any child from a disadvantaged background, such as my one-parent family living on a council estate, to be filtered out of the 11-plus passes regardless of their marks. Two assumptions were made: one, that an equal number of boys had to pass because there were allotted grammar school places for them, even though it was common for more girls to have higher marks; and two, that unless their marks were absolutely outstanding, it was believed that kids from disadvantaged backgrounds wouldn't be able to cope with academic rigour.

Maybe I failed anyway, but I do know now that I should have passed. I also believe that regardless of whether I passed or not, I should have had a decent school to go to. And so should all the other children I was at a rubbish school with. Heaven knows that I had no encouragement at home to do well. Once at secondary school, where girls like me were assumed to be destined for typing and marriage, I lost all motivation. Once I'd hit puberty and was having my shouting matches with Gran, I was only highly motivated to escape – from her, from school, from any rules of any kind.

In my mind, going to work full-time would mean being able to earn money and look after myself. It sounded great. I was among the last batch of British schoolchildren who could opt out completely and choose to leave school at fifteen without taking a single exam. Once I realized this was possible, I practically ticked off the days.

I and the other three girls in my preening, self-important little gang were very sure of ourselves. I don't think we were nice or kind. If I were to go back in time and sit next to Felicity Baines in class, I'm not sure I would have liked me very much.

'Hey, girls, what did you score in that English test. I came top,' I gloated as I stared at Jane Thomson, who was not the brightest button in the top stream.

We tormented Jane. In fact we bullied her. She was neither pretty nor smart. Or so we thought. We teased and tormented her and any other girls in our class who weren't, in our estimation, worthy of being in our 'in' crowd.

Elaine was an exception, and the nicest of us – not quite as cocky, and less ready to insult anyone we didn't think matched up to our standards.

'Nice' girls would not have accosted those boys on Valley Road that day. Elaine probably wouldn't have done it, either, except that she knew Dave and was in a position to introduce me to him. There was much giggling and flirting, and then girls and boys went their separate ways.

A couple of days later Elaine asked if I wanted to come round to her house after school.

'The blond one. He stopped me this morning and said I was to ask my friend if she wanted to go round and see him.'

I could hardly have got round there faster. Dave invited me into his house and I was swept away by the comparative luxury of it all – a record player and loads of records, a radio that he was allowed to turn on to Radio One whenever he wanted to. He could listen to the chart countdown on a Sunday evening and find out what was number one, ready to talk about it with his mates at school on Monday morning, whereas I had to pretend that I knew, or see if I could find out by some other means.

On that first evening he asked me what I wanted to do. I assumed he meant 'with the rest of your life'. So I started telling him that I wanted to be a secretary.

'No,' he said, stopping me in mid-sentence. 'This evening. What do you want to do this evening?'

It's a fact that if you spend years telling a girl she's a slut and a prostitute, the chances are that losing her virginity will not seem that big a deal. There are lots of other reasons why young girls become sexually active far too young, of course, but having seen hundreds of hormonal teenagers pass through my classrooms, I'd say almost all of those reasons begin with believing that you're unloved and unloveable. With Dave, up in his attic room, well away from his mum downstairs, I discovered, to a soundtrack of Bowie, Bolan and The Who, that sex was not the outrageously disgusting and dangerous thing that Gran's rantings suggested.

I was incredibly lucky. Dave was a nice boy, kind and caring. He was also a virgin, and he wanted a proper relationship where we spent time together and didn't play the field. For a girl like me with so little self-worth, my first experience of a lover could have been so much worse. I managed to avoid the dangerous glamour of all the terrible boys I knew who didn't care about the girls they dated and choose myself a good one.

Dave lived with his mum – she was on her own after a divorce, so that part of their lives was fairly familiar to me – and he had the whole attic floor of their Victorian house to himself. We were allowed to paint it whatever colour we liked. It ended up purple and black, very 1970s. And, of course, there was a television that we were allowed to watch, a treat almost as amazing as being Dave's girlfriend, which – despite all my posturing at school – was a privilege I couldn't quite believe had been granted me.

I still had to take the insults from Gran, of course, when I got home. This happened more often in the mornings these days, because to avoid her I began timing my arrival at home in the evenings to coincide with Granddad's return from his shift as doorman at the Conservative Club. This meant that, as I turned fifteen, I was regularly staying out until 11 p.m. – not good for my concentration in class. But the alternative was to obey Gran's rule that, even at fifteen, I should be in bed at 7 p.m.

If I couldn't meet up with Granddad, perhaps because there was some function on at the club and he wasn't off duty until the early hours, I'd sneak round the side of the house and tap on my bedroom window, hoping that Mum would come to the front door and let me in. If Gran hadn't been long in bed and that was too risky, she would open the window as quietly as she could so that I could climb in, although I didn't like doing this because it laddered my tights and risked ruining my precious clothes. This was the one time when I felt as though my mum and I had a real bond – partners in crime dedicated to outwitting Gran. I was still in for an earful in the morning, of course, if I didn't get out of the house and off to school before she came out of her room, but at least the night generally ended peacefully.

For a year or so, from just after my fourteenth birthday to a couple of months after my fifteenth, I was, despite my home life, a very happy girl who had the most fantastic boyfriend in the world. Being the cheeky, bolshie madam I was, I was delighted to be able to announce loudly in assembly the morning after I'd lost my virginity that I'd 'done it' with my boyfriend – a pretty shocking thing for a fourteen-year-old in 1971, but I didn't care who heard or what they thought. Who was going to say anything worse to me than what Gran had already said?

Then, as summer and freedom approached, everything seemed to crumble. Dave finished with me and quickly found another girlfriend. I couldn't accept it at all.

After two or three tearful scenes when I pleaded with him to go out with me again, he started avoiding me.

'Please, Dave. Just remember how good we were together. I'm so sorry that I've been so difficult. Can't we try again?'

'It's over, Flic. I can't do this any more. I've tried but you're just too much.'

'Please, Dave. I promise I'll try harder'.

'It's not about trying harder, Flic. It's over. Move on. I have.'

I was devastated. There were three days in a row when I stood on the pavement outside his house from morning until afternoon looking up at his dormer window, hoping that he would look out and see me and come down to tell me he'd changed his mind.

Eventually his mum, who had always been nice to me, came out to have a chat.

'You need to move on with your life, lovie,' she told me. 'You and Dave have had some lovely times together, but he isn't going to ask you out again. He needs some space – the two of you are too young to only be with each other.'

I became dimly aware that I had been a very needy girlfriend indeed, and I had scared him. I had gone round to his house at almost every opportunity because it was so much more wonderful than being in my own home, and I was besotted with him and besotted with the whole business of feeling loved after feeling very unloved for so long. Needless to say, Dave had never come to the prefab. I hadn't let him.

There was something more, however, and it was something a lot less forgivable than my clinginess. It didn't happen often, but there were times when I found myself baiting him quite deliberately, trying to make him angry. I wanted to, needed to – it was what I understood relationships to be and it made me feel in some funny way more comfortable. It was always over the most trivial things, like which friends to go out with or where to go, or about him choosing to go out with his mates rather than me, or – and this was a real bone of contention – deciding to do his schoolwork instead of spending time with me. I, of course, wasn't doing any schoolwork. I could never take no for an answer and sometimes I would nag and goad until he lost his temper, at which point I'd act hurt and offended.

Dave was a really nice boy whose mother treated him well, and he had seen nothing in his life of the kind of treatment I'd been living with for all my fifteen years, yet there were a couple of times when he felt driven to slap me on the face. My technique combined Gran's verbal abuse with Mum's whiny, needling method of getting her own back. I said such awful things about him, his mum and his life that I can't even allow myself to remember what they were, but they were horrible enough, obviously, to make him so furious that when I wouldn't shut up, he slapped me to make me stop. It only happened two or three times, and each time he was full of remorse. 'I'm so sorry, Flic,' he'd stammer, horrified at what he'd done.

But I loved it. It satisfied something very deep and dark inside me when he apologized, promised he wouldn't do it again, wanted to kiss and make up. I felt as if I was getting everything I had ever wanted, including all the apologies owed me by my grandmother, none of which I would ever get from her, of course. It was not surprising that in the end Dave found me far too intense, too needy – emotionally greedy would be more accurate – and felt like he needed some air. I was just impossible to be around for any length of time.

I was still wallowing in the heartbreak of it all a couple of months later when there was a knock on the door of the prefab. I answered it, as I usually did – there was no question of Gran getting out of her chair for the door – and saw a police officer standing there. I was aware of Mum somewhere behind me trying to vanish into the back of the house like a toad trying to scramble under a stone, which was odd because she didn't generally react to what was going on around her.

'Hello, love. Is your mum in?' he asked.

'Yes, I'll just get her.'

I found Mum sitting on her bed. She wouldn't look me in the eye and refused to come. 'Ask him what he wants,' she said.

Back at the door, I announced: 'She's poorly, she can't come.'

The officer looked a little uncertain. 'It won't take a

moment, love.' He hesitated. 'I'm really sorry to bother you at all at a time like this, but it's important. It's about Major, and I just need to ask a couple of questions.'

'What about him?' Now the officer really did look uncomfortable. 'That's my dad. What's he done?'

'He hasn't done anything, love. Nothing.' Another pause. 'Could you just ask your mum again if I can step in for a few words? Tell her it's the Coroner's Officer.'

I didn't know much, but I did know that coroners and death went together. I went back to Mum and demanded to know what was going on. 'He's still here, and he won't go away.'

Mum couldn't look at me. 'I'll come and speak to him,' she said at last, as miserable as I'd ever seen her.

It turned out that she'd known for two or three days that Dad was dead. She had been the one to find him collapsed on the floor in his kitchen. I had been vaguely aware that she had gradually stopped going round there quite so often, wasn't quite so fast off the mark after tea to get out and over to his flat. I suspect he'd told her not to come when he was feeling ill. Finding him like that when he had been dead so long can't have been nice for her, but I didn't think about that. I decided to be unreasonably furious with her for not telling me, for leaving it to the Coroner's Officer, waiting till he came round to discuss procedures and next of kin with her. Dad's death was sudden, unexplained and unwitnessed, so there was going to have to be an inquest. Quite when she would have got round to telling me otherwise, I don't know. It turned out he'd died of pneumonia.

A week later there was a funeral, organized by Dad's

eldest son, Andrew. As Mum and Dad had never married, his eldest son took on the next of kin role and came down from his Lake District home to bury his father. Andrew had discovered that kids had broken into Dad's flat and stolen everything, including my precious Monopoly, my Spirograph and my Tiny Tears doll. I cried for the toys, strangely enough, even though I was a sophisticated know-it-all teenager. I wasn't sure I felt anything for the man, but I did feel guilty about the way I'd brushed him aside on the street when he'd asked me to visit him. I also felt guilty about not feeling more upset than I did.

Andrew stayed for a couple of days after the funeral and we talked lots about our different lives. He told me about his children and wife and I could see he was happy. We took ourselves into Scarborough town after the funeral and he bought me a silver crucifix from H. Samuel's to keep me safe. We said we'd meet up again and that I should visit him on his farm. But somehow it never happened.

I was, all in all, in quite a state. I had a broken heart and a dead father I didn't seem to care enough about, and I had lost face in front of the other people at school when I lost Dave. His grammar school was literally next door to our comprehensive school, and everyone knew he'd chucked me.

If I needed any other reason to leave school as quickly as possible and get out into the world, Gran gave it to me. It was a matter of weeks until the end of the summer term, my last term at school, and I had decided I would go to secretarial college for a year to acquire some skills instead of getting a job straightaway, and save up from my Saturday jobs for a month's advance rent on a flat of my own. I persuaded myself that this was the sensible thing to do, even though it would delay the day when I had enough money for rent and therefore meant I had to carry on living at the prefab. Not full escape quite yet, then, but it was within sight.

My gang of friends was going out, properly, to a nightclub, to celebrate the coming of summer and the approach of the end of school and, as we saw it, of being a child. I had bought a long frock, a Laura Ashley-style print with frilly bits and a low neckline. I was all ready to go to Elaine's, made-up and beautifully dressed, feeling happy despite my recent troubles, and went into the living room to say goodbye to Granddad and Silver.

At which point Grandma came out of the kitchen with a pan of hot water and threw it over me – over my hair, my face and down my front.

Fortunately it wasn't scalding, but it was hot enough to hurt. I stood there speechless for what felt like half a minute. Granddad's mouth was wide open. I was so shocked, I couldn't quite move into shouting mode.

'What did you do that for?' I eventually asked her, gasping.

'You're a slut, dressed up like that. You're no better than you should be,' she screeched.

I looked at her, feeling totally in control. I picked up my coat and my bag and said simply, 'I'm going now,' and walked out of the door. At that very moment I knew it was the end. That tomorrow I would leave and never come back.

I heard Granddad's weary voice behind me saying, 'Elsie, Elsie. Oh God, Elsie, what have you done? You've gone too far this time. Why did you do it?'

I went to Elaine's, soaked and bedraggled as I was, and they dried me out. I re-did my face and defiantly insisted on going out rather than letting Gran defeat me. For the first time I opened up to them about my home life. I told them I couldn't stand it any more. I was tired of fighting. I would get a bedsit. I'd find a floor to sleep on. Elaine's mum, seeing that I was serious, told me to come and stay with her and Elaine, rather than do anything risky.

'Until you get on your feet,' she said. 'You might even decide you want to go back to your mum once things have calmed down.'

She had no idea, I thought, gratefully accepting the offer.

That night, at about 1 a.m., I snuck in through the bedroom window for the last time, exhilarated after a fantastic night out, and excited at the promise of somewhere to go to begin my life – my real life – away from Gran. I climbed into bed after getting undressed with the usual stealth, and lay in bed in the dark planning the next morning quite calmly. When I had it all sorted out in my mind, I had no trouble at all getting to sleep.

I ate the breakfast Granddad gave me that morning and went back to my bedroom. Gran was unusually quiet, and I had the sense that everyone, including the dog, was watching and waiting, wondering what I would do next.

For the first time ever, it was me, not Gran, who was the centre of everyone's attention.

While I was packing my stuff into an old suitcase, Mum came in. She sat down on the bed, put her hands in her lap and her head in the kicked puppy position, and cried.

'What's going to happen to me if you go?' she sobbed.

I looked at her coldly, thinking that if I could do it at fifteen, why couldn't she, a grown woman, get it together sufficiently to do the same. Putting on my coat, I walked back into the living room. This was a scene I had been fantasizing about for months, possibly years, and I was going to milk it.

'I'm leaving,' I announced.

Granddad was at the table, staring down at his paper, but I could see how upset he was. He'd obviously been expecting it. I put my arms round his shoulders and squeezed him, promising to come back to see how he was, and then I knelt down and wrapped myself around my beloved Silver. Leaving my lovely dog behind, knowing I would probably never have the chance to play with him again, was the only part that brought me close to tears.

Gran sat silently next to the fire, in front of the telly, refusing to notice me. I hardened my heart and did much the same, refusing to let the fear show. I refused even to let it take hold inside me.

And I walked out into the street.

I was going out into the world. I could get a job and pay my own way and have fun without having to ask permission or care about what other people thought, as long as I didn't break the law. I didn't know then that I was getting a chance at independence that few women in my family had been allowed. All I knew was that I intended to take full advantage of everything that was on offer. I was finally free.

Chapter Six

EMILY AND BILL

When Emily married William Swann a few days before Christmas in 1881, she probably thought she had grasped freedom too as she went off to live in the newly rented house in Ardsley, near Bill's parents, Alexander and Ann, and the other three Swann brothers.

There was a rapidly growing clan of Swanns in this district, even though the family had not been in the area for more than a decade. Bill had been born in York and his older brothers in his parents' native north-east, near Sunderland, traditionally the heart of England's glass-blowing industry. In the mid-1800s when Bill was born, glass-blowing was an up-and-coming trade and new glass-blowing enterprises were springing up wherever there was coal for the furnaces, canals to take the glass products to their markets, and plenty of new industrial communities full of people wanting to buy things from shops in glass bottles and jars.

Maybe Alexander Swann had heard that the wages were better outside Sunderland where glass-making shops were two a penny, or maybe he just wanted to get his family out of an area where new industry and the old-fashioned behaviour of sailors home from the sea had combined to create a region that was increasingly notorious for its hard-drinking, handy-fisted men and grinding poverty. It's also possible that he was invited to take his skills to a different part of the country. The Wearside newspapers frequently carried adverts placed by employers from outside the area hoping to lure skilled glass-blowers to their factories, where they might put together a pool of experts who could then train their own local workers.

The Swanns were regarded as foreigners, even though this was an era when the community in and around Barnsley was in a perpetual state of flux, and families were constantly coming and going according to their rapidly changing fortunes and the precarious supply of work everywhere. But then the Hinchcliffes weren't thought of as locals either, and they had moved in from a village only seven miles away on the north-western edge of the town.

Alexander, Ann and the older Swann boys still had the strange clipped consonants and distinctive vowels of their native Wearside. The parish records show that the family and its trade of glass-blowing went back at least three generations there, but there's also a suggestion that these Swanns had come from Ulster at some point in the 1700s – perfectly likely, since the Irish were and remain the largest ethnic minority in the north-east. Glass-blowing was regarded as thirsty work, and beer seemed to be the cure for it. Whether or not this was the root of the Swanns' rather uninhibited approach to life, they were considered a rather wild lot compared with the Barnsley miners. That might be exactly what Emily Hinchcliffe loved about them. She had a share of wildness herself. Although there are no youthful pictures of her left, all the evidence suggests that she was a strikingly beautiful girl. No wonder she and Bill were drawn to each other, and no wonder everyone around them, especially Emily's family, shook their heads and said that no matter how handsome a couple they made, nothing good could come of a union between two such wilful youngsters.

On the face of it, Emily's marriage to Bill began on a sound financial footing. Emily had employment, and although she would have to give that up as soon as the first child came along, it gave her some income for the time being with which to prepare and furnish her first independent home. Bill worked in one of the few trades where wages were generous. Not only was it an absolutely essential job, but it was also difficult to learn – it took a full eight years' apprenticeship just to become a 'footmaker', the lowest rung on the glass-blowing ladder, and many more years to get to 'servitor' or fully fledged 'workman'. The footmaker offered a small piece of molten glass – a foot – to the piece the workman was making, to help him keep his hand and his spinning steady. The last part of the process was cutting off the foot, and this, along with the wielding of any smoothing irons or moulds to print an embellishment on the glass, was done by the more skilled servitor.

In the 1880s, a time-served footman could earn about 35 shillings a week and a servitor between 45 and 50 shillings; a workman could earn as much as 60 shillings – or £3 – a week, which compared very well with a fit young collier's average earnings of about 50 shillings a week. Glass-blowing was one of the earliest trades to have powerful and well organized workers' unions that protected minimum earnings and regulated training, and not everyone could get an apprenticeship – you had to have family connections.

Like all other apprentices, Bill served his indenture out with his sponsors – his father and brothers – assigned to one of their 'chairs'. The 'chair' was the three-man squad in which the glass-blowers worked, and each chair generally trained one apprentice at a time. Bill would have fetched and carried, watched and learned until he was well grown enough, strong enough and trustworthy enough to take the blowing rod and have a go at spinning and blowing himself.

I want to be fair to Bill. His trade was a tough one in all sorts of ways. It had none of the physical danger of mining, but when I looked at what would have been required of Bill when he started work in the early 1870s, I had to admit that it was hardly an easy option.

The molten glass stood in four large pots, arranged around the searing red-hot heat of a bellows-fed furnace so that they could all be kept hot and worked together, one or two gangs of men in their 'chairs' to each pot. The pots, generally about three feet high and three feet in diameter, were made of fire clay and glowed as vividly orange-red as the molten glass when they were at full temperature. The men must have sweated buckets in the course of a day's work, hence the thirst.

It took so long to get the pots up to temperature and to

melt each batch of glass that the blowers had to work on rolling shifts, arriving whenever the glass was ready for them. A shift could begin at two in the morning, and that was generally the time the working week began on winter Mondays, since the furnace keepers were allowed to start their fire as soon as the sun had set on the Sabbath. Even the most ardent social reformers, worried about eleven- and twelve-year-olds working in the trade, found it hard to see how this system could be changed. Glass took a certain length of time to melt, and fuel cost money.

Bill would have worked six hours on and six hours off until the week's work was done, doing about eight shifts in all. For four solid days, working to this traditional pattern, glass-blowers worked and rested and worked again, never getting a full night's sleep until they knocked off for the week. During this period they wouldn't dare to sleep deeply even when they did rest, in case they didn't get to the next shift on time. With sleep patterns so habitually disrupted, a few pints of beer would have gone down very well when knock-off time came, and Bill and his colleagues, well paid as they were, would have had money to spare for such indulgence. No doubt the alcohol helped Bill get to sleep after four disrupted nights. Anyone who has ever done shift work knows how that feels.

This was a way of life guaranteed to create grumpy men, too tired to feel content, or too hung-over to be good company. Put a couple's first baby into the picture, in a tiny two-bedroom house with no running water, and tempers must have been short.

Bill Swann's own family described him as a headstrong

young man, and he had fallen for a girl who was his match in that department. If passion had brought Bill and Emily together, a stubborn refusal to give way on both sides began to drive them apart almost as soon as the ink was dry on the parish register. If Bill started out trying to be a model husband, it didn't last long.

Emily was free of her parents and the linen mill, but she probably hadn't bargained for servicing the very different kind of working routine from the collier's shifts that she knew at first-hand from her own family. She very quickly began to see a rather different Bill Swann from the handsome, exceptionally strong young man who had been such good fun, so generous with his money, and so passionate when he came courting her during his long weekends.

Before their marriage, Bill had shown every sign of becoming a well-off husband who had plenty of free time, and a willingness to spend his spare money on her. As time went by and the novelty of marriage and family life wore off, Bill began to rant about keeping the baby, Eleanor, quiet while he was trying to get some sleep between shifts. There were some days when he didn't come home for twenty-four hours after he'd completed his weekly cycle, and less and less of the money came home on pay day. Emily, never the shy, retiring type, did not let this pass without comment, I'm sure, and Bill started to get a little too handy with his fists when she wouldn't shut up about the unpaid rent, the lack of food and clothes, the difficulty she was having finding a coal merchant who would let her have coal on credit. The colliers' families around her got cheap coal or even free coal, depending on which colliery the husbands worked at. The Swanns had to pay full price, and Bill wasn't the man to save for a rainy day. He was taken to court for hitting a coal merchant about five years after his marriage, probably because the man wanted his bill paid and had the bad luck to call just after Bill had got home from the pub.

There was a fair bit of making-up, of course, particularly in the early days, and Charles Henry arrived almost a year to the day after Eleanor, followed rapidly by Annie, Clifford, a third baby boy who died in infancy, and Frances, all two years apart, just like her mother's children. However, whereas Hannah had lost at most two or three babies and one half-grown child out of a brood of fifteen by the time she was delivering her last child, Emily had lost five out of eleven children by the time she was in her early forties. She might not have been as capable a manager as Hannah, but it seems that a greater difference was that the Swanns were constantly short of the necessities of life, including a decent house to live in.

It is indicative that Emily gave up her first-born Eleanor quite early on to make her home with her grandmother Hannah and her aunts. It was quite common for large families of the time to send an older child to live with its grandparents, but it was usually for mutual benefit – the aim was not only a better life for the child, but also company and domestic help for the older generation. For that to be possible, the child obviously had to be older than five. The fact that Eleanor was so young, no older than five, when she went to live with Hannah says clearly that this was a one-way act of charity towards the Swanns. The

Hinchcliffes were taking the burden of at least one hungry mouth off their hands, and probably protecting a favourite grandchild from the horrors of her parents' house. I wouldn't have been surprised to discover that they wanted to get their hands on Charles Henry too. The chances of that, however, must have been remote. Even a man as heedless of his wife and children as Bill Swann must have hoped, like his father and grandfather before him, that Charles was a son to whom he would be able to pass on the mysteries of the Swann family trade.

There was another important difference between Hannah's family life and Emily's, and that was that John Hinchcliffe had never been prosecuted for assaulting his wife. Bill was charged and convicted of causing Emily significant injury. That isn't to say that John definitely never struck Hannah. John had, after all, married at a time when the law looked at a married couple and saw only one human being, the husband. A wife had almost no legal identity at all. But what we can be sure of is that, unlike Bill, John always kept his family well housed, and that he found the pennies to send his children to elementary school in an era when he didn't necessarily have to. Even the resourcefulness of a woman like Hannah couldn't have compensated for the kind of behaviour that Bill Swann inflicted on his family.

Women's lives were beginning to change, little by little, towards the end of the 1800s. During the 1870s, wives had become entitled to be the legal owner of any money they earned instead of being obliged to regard it as their husband's property, and for the first time the law recognized their right to support from their husbands if they were deserted. Shortly before Emily was born, it had become possible for wives to seek a divorce if their husbands were violent. A woman in Emily's position could not possibly have afforded to do such a thing, of course, and the reality was that everyone carried on believing that a man had every right to hit his wife – it was accepted without question that he could justify even the most severe beating if she had not done as she was told. Even so, men who routinely used their fists on their wives were not admired. They were, in fact, universally despised by their neighbours. But it was rare for an outsider to intervene, and when a wife was seen as disloyal or even just a bit too openly critical of her husband, it was often felt that she was responsible for provoking the attack.

So if he was charged, Bill Swann's attack on Emily must have been particularly vicious. The precise details of his conviction for 'aggravated assault' against her are lost. Aggravated assault in this context suggests much more than a random act of violence. Bill must have used a weapon of some kind on her – a pot, a chair, a ladle, maybe even the poker from the range – and his attack must have been sustained. It is also clear from the comments of a local police officer that this was not, by a very long chalk, his first serious attack on her, and that he was prosecuted as a last resort because it was felt by senior officers in the area, to whom he was well known, that he had to be stopped in his tracks before he actually murdered Emily. The police of the 1890s did not usually get involved in domestic disputes, but by this time Bill Swann was well known for his temper.

Bill appeared in court no fewer than twelve times. The law-abiding Hinchcliffes must have shaken their heads a great deal over the shame he was bringing on the family. The local newspapers reported all court proceedings in careful detail. All his offences had something to do with his excessive drinking and his total lack of self-control. There were the two convictions for assault on Emily and the coalman, and three for being 'drunk and riotous', which was a much more serious offence than being drunk and disorderly – for which he also had a conviction – because it involved causing damage to property. Bill seems to have done this often in the local pubs when he was refused more drink.

He also had a number of convictions for illegal gambling, and one brought under the Poor Law Act which was a nineteenth-century version of modern-day benefit fraud, when he claimed help from the workhouse guardians by posing as an unemployed itinerant although he had a perfectly well-paid job. I assume he needed the money to pay for his gambling and drinking.

Even though he came back before the magistrates again and again, the punishment for his wrongdoings was only ever a fine. Unless they were dealing with an offence of theft or burglary, magistrates took the view that a man who still had a job was best kept out of prison so that he could continue to work and feed his family. So went the theory.

To paint a more graphic picture of the unequal battle that was going on in the Swann household, Bill Swann was about five feet six inches tall and could, for six hours together, manipulate as much as nine pounds of glass well beyond arm's length on the end of a five-foot-long metal rod. Try slinging three bags of sugar in a towel off the end of a broom handle to get some idea of the strength and stamina this involved. Colliers were broad in the shoulder, but no one messed with a glass-worker at closing time. Emily, by contrast, was four feet ten inches tall and weighed about eight stone. She must have been very badly injured indeed to induce someone – perhaps one of her sisters or a brother-in-law – to go to the local magistrate and lay a complaint.

Bill was only fined, as was to be expected, but one thing that can be said for him is that he went back to work – he always went to work, no matter how hard he had been partying – and had the fine paid in short order. Perhaps he was even contrite and asked for forgiveness. Perhaps, for a while, there was a flare-up of the passion the pair had once clearly had for each other. Or maybe he just went home and resumed his place as head of the household, expecting obedience, passive acceptance of whatever he did, and his dinner on the table. Emily would have had no means of getting rid of him without putting herself and the children in the workhouse.

As if that wasn't bad enough, Bill Swann is also described in official documents as being frequently 'lost in debauchery'. This could simply mean that he drank to excess without inhibition, but in Victorian times it was more often a veiled way of saying that he used prostitutes. If he did, then he did it often, and everyone in the district knew about it, adding to Emily's many humiliations.

It seems that, just like me, Emily didn't do obedience or

passive acceptance. Bill Swann was an irresponsible, selfish and vicious bully, and Emily's refusal to take his treatment of her meekly and be the submissive wife, which was at odds with the attitudes of the society she lived in, meant she had to pay a price. She became a nagging wife, at times as foul-mouthed as her husband, and the fights that took place in her kitchen as the children cowered in the corners echoed around the neighbourhood daily.

Within a few years of their marriage, instead of moving to a larger house with better facilities to accommodate their growing family, the Swanns actually moved down the social scale. It should have been possible, as Bill's wages increased and he became more skilled and got a chair of his own, to graduate to an easier life. Instead Emily had to leave the heart of Ardsley, where the presence of his family, wild as they were, helped keep him in some kind of check, and take a small stone terraced cottage in Gordon Street. It was still officially classed as Ardsley, but was exactly halfway between the moor-top village and Barnsley town's boundary. It was an isolated spot, particularly for a woman with a growing brood. By this time – 1891 – Emily had five surviving children, having lost at least one baby and possibly two others shortly after their birth. Gordon Street was not isolated enough to keep Bill out of the pub or out of trouble, however, and for him the move only meant an even better excuse not to go directly home after a shift.

The Swann children were required by law to attend elementary school until they were ten, and should have stayed on until they were thirteen if they hadn't passed a basic literacy and numeracy test. It's a fair bet that Emily had to explain to the local Attendance Officer why her oldest son had vanished from his classroom some time before his official school leaving date of 1892, but these officers had few powers and the poorest families took little notice of the reprimands they got from them. Bill would have wanted Charles in the bottle factory with him as soon as possible, if only so that he could have a few more shillings to lubricate his own leisure time, and Emily would have been grateful for any extra cash that the boy might manage to bring home. Employers who had children under the age of thirteen working for them were now required to have a certificate to show that the child had reached the basic educational standard. In practice, however, a boy like Charles could get casual work, their parents would be paid cash in hand for it, and they would slip under the radar of officialdom quite easily.

Charles's prospects of decent work were blighted by the hardships of his early family life and his father's behaviour. By the time he was old enough to be apprenticed, there were few apprenticeships to be had. Bottle-making was beginning to be routinely mechanized, and while it was still possible to sign indentures, Charles had the additional problem of finding a respectable sponsor. Bill Swann, even in the work-hard, live-hard world of the glass-blowers, was not seen as the kind of man who could be allowed to have the responsibility of training an apprentice, and Charles Swann's uncles had their own sons to find apprenticeships for.

By the time Charles was nineteen, his father had been demoted to a glass-bottle maker rather than a blower. This was still a fairly skilled job but involved the use of moulds and presses, which was much quicker than the old-fashioned process, and doubled the number of bottles one blower could produce. It was a step down from the trade he'd been trained in, and the quality of the product was inferior, meaning not only would he be paid less but he would have lost status amongst his peers. Charles, meanwhile, was a glass-bottle gatherer. 'Gathering' the right amount of molten glass from the crucible to hand on to the skilled blower would once have been an important step on the way to a full trade. By the time Charles was doing it, it was little more than an unpleasant labouring job which involved spending a full shift in front of the furnace dropping globs of glass into the moulds of a bottle-pressing and -blowing machine.

The family was barely hanging together as the 1900s began. Annie had left her parents' house before her sixteenth birthday, another daughter spirited off by the Hinchcliffes before too much damage could be done, according to a neighbour, who told the police that 'the older daughter' had gone to live with her grandparents in Barnsley. The next we know of Annie is that at the age of seventeen, she was living and working in Bradford and about to marry twenty-two-year-old Harry Middleton, a Bradford-born mill hand. In 1901, that left Charles, working at the glass factory with his father, and Frances, aged eight, Ernest, four, and Elsie, the baby of the family and my grandmother-to-be, who was three. It looks as if they were depending largely on whatever Charles or their mother could earn. There is no record of what kind of work Emily managed to find, but I know she was working because her children testified to the fact that she had been forced to leave her babies with family or neighbours while she tried to earn some money.

Census records for that year show that the family had moved yet again. They were now in a tiny house near the Aldham glassworks on the edge of a market town called Wombwell, south-east of Barnsley. The pressure on Charles to stay and help feed his three youngest siblings must have been great. His Hinchcliffe aunts had been in a similar situation, but at least they had had the comfort of knowing that their situation had been thrust upon them by tragedy. Charles was having to make up for the shortcomings of a father he loathed. He would be gone as soon as he could honourably escape.

All his married life Bill carried on dipping deep into the family finances to fund his drinking. For her part, Emily, small, fierce and full of fire, never tired of giving him hell for being such a terrible disappointment as a husband and a father. Her mother Hannah later summed up her daughter's unhappy marriage in a single bleak sentence: 'It was as if they each had hold of either end of a rope, and neither would give over pulling against the other all their married life.' The consequences were to be disastrous.

Chapter Seven

FREEDOM

'Felicity Baines! Will you please concentrate!' Miss Drew bellowed.

'But miss, I just don't get it,' I answered back cheekily.

Most of the class were studiously practising their shorthand, while I gazed out of the window wishing I could be outside in the warm September air. Besides, how could I take Miss Drew seriously when she wore a hand-knitted twin set with matching pearls and tidy front-laced brogues. She didn't possess an ounce of fashion credibility.

On my first day, sitting in the new classroom at Scarborough Technical College, I'd been so excited, convinced that this secretarial course would change my life for ever. Soon I'd have a job that would give me enough money to buy the trendiest 'gear' that Scarborough could offer and enjoy the seaside night-life. It didn't take long for me to become mind-blaringly bored. Shorthand had no hidden pleasures for me. It wasn't that I didn't get it. I just didn't see the point. I felt they were ridiculously strict about attendance and homework and typing speeds.

I could see and feel Miss Drew's complete exasperation

as she tried to teach the class to type. Rows of girls were rattling away on their new Olivetti typewriters, worrying more about ruining their beautifully manicured 'luscious red' Rimmel nail polish than mastering the keyboard.

'Balance your left hand over the ASDF keys,' she would grumble at us, 'and your right hand over the LKJH keys.'

Our hands were like spaghetti, and we collapsed in fits of giggles as we tried to step them up to the top row of keys, down to the bottom and back to the middle, moving uncomfortably like side-winder snakes lost in transit.

Like my great-grandmother Emily before me, I was discovering that freedom wasn't delivering all that I'd dreamed of. The morning I walked down the valley to Elaine's house with my suitcase had felt fantastic, so right. It was to be a new beginning. My feet seemed to fly, until I entered the old railway tunnel where I had enjoyed hollering 'helloooooo' as I walked through with my granddad and mother on many a sunny summer trip to the beach. For a moment, the tears welled up in my eyes as it sank in that I was leaving the only home I had ever really known. But as I turned the corner to Elaine's modern detached bungalow, I couldn't help but feel relieved. Here, I knew, I'd found a safe haven.

For the first few months after leaving the bungalow, however, I found that living with Elaine and her mum took a bit of getting used to.

'Felicity, I hate to mention this, but you are very untidy,' Elaine's mum said very cautiously one Saturday morning. 'You just throw your clothes around and expect other people to pick them up. Your make-up is spread out along the bathroom window sill. And you haven't offered to take your turn with the cleaning yet, and you have been here well over a month.'

I was mortified. It hadn't occurred to me that I should help out. Quarry Mount may have been my prison, but it was a prison where everything had been done for me by my granddad and my mother, and I now realized that I had a lot to learn. I had lived a very selfish, only-child existence without even realizing it. From that day until I left Elaine's house, I felt that I had let myself down. I had believed that I had joined them as a guest, when in fact they had wanted to embrace me as a part of their family.

It was even harder to get used to the idea that no one was looking for a fight. All my life I had been on the alert for the mood swings of one person, and only one person, and learnt how to protect myself as far as possible when she erupted. Now I was living with people who were polite to each other and to me, and I felt that I was treading on eggshells in my efforts to pay back their kindness. Some nights I would go to bed and lie in the dark feeling anxious without knowing why.

Looking back, I see that I'd lived an almost feral existence up to this point, and I simply didn't understand the social interplay of polite society or the social cooperation that goes on in a family. I didn't know how to read other people, and my lack of empathy for others was to have near tragic results.

When I moved into Elaine's house that summer, just as we left school, she was seeing a lad called James. He was a good-looking guy, and he knew it. I was blown away by his long, blond curly perm, the coloured blue lenses of his trendy John Lennon-style octagonal glasses. He always wore bleached Levis, which I thought made his long, slim legs look incredibly sexy, along with a faded blue denim shirt and a bedraggled Afghan coat. He came from somewhere near London and didn't speak like the rest of us. We thought he was rather posh.

By Christmas I was bored rigid by the secretarial course. I decided I'd had all I could take of classrooms and it was time to get a life. The worst bit, leaving home, was over. Getting a full-time job ought to be a piece of cake by comparison.

I walked out of the college and into my first job at the local solicitors Pearson and Whitfield, earning the enviable amount of £6.50 a week. I went out on the town for the Christmas celebrations with Elaine and James and had a great time, and then, out of the blue, James ended his relationship with Elaine, and she was devastated.

I was well aware how upset Elaine was because we talked about it long into the night, as you do when you're a teenager and your best friend is nursing a broken heart, but I didn't really take on board how badly she had been hurt. I didn't even make the connection between what she was going through and my own experience less than a year earlier when Dave had dumped me. I tried to understand how she was feeling, but what I really wanted was to make her smile again; I wanted us to laugh the way we used to when we'd rush home from school to her house to watch *The Partridge Family* and curl up and listen to our favourite

David Cassidy albums, or learnt to twizzle and turn to The Shadows' 'Apache' and 'Foot Stomp', using the crystal doorknobs on her dining-room doors as our jive partners.

As we curled up under our counterpane in her bedroom, I asked her to tell me what had gone wrong.

'I told James I didn't trust him,' Elaine said, choking back the tears.

'Why did you say that to him, Elaine? You know how he hates anyone who challenges him.'

I actually knew the answer before she cried out, 'I caught him kissing another girl. I can't take his flirting ways any more.'

'Well, you know what he's like, Elaine. Forget him!' I said bluntly. It seemed quite simple to me.

I hardly gave it a thought, therefore, when a few weeks later we were out with a group of friends and James turned up, and I ended up spending most of the evening talking to him. He was a challenge. A good-looking boy with attitude – who couldn't be trusted. But I believed that I could be the girl to change him for ever. My lack of empathy for Elaine, combined with the colossal self-obsession that comes with being sixteen years old, helped me arrive at the conclusion that it wasn't wrong to fancy him now that he was free. He wasn't going out with Elaine or anyone else, and I wasn't doing it behind her back. So that was all OK then.

We spent the night at his flat on the Esplanade. And what a night. James taught me that there was far more to sex than Dave and I had enjoyed in our tentative virgin fumblings. I should have wondered where a boy of seventeen had gained such experience, especially bearing in mind what Elaine had gone through. But common sense had never been my forté.

A couple of days later I came back to Elaine's house after a night out, fuzzy from a few too many drinks, to find her sobbing uncontrollably. She was distraught – I'd never seen anyone so upset. As I tried to discover what had happened, she admitted how hard it was to know he'd found someone else and clearly didn't care. It sobered me up fast but I still wanted to believe I hadn't done anything wrong. I hadn't stolen him from her, after all.

However, I did have some sense of what it might be like to be on the wrong end of such treatment from your supposed best friend, because when it became clear she wasn't getting over the break-up, it seemed the decent thing to do to remove myself and let her mum get on with helping her pick up the pieces. I found myself a bedsit and moved out.

I did go to visit her, even though I was fairly sure that she didn't want to see me, because I wanted to find out if there was any way I could make things better.

The atmosphere was uncomfortably frosty and I left with the devastating feeling that I'd lost my best friend. But I couldn't see that this was any reason to stop seeing James. She moved away quite soon afterwards, and I never saw her again.

So I made a life for myself that looked sound enough. I had found a very poky bedsit. I had a job that would pay the rent. I had some new, fun friends to go out and be a teenager with, and there was plenty of partying. With the final refinement of being able to run my own life, with no grown-ups trying to tell me what to do or what time to be in, everything looked terrific on the surface. The girls I knew were seriously envious of me.

At first, while James was still living at his mum's on the other side of Scarborough, I spent a lot of time over at his house. His family had moved all over the place while he was growing up as his dad had been in the army, and for a while they had been stationed in the north. When his parents split up, his mum Monica had decided to settle in Scarborough. She and James were very close and I got on really well with her. As I spent more and more time with James, often at his house, I felt as though I had found not only the affection of the romantic and physical kind that I craved, but a surrogate mum too. This was an added bonus. I had never really been mothered before.

James quickly became hugely important to me, the soulmate I'd hoped I'd find one day. We had heaps in common, and I felt that he understood that I needed to move on from a very damaged childhood. I think James had told his mum about my background, and I found that I could talk about anything to her. Monica was very tolerant, happy to let us share a room when I was staying there in an era when many parents were still quite prudish and strict about that sort of thing. I had the idea that she was keen to do nothing that would drive James away, having already struggled to sustain her relationship with him after a broken marriage.

Then James decided that it was time he stopped relying on her so much, and he rented a flat on the 'posh' north side of town in what had once been a very large house on

Scarborough's own Trafalgar Square, overlooking the county cricket ground. We soon discovered that another flat directly upstairs from his had become vacant, and thought this was the perfect solution. Even in the mid-seventies, few private landlords would have tolerated a teenage couple moving in together. A flat each would make it possible for us to appear to be living separately while getting away with a form of living together. The landlady was suspicious, of course, and the fire escape that ran past both our windows got us out of a couple of scrapes when we suspected that she was waiting for one of us to come out of the wrong flat in the morning as we set off for work. But we were both responsible about getting ourselves to work and paying our way, so no one had any gripe with us over what we did or didn't do.

It is hard to put into words what it was like suddenly to have command of all the little pleasures of life – eating what I wanted when I wanted or not eating at all, shopping with my own money, walking in through my own front door with my own key at any time I liked, getting affection, attention and lots of sex on tap, drinking alcohol and getting tipsy if I felt like it, making new friendships with people my own age, midnight skinny-dipping, going to bed at dawn. I was captivated by the smell of my own home. When I walked through the door, there was always a lingering scent of the musky joss sticks I burnt on the fireplace much of the time, so different from the stifling, gas-fire-heated air of Gran and Granddad's prefab, which smelled only of being locked in.

All through my childhood I had been cut off from almost every kind of joy, even quite mundane things like cuddles. Nobody had ever said they loved me. After all the years of powerlessness that had characterized my life, I found myself, almost overnight, transformed into someone who seemed to be indescribably powerful. I became aware of the fact that I was an attractive young woman, and began to grasp how this could be used to manipulate other people, and in particular how to use the power it gave me over men. But I only half believed that this powerful someone was me, which meant that I was quietly amazed when people did what I wanted them to do, and felt overly, bitterly betrayed when they didn't. And when I felt betrayed, I could out-gran Gran in my rigid refusal to forgive and forget.

While things were going well during those years between fifteen and seventeen, it seemed to me that all the unhappiness of my childhood was gone for ever. There were summer evenings when I would walk out into the warm rain with James, dressed as skimpily as I could manage in the halter-neck tops that were so fashionable at the time, with the deliberate intention of getting drenched. It was a wonderful thing to know that it didn't matter to anyone but me because I'd be drying my own clothes – a wonderful thing to get wet through on purpose, and feel more alive than I had ever known I could feel, to laugh with James who told me he loved me often. I was completely, utterly and totally in love with life when I first left home.

When the weather was good at the weekends, we could walk hand in hand through the old Victorian churchyard on the headland under the old Scarborough castle, where Anne Brontë is buried, and I'd make up stories about the unknown people buried alongside her. When it was too blustery and wet to go walking, we would hunker down together in one flat or the other, reading novels to each other, cooking Sunday dinner, playing at house and being in love. I knew that I wanted to spend my life with James, and was sure we would eventually marry and have children.

We were, of course, typical teenagers and there were times when we were as daft as brushes. My favourite drink quickly became a lethal mixture of whisky and ginger wine known as a Whisky Mac, a name which makes it sound a lot more harmless than it really is. Not only could I put away a staggering amount of the stuff, but I could also be daft enough – as we all could – to go swimming at closing time. I had James to go out with, of course, but I also got to know a crowd who regularly went to Emma's, the night-club where we locals did our partying, avoiding the tourist traps. Sometimes, in the early hours of the morning after the club had closed, we would climb over the wall of Scarborough's famous outdoor pool on the front, and go skinny-dipping in the warm water. It had a ludicrously high diving board that few of us would attempt, even when we were drunk – we weren't quite that daft – except for James, and he really was good at it. It was a fabulous thrill to watch the pale streak of his naked body slicing through the dark into the inky water with hardly a splash.

And sometimes we would decide to swim in the sea off the North Bay beach. In the dark, and drunk, and sometimes in quite big swells, this was scary and exhilarating and really very silly. But we were teenagers and we were immortal, and we were fortunate to live long enough to be able to look back and be astonished that none of us had ever drowned.

Despite all the nights spent partying, I always got up in the morning and got to work more or less on time, though I suffered an occasional talking-to from the boss about my timekeeping. I had discovered that I rather enjoyed hard work, particularly when I was challenged to stretch myself. I was, I have to admit, something of a madam at Arundales, the car sales showroom where I had been taken on as the office junior soon after moving into the bedsit. It took me a while to notice that Neal, the owner, had decided to ignore my complete lack of exam certificates. My responsibilities expanded almost by the day, and within a year or two I was pretty much running the accounts department. All in all – outwardly, at least – I thought rather highly of myself as I flirted my way around the place, always perfectly turned out and in full war paint, thoroughly enjoying strutting through the workshop past the lads in my miniskirts and platform shoes.

It wasn't all about looking good, though. Much of my new-found confidence came from the fact that Neal was a visionary man who had decided that I was worth spending time and training on, and who was installing the first computer system ever seen in a business in Scarborough. He had me trained not only to operate it but also to program it. I dimly realized that this was the kind of experience that was going to give a girl of my age and background a CV to die for, though deep down I didn't have the confidence to believe I could really achieve anything.

That winter, James, whose work as a lighting engineer at

one of the theatres was seasonal, decided he was fed up with sitting around on the dole once the tourists had gone and decided to become a Betterware salesman, earning commission by going door to door with catalogues selling household equipment. It was a sensible attempt on his part to be self-sufficient, even if he wasn't exactly one of life's natural salesmen. My reaction was less sensible. I had to leave him lying in bed in the morning as I went out to work, and pass him in the evening as I came home and he was on his way out to do his rounds. It seemed to me that it was terribly glamorous to be able to lie around during the day when most people had to be in their offices – and there was something irresistibly erotic about being able to make love as much as you fancied in the afternoon – and I thought to myself, 'I want to do that.'

Blind to which side my bread was buttered, I handed in my notice. Neal tried hard to make me see sense, but he had worked out by now that the harder I was pushed, the more entrenched my decision was likely to become.

'Why do you want to be someone else's saleswoman when you'll probably end up ruling the world if you stay here?' he asked. I had no idea what he was talking about. I was just short of seventeen, and he must surely know that, like all teenagers everywhere, I felt that I already ruled the world.

I quickly began to see what he meant as the novelty of going door to door with James selling plastic household stuff that no one really needed quickly wore off. It took a little longer to tire of the exotic afternoon love-making in James's flat, as it was rather fantastic, especially when the weather was good enough for us to throw open the balcony windows that overlooked the cricket ground so we could feel the wind on our bodies and smell the salt from the sea – it was every bit as good as making love in the open air. But I made few sales, earned a derisory amount of commission and ended up having to sign on the dole for the first and only time in my life.

I hated the sense of being monitored by authority. I had effectively lost the independence that I loved so much. After three months, I put pride aside and went back to Arundales to beg for my old job back. Lucky girl that I was, Neal said yes. I consoled myself with dashing back home at lunchtime to have some daytime nooky, with the added frisson of a frantic time limit. There was never time for lunch, but I can't say that I minded.

I never felt I could take James for granted. Although we were very much together, he remained a bit of a player, excitingly dangerous. He was a long-haired prog-rocker, well into his Led Zeppelin, Bad Company and Hendrix. I was more into the 'now' music of the time – The Stranglers and the anti-Nazi league supporting bands like Tom Robinson. We had one of the north's coolest music venues right on our doorstep – the Penthouse – where every top-flight band of the era played.

James and I had two quite different sets of friends, which we mixed together quite nicely from time to time. But there were nights when I'd be off at a gig he didn't care for with my more clubby mates, and he'd be in a flat somewhere with his long-haired lot smoking dope. Drugs were never my thing. If I had taken any of my grandmother's mad rants to heart, it was her railing against the imaginary drug dealers in our street – one of her favourite pastimes. Of course I could not be with James all that time and not try a spliff just once, but I never wanted to do it again – I really disliked the sensation of being stoned. Since freedom from the past meant feeling entirely in control of the present, handing over control to a drug was never going to be my idea of fun.

But there were other contrary forces at play within me, and the better things were, the more likely I was to find a way of sabotaging them. It wasn't conscious, but it was a sort of pattern. There were times when I deliberately provoked James, trying to create conflict where there was no need for any.

He had kept in touch with an ex-girlfriend from Boston Spa and she used to write to him. I was choked with jealousy whenever I saw her handwriting come through the letterbox. Most of the time I managed to hide it, but on one occasion I taunted and taunted him – much like I had done with Dave – about wanting to see the letter.

'Come on, James. You can't love me if you don't show me,' I declared stormily, feeling a niggle of doubt as I remembered Elaine challenging him about kissing a girl at Emma's.

James was incensed, especially when I tried to grab the letter out of his hand. He was a lot taller than I was, and taunted me by waving the letter in the air.

'You're so disloyal. You must be if you won't let me read it,' I whined. Even though I sensed his fury, I carried on taunting him. 'You could never be faithful to just one girl, could you?'

He snapped and knocked me flying on to the small single bed. I felt the sting of his hand on my face as he stormed out of my bedsit. I had pushed him too far. James was not a violent man, but I had goaded him until I'd got the reaction I had wanted. In tears, I nevertheless felt a strange sense of satisfaction.

On that day, as on several others over the next few years, James stormed out, furious with me and with himself, and later came back asking for forgiveness. It was a sick pattern. This was me at my worst – wanting my own way, wanting a reaction, wanting to be punished for it, and wanting the making-up that came afterwards.

Then came the evening when we had a row over who would put money in the meter. These were the days when rented flats had coin meters for the electricity and they were often set by the landlord to give a profit on what it actually cost to run the cooker or the fire. Our meters were outrageously expensive. Our 50ps never seemed to last very long, especially when it was cold and we had the three-bar electric fire going. Neither of us had much money, but I was convinced that I was better at handling it than James. This was probably true, but I doubt whether I was being fair when I began to accuse him of leeching off me. He called me a tyrant. The argument took off, and he stormed out, leaving me in a cold, dark flat while he went home, I assumed, to his mum's, where the warmth and light were free. I had no mum to go home to. He knew that.

I was livid, so I went out too, my heart full of furious

self-pity, to see Joan, a friend from Arundale who was a few years older than. She dried my tears, offered me her dressing table so that I could repair my make-up, got her coat and bag and took me straight down to Emma's.

'What you need isn't 50p for the meter,' she declared. 'What you need is cheering up. You can spend a pound on buying yourself a drink, and then you can enjoy the free heating in Emma's – much better value.'

I decided she was right – and I did the job thoroughly! We met up with our usual gang, which included a big crowd of gorgeous young men, among them a particularly predatory character called Robert, who always had a beautiful girl in tow – a different one each time we saw him – and who had a reputation for being the worst possible boyfriend material. For a long time he had been trying to get alongside me, and I'd always fended him off with the steady boyfriend defence. I found him attractive, if only because he seemed very dangerous indeed, which is always fascinating, but until this point I had enough sense of self-preservation to realize that James had qualities that could beat this kind of character hands down.

On this evening, however, I was in betrayed mode. I was the deserted one. James had walked out, not caring what happened to me, therefore I owed him nothing. So I did what I was to do many more times over the years when I felt I'd been let down – I brought the axe down on James. I found that I could coldly cut any consideration for him or his feelings right out of my emotions.

I homed in on Robert, who seemed every bit the Byronic hero. He must have thought all his Christmases had come at once, and he spent the whole evening with me. Then I took him home to my flat because at that moment a mad fling seemed the perfect way to get even.

'I have wanted you for an eternity, Flic,' Robert told me in his suave manner, expertly undressing me.

We were in bed when we heard a loud hammering at the door. How annoying. It might have been revenge that was driving me, but all of a sudden I was looking forward to this new experience. I wanted to taste the joys of illicit love and so did Robert.

'Who's in there? Flic, I know there's someone with you!' James yelled.

But even if I wanted to get even, I didn't want to get caught. Nor did Robert, who shot out of bed and desperately tried to pull on his trousers.

'Use the fire escape,' I begged him in a panicked voice, pushing the window open.

He was only too eager to leg it, scrambling out and clattering down the stairs. Unfortunately James had worked out what was going on and shot downstairs to his flat, hoping to intercept him on his part of the fire escape, but leaping to the ground just feet behind Robert into the ginnel that ran along the side of our block between Trafalgar Square and the cricket ground.

Robert ran off through the streets of Scarborough, frantically trying to shake James off. Fright made him faster than James's fury made him, though. James was left behind, shouting, 'Who is it? Whoever you are, I'll bloody find you . . .' He haunted the streets for the next few days looking for him, but Robert had gone to ground. I didn't see him in the usual places for a long time afterwards.

James came back to the building and hammered on my door again. I had to let him in.

He stood in front of me, gasping for breath, beside himself with fury and hurt.

'Why did you have to do that to us?' he asked.

'You left me!' I shouted back. 'You left me cold and alone and in the dark – what did you expect? You were fine with Monica, but what about me? You didn't care about me when you walked out, so why should I care about you? I would never do that to you. But you didn't think twice.'

'I came back, didn't I?' he yelled.

Then the fight seemed to go out of him, and he slumped down on to a chair and put his head in his hands.

'I was just angry. It didn't take me long to realize I shouldn't have left you alone. I love you. I only love you. I know I treated you badly and I shouldn't have gone off, but why did you have to do *this*?'

After a night during which I doubt James slept much, I went off to work feeling . . . not all that guilty. I was enjoying the drama, the emotional upheaval, having the control and power back, and I could already see that the attention I would be getting from James would be intensified. I was in high spirits. I had plenty to tell Joan once I got into the office.

'Flic! How did it go? Come on, tell all. All of the details, please!'

Joan was on to me before I'd got my coat off. She had always said that my relationship with James was like the

10cc song 'I'm Not In Love', both of us trying to pretend that there was nothing much going on when in reality we were besotted with each other, but neither of us wanted to admit it.

'He caught me just as it was getting interesting. Oh, Jo! He came back . . .'

'Bloody hell! No! What did he do? Did James hit him? I can't believe it. Flic, how awful.'

'No, he didn't hit him, I threw him out of the fire escape before James could get to him. But James searched the streets for him – what a laugh!'

After a few days, James's anger ran itself to a standstill, and when that happened, he broke down in tears in front of me. We got back together and the making-up was wonderful, but the truth was that after this episode he found it difficult to trust me.

Just as the cracks began to appear in this part of my life, along came the first signs of something even more worrying. I had fondly imagined I was free of my troublesome family, free to enjoy the bits of it I liked best. I had kept up contact with Granddad. Because he was still working as doorman at the local Conservative Club, which was just around the corner from all of our usual night-club haunts, I often used to call in to see him and get a welcoming kiss and hug. Granddad had been thrilled to discover that my new home had a grandstand view of the cricket ground, and he had turned up at Trafalgar Square often throughout the long, hot summer of 1973. He and James got on well, and we had some gloriously happy days when Yorkshire were playing there, sitting him in front of the open French windows while we kept him supplied with refreshments – the grandest seat in Scarborough.

'This is grand, lass,' he would say, grinning from ear to ear. I loved the fact that I was able to do something nice for my beloved granddad, and never gave a thought to the passing of the years, or the fact that he was now over seventy.

He began to turn up in the Square having forgotten why he'd come. There were times when he couldn't even find the flat and neighbours had to bring him to us. At first, knowing nothing about memory loss or old age, I thought of it as something that happened to all old people at some point, though I was petrified to think of him travelling the six miles between Quarry Mount and the centre of Scarborough and forgetting where he was halfway through the journey.

Then one day, after he'd been handed over to me by a lady from across the road, he asked, 'Where is everyone?'

'What do you mean, Granddad?'

'Where's your mother? I've come to collect her before she gets into more trouble.'

I phoned my GP and he came out to have a look at Granddad. I didn't know what was happening to him and I felt very frightened indeed.

'It's the beginnings of senility,' the doctor told me. 'His memory is going. It will get worse as time goes by, bit by bit. There's nothing that can make it better.'

This didn't sound too bad. I was quite relieved. At least

I knew he wasn't hallucinating and nor was he about to go completely bonkers.

In the mid-1970s, no one I knew had any idea what senility – or rather dementia – was, how terrifying it could be for the sufferer and how draining for the people who had to care for them. I thought that forgetting why you'd set out to see your granddaughter wasn't much more alarming than forgetting the shopping list. I had no idea how completely the disease would rob me of my lovely granddad, long before he was actually dead.

When I had first left home, it had taken me many months to pluck up the courage to go back to the bungalow and it had felt very strange the first time I walked down the little unkempt pathway to the kitchen, where I saw my beloved Silver through the window, beginning to threaten a bark. As I knocked on the back door, I looked across to the old allotment and into the overgrown space that had once been my place of solace; my secret garden.

Granddad came to the door and welcomed me inside. I shivered as I walked past the cooker and saw the pans lined up ready for dinner. I hadn't ever forgotten Gran throwing the scalding water over me and my vow never to come back to this house again. But as I stood in that very kitchen, it now seemed so small and unthreatening.

'Sit down, love,' Granddad said, smiling from ear to ear and pulling out a chair for me while Silver jumped around my legs. Mum was already sitting at the table, smiling shyly.

I was treated as an honoured guest by the two of them – the best mugs, biscuits on a plate. Gran was in her usual spot on the sofa by the fire, watching her television. She didn't speak; I didn't acknowledge her. When it was time to go, I hugged Granddad and Mum and petted the dog. I felt deeply sad about leaving them behind – if only I could take them away with me. But I knew now that I could always come back if I was needed.

Further visits followed the same pattern. Gran and I completely ignored each other – pride on her side, triumph on mine. I felt able to come and go as I pleased, and hoped that what had happened might make Gran behave a little better than she might otherwise have.

It was as I was adjusting to all this that, out of the blue, James took the momentous decision to make the break from Scarborough. He had been working at the Mecca in Scarborough and asked for a transfer within the company across the county to Bradford. He said he was fed up with being laid off in the winter and fed up with small-town seaside life.

How I fitted into all this was something he left up in the air. He never actually said 'it's over', but in the weeks after he moved out I was absolutely beside myself with grief. It came as a terrible shock to me to discover that I cared so much. I had imagined that I could take him or leave him, and had frequently told myself that there were plenty of other fish in the sea.

'It's not personal,' he insisted. 'I just need to get out of Scarborough. You can come over and see me in Bradford if you want. We could both do with getting out of here.' Hardly an invitation to make me feel he couldn't live without me.

If he were being honest, it was personal. Sure, there were obvious advantages in not being stuck in a northern seaside town where he could only work regularly between Easter and autumn. But I also knew that a big part of it was that I was difficult to be around. James, I suspect, felt instinctively that a move out of Scarborough might be good for him and, as a welcome side-effect, for our relationship. But even if that was what he had in mind, there was no way I was going to acknowledge that he might be right.

Heartbroken, I gave notice on my flat in Trafalgar Square shortly before he moved out of his. I couldn't bear the thought of living there after someone else had moved into his flat. I found digs about half a mile away, with Jane, a friend I'd met at the Penthouse, at the top of a house in Nelson Street. It was a come-down from Trafalgar Square, just the top floor of a little terraced house that had been converted into a bedsit and tiny galley kitchen by the old lady who owned it, and she still lived downstairs. There was one bathroom and loo in the whole house, and two single beds crammed into our dormer room.

She was a potty little old woman and was always complaining about the 'comings and goings', as she put it, of us girls coming home late and getting up late in the morning. She was in her late seventies or early eighties, so it was a completely impractical arrangement and a mismatch of lifestyles, but we had nowhere else to go and she was happy enough to take our rent.

James and I were no longer an item as far as I was concerned, and at first I didn't go and see him in Bradford at all. He called round to see me when he was back in

Scarborough, and sometimes he would stay over for a couple of days – I'd have to sneak him in past the old lady – and we would take up with each other again. I'm sure both of us knew, really, that it was over, but we weren't quite able to let go.

It was a miserable business, being immersed in a mass of feelings that had no future, and didn't even have a proper place in the here and now, given that he was living so far away. It took me years to get over James. I hadn't realized how deep our love had gone. Eventually, after about a year, I took refuge in an affair with a man who was completely unavailable.

Jonathan was a sales rep in his late twenties who lived in Lincolnshire, but travelled up most weeks and would stay in Scarborough overnight. He was married, but had no children, and he didn't mind a bit of company when he was on his own in the boarding house during the week. He was different from the lads in my usual crowd, wore immaculate suits and, being ten years older than me, loved The Beach Boys and The Who.

He was undeniably flash, but I loved it. I especially loved his shiny black Jaguar, and on long summer evenings after work he would drive me out of Scarborough in it, up on to the North Yorks Moors above the coast and we'd fly across the heather-misted tops, past the golf balls of the Americans' Fylingdales Early Warning System, racing around Goathland as if it was a rally circuit. Thankfully, we never hit any sheep. We drove over to pubs and clubs in Whitby, where we weren't likely to be recognized, and spent odd nights in his hotel room.

It was exciting, but I never for a moment pretended to myself that there was any future in it. I had lost the stability of James, and I was watching Granddad wander ever deeper into the fog of his lost memories every time I went to see him. With everything so uncertain, I found myself casting around for something that might make me feel as if I had dependable roots.

The best thing I could come up with was to go to Wakefield to visit Granddad's family. I had already been in touch with them. Soon after leaving home, I had asked if I could come and visit, and I'd been going sporadically ever since, making my own family, rather than just borrowing James's mum.

Aunt Rene, Granddad's brother's daughter, had a son, Carl, who was a little older than me. Then there was Uncle Ted, his sister Alice's son, one of the few relatives who had ever turned up in Scarborough when I was a child to visit with his wife Mavis. Not that they ever came to the house – that must have been because of Grandma – but Mum and Granddad and I would meet them in town when they came through for the day. They had a daughter, Sheila, a little younger than me.

What I liked about them was that all of them were quite normal, certainly when you compared their lives to mine in the prefab. They were wonderfully welcoming and took me to their hearts, and when my relationship with James crumbled and I turned to them, they became a vital part of what propped me up. They gave me a sense that I was being thought of somewhere by someone, that I was important to them, that I could always go to them. And they rarely asked too many questions about Gran and Mum, or about what had gone on when I was growing up.

I spent quite a lot of time with them, enjoying the adoration of my younger cousins, who thought I was terribly grown-up and sophisticated, and the warm northern hospitality that the various aunties smothered me with, mothering me as if they sensed what I had missed.

But it was impossible to keep papering over the cracks. I went round to the bungalow one day to make one of my regular checks and discovered that Granddad had his suitcase packed. He told me Gran was throwing him out.

Later, when I spoke to the Social Services myself, I was told that Gran had called them to say she wanted him out and would put him out on the pavement if they didn't come and take him.

'Didn't you think it might have been better to take her rather than him?' I asked the woman on the phone.

'It doesn't work like that, Miss Baines,' she said, a little annoyed. 'We can't make people go where they don't want to go, or make them leave their homes.'

'But you can let a mad old woman force an old man who's never done any harm out of his home?'

She sighed, probably all too accustomed to being caught in domestic cross-fire of this kind.

I did not take into account how increasingly difficult Granddad might be to live with as the dementia took hold, because I didn't understand the condition, and I hadn't had to live with it day in, day out. I thought only of the day when Gran had sobbed her heart out as the men with the green ambulance tried to take her away, and how Granddad had rescued her. She was repaying him now by throwing him out because it didn't suit her to have him around – or so I saw it. The only place Social Services could offer him at that moment was in a home for the elderly in Filey, several miles down the coast. He wouldn't last long in a place like that. I knew it, and I was sure Gran knew it too.

I didn't think I could contain my anger, it was so extreme. I shouted, '*You can't do this, you selfish woman. You owe him his home, at least, after all he's done for you!*'

But she did what she always did. She sat quietly, staring ahead, even when I stood between her and the telly. She blinked a little as I banged my hand on the table, but otherwise refused to acknowledge that she heard me at all. I shouted at Granddad, and at Mum too, for all that was worth, but the biggest problem turned out to be that Granddad himself was determined to go.

'She wants me gone. I'm going. That's that,' he said, also staring out of the window, refusing to look at me, or Mum, or Gran.

'You can't go! This is your home too,' I told him, almost yelling in his face because I was so exasperated that he wouldn't stick up for himself and fight back.

He said quietly, 'I can't stay. She's sold my bed.'

Well. Of all the spiteful things she had ever done in her life, didn't that just take the biscuit.

Chapter Eight

A HARD LIFE

Hannah Hinchcliffe had witnessed the passing of three-quarters of a century, and she'd seen her family through some very hard times. As the nineteenth century drew to a close, things were about to get harder than ever.

She was already worried about the state of Emily's marriage and the fate of her Swann grandchildren, and about the health of her own son William, who, although finished with the pits and living out at Cawthorne with his family, was having the same problems with his chest that his father had suffered from. Twenty-five years of pit work was inevitably catching up with him as he neared sixty. Her youngest son John's marriage was also giving cause for concern.

John had married late compared to the young men of the Barnsley mining community he'd grown up in, at the age of thirty, and had chosen a woman ten years younger than himself, Birtha Ann Dale, the daughter of a station master. Like John, she worked at the Co-op in the fabric and haberdashery department. John and Birtha set up home together in 1891 and produced four children within six years, although one baby died. It was generally agreed in the family that, young as she was, Birtha ran her home like an army general and John did as he was told. Unfortunately, she also seemed to be regretting her choice of husband, despite his pliable nature. Every time the Hinchcliffes saw her, she had some fault to find with him.

'Many worse couples have rubbed along together,' said Hannah's eldest daughter Elizabeth whenever her mother started fretting about John, as she did increasingly frequently. The Hinchcliffe women agreed that his wife ought to be grateful that they had few enough mouths to feed, and that John had steady work. In the summer of 1897, something quite shocking happened. Birtha threw John out of their house. Even Emily, with all her troubles, had not attempted anything so drastic. John might not be the kind of man to set the world on fire – and a good thing too, if one considered what the exciting Bill Swann got up to – but he was a reliable worker and brought his wages home.

He arrived in Havelock Street one morning in a state of some agitation, saying that Birtha had told him to get out of the house with just the clothes he stood up in, and never to come back. Hannah, always ready to defend her children, first sat him down by the range and gave him a hot, strong cup of tea. She then put on her black bonnet, took up her warmest woollen shawl to put around the shoulders of the black widow's dress that she always wore, and set out to ask Birtha what was going on.

'I won't have him in the house,' Birtha shouted. 'He's not in his right mind. No woman should have to put up with it.'

'Has he used his fists on you?' demanded Hannah.

'Nay. But he's talking filthy talk. You're his mother, and an old lady, and I won't tell you the things he says. But no wife should have to put up with it. I'm a decent woman and I'll not have him back in the house.'

Exactly what had tipped John over the edge is not clear, but over the next few days Hannah could not deny that he had lost his grip on reality. The 'filthy talk' that had so outraged Birtha was John's conviction that he had venereal disease – the Victorian name for a sexually transmitted disease – and he believed his wife had given it to him. Birtha had taken umbrage at this; Hannah's instinct was that there was no smoke without fire. John might not be in his right mind, but the gossip was that Birtha was taking more interest than she should in another man. However, there was no proof of this, and while violence, for instance, was rarely a valid excuse for excluding a husband from his family home, the kind of slander that John was directing at his wife certainly was.

Hannah wasn't able to make Birtha take her husband back, but she did at least hint to those treating John for his mental derangement that he might have some reason for his behaviour by telling them that Birtha was now living with another man.

In the late spring of 1898 he disappeared altogether. Hannah asked for him at the town workhouse, thinking that he might have taken himself there as a pauper rather than suffer the indignity of returning to his mother's house permanently, but there was no record of him. Six months later he turned up at the Leeds Union workhouse, about twenty miles away. No one had any idea how he had got there. Hannah believed that he had probably gone there to look for another job, well away from Barnsley. He was still not making much sense, however, and he was taken to the workhouse infirmary by a police officer who had found him wandering the streets of the city centre talking nonsense to passers-by.

'He has delusions that he has money here in the care of the attendant,' wrote Mr Allen at the Leeds workhouse. 'He also believes that his mother has called and left him five shillings, and that he has got cured here of venereal disease. He has exaggerated opinions of his own strength and capacity, thinking he could lift a 20 stone bag of flour [about 130 kilos] and play difficult pieces on the organ.'

He was taken to Wakefield Asylum on 1 June 1898. The picture of John taken on his admission to the asylum shows a man in good shape for a thirty-seven-year-old who hasn't had a life of ease. He had, of course, always worked indoors, which helped. His large, clear grey eyes look into the camera with disarming directness; he is a rather attractive man who certainly doesn't look old before his time. He looks tired, though, and sad rather than mad.

However, his personality was in a fair bit of disorder.

'He has been strange in his manner and cannot pay attention to his work these last six months,' Hannah told the admissions officer.

'Where have you been living?' asked Dr Hearder, who examined him when he first arrived at the asylum.

'I've worked in Barnsley *and* Leeds,' John replied,

smiling and tapping his nose in a confidential manner, as if this was secret information that shouldn't be shared too widely.

'So you've worked in Barnsley and Leeds, but where were you living before you went into the workhouse?' asked the doctor.

'Well, I'm from Barnsley.'

'So you've been living with your mother?'

'Nay, I've not lived with my mother these six or seven months.'

'I see. Where did you come from to here, then?'

John looked at the man as if he was mad. 'From Barnsley. I've already told thee.'

'Were you living there with your wife, and not your mother?'

'I've not lived with my wife this twelve-month. She gave me the pox. I wouldn't live with her. A man can't live with a woman that has the pox.'

'Where is your wife now?'

'With her mother.'

'I've been told that she is living with another man,' said Dr Hearder.

John looked at him, knocked off balance for the first time in the conversation. Up until this point, reported Dr Hearder, he had seemed rather self-satisfied, like a mill owner condescending to talk business matters over with his foreman. This tired man, with all his 'thee's and 'thou's, his shirt collar skewed halfway round his neck and knotted with a coarse worker's neckerchief, must have appeared quite incongruous as he patronized the well-educated, well-spoken doctor in front of him. Though he was driven beyond reason by his circumstances, he was probably dimly aware that he wasn't making much sense, and was trying to construct some sort of respectable front to present to the world.

John managed to pull his tattered, cock-eyed dignity tightly about him again, and answered with a dismissive wave of his hand: 'Nay, I don't know, and I don't care.' Then he yawned.

Although he had been at the asylum barely a couple of hours, he insisted that he had arrived there a fortnight ago, having 'finished my time, you know', as if he had been in prison. In his befuddled state, it is perfectly possible that he had mistaken the grim Leeds workhouse for a gaol.

'His expression suggests weak-mindedness and he is rather self-satisfied. It is very difficult to get a direct answer from him. He is an imbecile of fairly high grade. Prognosis: Bad for complete recovery.'

I was startled to see this bald statement about John's condition in the asylum case books. I went to the medical reference section and discovered that imbecility was a strictly technical term used by doctors to describe 'a person of moderate to severe mental retardation, having a mental age of from three to seven years and generally being capable of some degree of communication and performance of simple tasks under supervision'. This was John's diagnosis, and its cause was described in his case notes as 'congenital' – he had been born this way.

This couldn't be true. The Co-operative Society was an enlightened employer for the times, but in the nineteenth century even they did not have the kind of employment access policies that would have allowed someone with such severe learning difficulties to work there for twenty years. Equally, no Church of England priest of the 1890s would have allowed someone of obviously limited understanding to marry, on the grounds that this would have been as immoral and wrong as allowing a child to marry. But these were the days before Freud and psychoanalysis, and by and large a person's state of mind was considered an innate part of the way they had been made, whether by God or by nature, even where the behaviour was completely out of character. So the doctors at Wakefield asked John and his family almost nothing about his background and home circumstances beyond recording that this attack of confusion had been brought on by 'trouble in his marriage' and the loss of his job – although the second had clearly been caused by the first.

They did, on the other hand, measure his head very carefully. Phrenology, the idea that someone's mental faculties could be judged by the size and shape of their skull, was still very influential in psychiatry at the end of the 1800s, even though an eminent French physiologist had scornfully described it as a 'pseudo-science' fifty years before, and there was no evidence that it had any therapeutic value even after almost a century of research across Europe.

As it turned out, John's emotional problems were the least of his worries. When he was examined by the doctors on his admission to the asylum they found, firstly, no evidence that he had ever had venereal disease and, secondly, that he had a 'rather harsh' sound in the apex of his left lung when he breathed in. Elsewhere, in a brief note on family medical history, one word is entered: phthisis, the Greek word for consumption. This was what was on his father John's death certificate. It had taken a very long time to kill him, and it was probably the same disease that was making William so ill towards the end of the century. We know this disease as tuberculosis.

TB was everywhere and there was no cure for it. No one knew what caused it, but it was known that people susceptible to breathing problems, from asthmatics to miners, were more likely to be victims. It had obviously taken hold at Havelock Street. Yet even though it is and was a highly contagious disease, all the Hinchcliffe women seem to have escaped. Hannah, her daughter Elizabeth, who was still a regular visitor to the house, her spinster daughter Annie and her granddaughter Eleanor were all spared.

In the asylum John went into decline. His health worsened and his mind showed no signs of recovery. Sometimes he sat all day with a Bible in his hands rather than show himself willing to help with the routine housekeeping tasks that the inmates were encouraged to occupy themselves with on their wards. He never graduated to the more interesting work off-ward that was available for recovering patients. He was 'excitable' and 'obstinate', and frequently 'troublesome' – which seems right, because it's hard to see how the Hinchcliffes would have proved themselves such extraordinary survivors without these qualities.

For some reason, early in 1899 he started refusing to eat – the case notes record only the facts as observed by the

A newspaper illustration of the explosion at the Oaks Colliery in 1866. This second explosion killed many of the rescuers searching for the miners.

The public outpouring of support after the disaster was immense. This cartoon shows the spirit of Britain, helping the widows and orphans left behind.

The official court photograph of Emily Swann, my great-grandmother (left); John Gallagher on leaving the army (middle) and after his arrest (right). The years in between don't seem to have been kind to him.

PRISONERS IN THE DOCK.

The court illustration of the 'prisoners in the dock', from the local paper of the time.

Left John Hinchcliffe, Hannah's son and Emily's brother, was admitted to the Wakefield Asylum on 1 June 1898, and died there two years later.

Below left My Gran, Elsie Swann, as a young woman. She was beautiful, but even then her years of suffering had left her cold and cruel.

Below right Albert Baines, my beloved Granddad, back in his army days.

My mum, Marjorie Baines, as a child. She looks so innocent here, but I can't help but wonder if her childhood was as lonely and harsh as mine.

There aren't many photos of me as a child, but you can see the family resemblance in this school picture.

Gran standing outside the prefab, on one of the rare days when she left the house. To me it always looked – and felt – like a prison.

Visiting Auntie Rene made me feel like I had a proper family. I loved seeing her and my cousins as a child, and when I was eighteen I decided to get back in touch.

These were very happy years. I was independent for the first time, with a lovely boyfriend and a good job. I felt like the world was my oyster.

Working in the bar (with perm!) gave me my freedom back during my first marriage. And this is where I first met Martin.

Though I never quite came to terms with the fact that my mum hadn't protected me from Gran, she was a wonderful and loving grandmother to my boys.

Me with my boys. A friend took this photo to mark new beginnings, soon after I went back to college. Having a family of my own started to help me move on from my past.

I was so startled when I realized Gran had come to visit me that I didn't run after her; I just took this picture. In a way this photo started this whole story.

Below Now, with my family's support, I have found a career I love in teaching. I feel like I've finally moved on from my past, and am ready to take on the world.

staff, never any comments from the patients. Reading between the lines, he had taken to his bed because he had a painful and embarrassing problem with his bottom and he was fed up of being constantly examined and messed about with. He is described as 'extremely troublesome, always meddling with the dressing', and then 'will not allow anything to be done to him surgically and he also refuses his food'. This is followed by the dreadful conclusion 'has to be tube-fed'. This was a painful and insanitary business, particularly when done by force. John was fed by tube for much of the next two or three months and it seems unlikely that he submitted to it gladly. It's hard not to wonder why they didn't just let him decline, particularly since his lungs were obviously breaking down in the advanced stages of consumption.

He had a stroke in July 1899, probably because of his weakened, half-starved state and the strain that being force-fed put on his frail body, and then he became incontinent – or as the staff preferred to describe it, he had 'mischievous and dirty habits'. It was almost another year before he died, a macabre testimony to the ox-like constitution of the Hinchcliffes. The secondary cause of death is given as tuberculosis, but the first is 'general paralysis of the insane', which is how an inmate's refusal of reasonable medical treatment was generally described. It was some comfort to know that John was in a single room for the last few months of his life, rather than suffering and wasting away in full view of his fellow patients.

It's easy to judge harshly the attitudes of the asylum staff, but they were motivated by a wish to look after him and help him get better or, at the very least, keep him safe. What would have happened to him if he'd been left out on the street doesn't bear thinking about, and I was touched to read the detailed case notes which recorded that he wasn't left alone during his last days. He died at 10.45 a.m. on 22 June, 1900, in the presence of Attendant Barratt. He was thirty-nine years old.

This news was sent to Hannah on a standard printed form which baldly heralded the death of an inmate, leaving only two gaps for a name and a date to be filled in by the Asylum Superintendent. No other information was offered, not even cause of death or a formal word of regret. Hannah must have known that John was very seriously ill by then, and it is to be hoped that the letter didn't take her completely by surprise. She went to the corner shop to buy a few sheets of presentable blue writing paper, and sat down at her kitchen table to craft a reply. Her letter is business-like and to the point.

'I will come to collect my son on Monday next. I enclose a letter from his wife, Mrs Birtha Hinchcliffe, saying that she can do nothing for him and she leaves all the arrangements to me.'

She then put on her bonnet and shawl and headed over to Birtha's house to give her a second piece of blue notepaper. It looks very much as if Birtha's letter is written to Hannah's dictation, as it repeats her phrase 'I can do nothing for him' exactly. Birtha's writing is not as good as Hannah's. No reason is given why the dead man's wife, the mother of his children, wouldn't want to have some say in his funeral, and it was no concern of the Superintendent's.

He only had to make sure that whoever claimed the body for burial had the consent of the person's legal next of kin.

Hannah was helped to bring John home by the Co-operative Society, who offered charitable assistance to a former employee who had come to a sad and difficult end after many years of loyal service and also by a grant from the long-standing Oaks Fund. The Co-op's funeral service sent a hearse and coffin to the asylum to collect his body, and the Fund paid for a burial plot and a small headstone to save John from the indignity of a pauper's funeral. Without their help, John would have been laid to rest among the many, many unmarked graves in the asylum's corner of the Wakefield cemetery.

Over on the other side of Barnsley, careworn as she was with more immediate problems, Emily must still have felt the loss of her little brother. There was, after all, less than a year between them and the two of them had grown up practically hand in hand, with Emily doubtless leading the way into all sorts of mischief. She turned forty as John's last illness took its course, and from this point onwards her own life took a dramatic turn for the worse.

She had discovered that she was expecting my gran just as John was admitted to the asylum. The family life that Elsie was born into was undoubtedly hellish: a violent, womanizing, gambling father, not enough food or warmth to go round, and a mother who was rapidly losing the will to carry on holding it all together. She struggled on with help from her eldest son Charles, but the final straw came not long after Elsie's second birthday. Emily was arrested and charged in the summer of 1901 with the unlawful wounding of another woman. This was a serious offence – about as serious as Bill's conviction for his aggravated assault on her. He had been fined. Emily was sentenced to six months in prison with hard labour. There's no record of which prison, but the House of Correction in Wakefield seems likely.

In Victorian prisons, hard labour could mean a number of things. Inmates were often made to get into the treadmill, a human-sized hamster wheel, and turn it by walking for up to ten hours a day with only short breaks for rest. Sometimes the treadmill ground corn, but often it wasn't connected to anything and the only purpose of making it turn was punishment. Similar punishments included being forced to turn the handle of a crank that pushed paddles through sand in a drum, and being forced to carry cannonballs around the prison exercise yard, while in chains. I had heard in school lessons about oakum-picking, where inmates worked for ten or twelve hours a day teasing apart the fibres of old tarry rope, which made their fingers bleed. Whatever it was that Emily was required to do, it made my blood boil to think of this being added to everything else she had to cope with.

Emily had two previous convictions at the time, both of them within the previous two months, both for using obscene language. Again the court papers that would help to explain what was going on can't be found. However, Emily had reached the age of forty without having slanging matches in the street so vicious that the local constable felt the need to rein her in. Something was going on, and the only feasible explanation is that it was something Bill was doing. Another woman seems to be the possibility which fits the circumstances best, and one he had been seen with more than once.

The moment when Emily was taken to prison, sometime late in 1901, was the moment when her family fell apart for good. The three youngsters, Frances, Ernest and Elsie, were taken off by the Hinchcliffes. At first, all three went to Hannah and Annie in Havelock Street. Eleanor, aged nineteen, was already there, of course, and courting a colliery surface labourer two years older than her, Herbert Crossland from nearby Gilroyd. Annie was the only aunt still in Havelock Street, although Elizabeth, Frances and Clara lived nearby and could help out as needed. Charles, released from the duty of looking after his mother and the little ones, wasn't going to stay a minute longer in his father's house or his father's trade.

'Where will you go?' his grandmother asked him when he went over to Racecommon Road to let Frances and little Ernie know what he'd decided to do.

It's not hard to imagine him taking charge of the situation, because, in the years to come, he was to prove himself steady, reliable and hard-working, the very antithesis of his father. 'I'll go over to our Annie's in Bradford,' he said. 'She'll know where I can get a room, and she knows where there's work. When we can, we'll come and get Frances – she'll be getting her school certificate soon, and then she can come and live with us, and we'll start her in work. You shouldn't have to look after her now. We'll see her right.'

When she came out of prison, Emily was evidently too

ashamed to do the sensible thing and go to her mother's house and ask for help. Misplaced pride instead took her back to Wombwell, where she discovered that not only had Bill lost the house in Aldham View, but he'd managed to lose all her children too. In the meantime he hadn't had the marvellous time that he'd probably imagined he would have without her and the kids in his way. There was no one to order dinner from or to punish when it didn't materialize, or to make sure he had a bed to get into, and if he had a girlfriend I'll bet she went right off him once he started demanding domestic services and, I expect, cash handouts to finance his drinking and gambling. He was glad enough about Emily's return to go to the trouble of renting another house, although this time it was the very poorest kind of accommodation, a blind-backed terraced house right in the centre of Wombwell.

The stew of tiny brick houses crammed together directly behind the old market square which faced the fine new Town Hall across the main street was certainly convenient for the life Bill wanted to live. The area, just beyond the back yard of the eighteenth-century Alma Inn, had once been open ground opposite the medieval parish church, an airy square of garden with small-holdings facing on to George Street and Summer Lane on its northern and western sides. Wombwell had then become a boom town boasting two collieries, the canal, the railway and several glass-bottle factories, and this space had been filled with around sixty workers' cottages of the poorest kind, with communal privies that weren't properly serviced, and houses that had no yard or washhouse. You couldn't throw a stone from any of the houses without hitting either a pub or a chapel. There was the George on George Street, the Alma on Alma Road, the Royal Oak at the top of Church Street. The chapels of the Zionists, the Wesleyan Reform Methodists and the Primitive Methodists stood around the boundary of what was known as 'the square' – officially George Square – although there was no longer any open space in the area and the thoroughfares between its terraces were narrower than was usual. It need hardly be said that the people of the Square rarely patronized the chapels.

Emily attempted to get things back to something like normal. Now she went to her mother and sisters and took back Ernie and Elsie, although she had to accept that nineteen-year-old Charles and Frances, who was twelve, were gone for good. Frances had joined her brother and sister Anne in Bradford just as Charles had promised. Emily could have insisted that they brought her back, but Frances had a job in one of the woollen mills. Emily had the sense to leave things as they were for Frances's sake.

But she had been changed by her time in prison and she seemed to have given up on her self-respect. Bill soon went back to his old ways, and now she started drinking too. Down to just two children, she had the time to spare, the inclination to drown her sorrows and, possibly, a sense that there was almost nothing left to lose. Her reputation was shot to pieces.

Women did not go into pubs, but it was common for the women of the square to send one of their children to the off-sales window of the local pubs to buy beer by the jug. A few friends would chip in, and then the women would sit around the kitchen table having an afternoon drinking party. It wasn't the kind of thing that would ever have happened in Hannah's house, but Emily had by now moved herself completely into Bill's world, where notions of respectability were simply ignored and all that mattered was where the money for the next drink was coming from. Over the next year or so, she appeared in court four more times, either for being drunk and disorderly or for using obscene language. Then she was arrested for soliciting for the purposes of prostitution.

I feel so sorry for Emily. Bill's twelve convictions for consistent bad behaviour dated back sixteen years to his late twenties, and being taken before the magistrates made no difference to him. Emily's seven convictions were all gathered in the last two years of her life, between 1901 and 1903. For twenty years she had struggled and struggled to be a better human being than her husband, and in the end his many weaknesses had ground her down. If there was any member of her own family who offered help or refuge to her at this point, she didn't take it. Short of putting herself in the workhouse, there was unlikely to be any escape from George Square.

Even so, she needed something to live on. Bill was obviously managing to keep up with the rent, because this was the kind of property from which their landlord would otherwise have evicted them swiftly, but he gave her almost nothing to run the house on. With only the two small children to look after, she might have been able to think about going back to mill work and earning her independence that way. The sad truth was, though, that because she had been labelled a prostitute, she was now a woman of bad character, and few mill owners would allow her to work alongside women and girls who regarded their respectability as one of their most treasured assets. Emily found a solution. With none of the older children at home, she had a spare bedroom, and she decided to take a lodger.

John Gallagher was a coal miner from Middlesbrough and, although no one in the area knew it at the time, an army deserter. Rather than go back to his native Teesside, he had decided it would be safer to come to work at the south Yorkshire coalfield and wait for the Army to forget about him. Perhaps it struck a chord with Bill Swann at first that, like him, the new paying guest was from the north-east. He was twenty-nine, considerably younger than the Swanns, who were now both forty, and single. He was as fond of a drink as any other working man in the area – he had one conviction for being drunk and disorderly – and as careless with his money, since he had been known to pawn his best suit towards the end of the week when his cash ran out. But he differed from Bill Swann in one important respect: he believed that men should not hit women, whatever the provocation.

Perhaps Emily saw in the young north-easterner something of her Bill as he had been when she first met him. John was equally taken with her, even though she was twelve years older, but she was still a petite, doll-like woman with a few embers left of her old fiery self, and he was able to reignite them. To see her powerfully built husband with the overdeveloped shoulders and forearms typical of his trade battering this tiny figure was more than John could stand.

John hadn't been in the house for a fortnight when he got up from the table one evening shortly after Bill had come in drunk, as ever, and started threatening Emily. He didn't like the look of the meal she had given him. Bill belted Emily, and then John belted Bill. Bill staggered back, astonished, as John told him to pick on someone his own size. Bill had no choice, befuddled as he was, but to obey the younger man's command to lay off his wife, but he must have resented not getting his own way with his fists in his own house for the first time in his life.

A month or so later, Bill came home to find his lodger and his wife coming downstairs together. They were dressed, but this was just the evidence he needed to order Gallagher out of his house. The two men had a furious row, with Bill shouting that Gallagher was having relations with his wife under his own roof, and Gallagher calling Bill a coward who wouldn't dare raise his fists to a man.

'You're a snake in the grass,' a neighbour heard Bill Swann shout, along with some choice obscenities that the neighbour refused to repeat in an official statement. 'You'd better peg it, or I'll have the constable on you.'

John, preferring not to have the police look into his background, had no choice but to pack up his things and get out. He only moved about twenty yards across the Square, however, becoming the lodger of Emily's friend and neighbour Mary Ann Ward, a widow with a grown-up son and fourteen-year-old daughter who lived with her. Everyone in the area knew why he'd left Emily's house, of course, because plenty of people heard the argument, and those that didn't heard the rest from Mary Ann. She was one of the women who liked to have a gathering in her house with a few jugs of beer, particularly on a Saturday afternoon, which, for most people, was the end of the working week. Even the factories only worked a half or three-quarter day on a Saturday.

Bill Swann beat Emily up for the last time on 6 June, 1903, when one of Mrs Ward's gatherings was underway across the street. John Gallagher had been paid off from Mitchell's Main, the colliery where he had been working, the night before because he had decided to leave Wombwell and try his luck in Bradford, maybe in the mills. The party at Mary Ann's was a kind of leaving do. Gallagher paid for the beer and neighbours drifted in and out throughout the afternoon from dinner time until the early evening, when Mary Ann's daughter Rose was sent to get Gallagher's jacket and waistcoat out of hock from the pawnbroker's. The girl brought them back and put them on the table, and for some reason, Emily, who had been drinking through much of the afternoon, picked them up and walked out of Mary Ann's house and over to her own.

John followed her. Perhaps that was the idea – to get him alone one last time before he left the district and she was left stuck in her miserable marriage. No one except Emily, John and Bill witnessed what happened in the Swann kitchen when Bill came home having been drinking much of the day and once more found John in his house with his wife. Emily said she was in the kitchen and John was coming down the stairs when Bill walked in. What was going on was never fully explained by John or Emily, but they can't have got up to much – Mary Ann Ward said that John had been away from her house for only ten minutes.

Both John and Emily admitted that Bill had been angry when he saw John and had ordered him out 'with much foul language', and the young miner had pushed his way past to get to the back door.

Bill had waited until he was out of sight, and had then attacked Emily.

Emily fled the house and followed John back to Mary Ann's not five minutes later. 'Look what our Bill has done,' she said, uncovering her face to show that the left side was swollen and badly bruised and her eye was starting to close. It must have been a vicious blow to cause so much damage in such a short space of time.

John Gallagher jumped to his feet. 'I will give the bugger something for himself,' he said grimly, heading for the door. 'If he'll not kick a man, he shan't kick a woman.'

He walked out with Emily close behind. Five minutes later the two of them came back to Mary Ann's where John announced – after taking a long drink from the pitcher of beer – that he'd broken four of Bill Swann's ribs and would break four more.

A few minutes more, and the two of them then decided to go back to Emily's kitchen to see what sort of state Bill was in. Maybe they wanted to find out whether Emily was going to be able to go back home without being beaten up again. This time they were gone about fifteen minutes before they returned.

After spending a bit more time at Mary Ann's, Gallagher

resumed his farewell tour of the district. He went to the Royal Oak on the corner of the square, and Emily went home. Within minutes she was back at Mary Ann's yet again, even more upset than she had been after Bill had thumped her. She asked Mary Ann to come with her back to the Swann house.

Neither Mary Ann nor her nineteen-year-old son looked keen. They knew Bill Swann, and they didn't want to tangle with him when he was drunk and angry about being roughed up by his wife's young fancy man. Then, to their astonishment, Emily told them, 'I think my master is dead.'

She begged them to come, and eventually they did, reluctantly. They found Bill Swann battered and bloodied on the floor in the back kitchen with his head wedged up at a funny angle against a cupboard. The long iron poker from the range was on the floor next to him. He was most decidedly dead.

When the news was broken to Gallagher in the bar of the George, he decided to make himself scarce. He wasn't seen again until more than two months later, in August, when he was found living at his sister's house in Middlesbrough.

Men died in drunken brawls every Saturday night all over Yorkshire and indeed all over Britain, and generally such deaths were regarded as no more than misadventure, or manslaughter at most. Had Gallagher had the fight with Bill outside the George, it's entirely possible that the world would have heard no more of it. The problem was that this brawl had happened in the man's own home and at the fists, it was said, of his wife's lover. Those facts turned Bill's death from a piece of sordid drunken violence – his, as well as his attacker's – to a sensational national scandal. In the version which was reported in newspapers all over Britain, Bill was transformed from selfish bully into an innocent victim, a hard-working man who had died at the brutal hands of his disloyal wife's inebriated younger lover.

An inquest had to be held, of course, and in an irony that was probably lost on the thousand-strong crowd of ghoulish onlookers that gathered in the street outside, it was held at the Horse Shoe Inn on George Street where Bill had spent a good deal of the money that should have gone home to his wife and children.

When the inquest jury returned a verdict of wilful murder, the foreman asked whether John Gallagher alone should be blamed for the fatal attack. 'For might it not also be thought that the dead man's wife, by her willingness to look on and even to encourage the man to attack her husband, should also be considered culpable for her husband's death?' the foreman asked.

The coroner, local lawyer David Wightman, replied that it was no part of his job to tell the police or the Crown who should be brought to trial for murder. Having stated his legal position, he went on to make it very clear indeed that he heartily agreed with the jury that Emily was as guilty as Gallagher, concluding: 'I shall make sure to write to the appropriate authorities to be certain they are aware of the views of the members of the jury on this point.'

From that point onwards, Emily Swann was as good as dead herself.

Chapter Nine

LONDON AND LOST OPPORTUNITIES

I have a snapshot in my photo album that draws me to it like no other. I doubt whether anyone else would look twice at it; for me, however, not even the fistfuls of pictures I have of my three boys at every stage of their childhood hold quite the fascination that this one does.

Like the snaps everyone of my age took on a pocket Instamatic camera in the 1970s and 1980s, the quality isn't very good. There's a greeny-yellowish tinge to it, and everything's a bit fuzzy. The picture was taken through glass, from the third-floor bedroom of the place I was sharing at the time with another girl. I was eighteen.

In the street below, lined with narrow Victorian terraced villas, a grey-haired woman is walking away from our house, apparently oblivious to me and my camera high above her, although I know that I must be in her thoughts. She is obviously elderly. She is wearing a beige mac that is a shade too big for her shrunken frame, and her shoulders have rolled forwards with age. The grey hair is an unruly thatched bob. There's lots of it, but it looks coarse and bushy, like clumps of grubby horsehair sofa stuffing. When I looked at the picture after it came back from the developers, I found myself thinking – so that's what happens to our thick, glorious, flame-tinged hair when old age robs it of its colour and softness. My hair will be like that one day. Because the woman in the photograph is Elsie, my gran. My abuser. The woman who made the first fifteen years of my life an absolute misery. And only seconds before I took this picture, she was gazing up at the windows of the house where I was sharing the upstairs flat with my friend Joan from Arundale.

If she knocked on the door that day, I didn't hear her. If she rang the bell, she would have had no way of knowing that it didn't work, that we couldn't have heard her, that our friends never bothered with it – they simply pushed the front door open and hammered on the door at the top of the stairs if they wanted to rouse us.

I had no idea whether she had come all the way into Scarborough – a six-mile bus ride – with the intention of speaking to me, or whether she'd come on some mad voyeuristic impulse just to eyeball the street and the house where I lived. I was frankly amazed that she knew where I lived, and so shocked when I happened to glance out of my bedroom window and see her white moon face staring straight at me that the first thing I did was rear backwards to get out of her line of vision.

My stomach flipped over with the sick fear that the sight of her still could trigger automatically, despite all the bravado of the shouting matches I'd had with her before I left home, and I hung back in what I hoped was the shadow of my room, just standing there gasping. It took a few moments to remember that I was – in my own eyes at least – a grown-up, an independent young woman with a job and a home of my own, and she no longer had any hold over me. And as my breathing steadied, in place of the fear came disbelief, and then curiosity. I asked myself, what on earth is she doing here? I hadn't seen her for months and, even when I had, it was only as the inevitable side-effect of going round to the prefab now and again to check on Mum and Silver.

I also went down to Filey to see Granddad whenever I felt I could bear to see him in the old people's home, which he clearly hated and where he seemed to have lost his identity, never mind his memory. Despite all my strutting about Scarborough being my own mistress, I still felt compelled to keep an eye on them all. In some odd way, now that I had broken free of them, our roles seemed to have been reversed and I sometimes felt as if I was a neglectful parent who had left the children home alone. None of which helped to explain why, after all this time, after all the foul-mouthed abuse before I left home and the frosty refusal to know me ever since, my grandmother had done the thing she dreaded most and left the safety of her chair by the gas fire to come and stand outside my flat. What can have been going through her mind?

At this point any normal person would have run down the stairs and into the street to find out. I could have run after her, taken hold of her arm like the grown-up I imagined I was, and asked her to come back. Maybe even got her to sit down in my kitchen, having come so far, and have a cup of tea. But neither she nor I were quite what you'd call normal, and nor was our relationship. A cup of tea? It was inconceivable that she could do anything so ordinary, or that it would occur to me to try to persuade her to do it.

Instead, as she turned away and broke the spell that had kept me rooted to the spot, something made me run to my dressing table, pick up my camera, shoot back to the window and take that picture as she walked away. It seemed urgent and vital to have tangible proof of this extraordinary event. I had no idea what I was likely to do with the evidence of it, but this was the day that my gran had actually come looking for me, as if it mattered to her where I lived, and it needed to be recorded. It was never referred to by any of us when I visited them afterwards – not me, not my mother, not her.

This concrete evidence of my grandmother's strange, unexplained visit was a picture of one missed opportunity representing many. It was a snapshot of my state of mind at the time and how it was to remain throughout my twenties and early thirties – I was transfixed by my past, which returned, unasked, time and time again to influence my choices – usually for the worse. It is compelling evidence of how well I had learned the family habit of coping with the past by not quite looking it in the eye. This, as I later discovered, had been my grandmother's downfall. It kept her doggedly, fearfully silent about her family, her parents, and particularly her mother.

*

I had moved into this new place in Bellevue Road a few months after Granddad had been carted off to the Silver Birches home in Filey. I didn't seem to be getting on so well with my flatmate Jane at Nelson Street, though I had no idea what it was I'd done to offend her. Perhaps it was the strain of being crammed into a tiny dormer conversion, with hardly room to swing a cat. Perhaps it was our landlady, who still observed our comings and goings like a hawk, always on the watch for us bringing in men. We learned that she was telling any of her neighbours who would listen that we were little tramps, out at all hours with men and up to no good. Jane said that the stories she told about us were more scandalous than the *News of the World*.

'Where've you been, coming in at this time of night? I've been waiting for you. We're respectful people round here. The neighbours are talking,' she would say, catching us as we came in.

'Mrs Bennett,' I would reply, feeling completely exasperated with this annoying woman who seemed to have become our prison warder. 'We pay our rent. We respect your premises. Don't you think you should let us be?'

To be honest, there was too much going on for me to care very much about any of this. For a start, I was determined to be out enjoying my freedom from James, blast him, and often went on from Emma's when it closed at 2 a.m. to the gay club that stayed open until 4 a.m., grabbed a few hours' sleep and rolled into work late.

'Why on earth can't you get into work when everyone else does?' pleaded my boss Neal, who was at his wits' end with me when my timekeeping got really bad. The other staff noticed and, not unnaturally, got pretty fed-up that I appeared to be getting away with it.

And Mum was calling round constantly. The old landlady was beginning to make sour remarks about how Mum should be paying rent too, given how often she was there. I could guess that it was almost unbearable for Mum back in the prefab, with Granddad gone and no company except for her mad, unpleasable mother. The problem was that there was hardly enough space in the bedsit for Jane and me, and there was absolutely nowhere for her to sleep over. A part of me was inclined to be tough on her for not having the gumption to get out of her mother's house and get some independence, just as I had done, and I was still very bitter about the fact that she hadn't had enough strength of mind to do this for the two of us when I was young.

I got particularly exasperated with her over my eighteenth birthday, which came round in February 1975. I invited her to come out for a drink with Joan and me before we went on to meet our mates in the club in town where we were intending to have a full-on birthday blowout. While we were in the pub, Mum got chatting to a bloke who was sitting at the table next to ours. He was about her age, maybe a bit older – impossibly ancient as far as Jo and I were concerned. We were having quite a nice time until I noticed uneasily how well Mum and this bloke seemed to be getting on.

'Mum,' I said finally. 'Sorry to interrupt, but Jo and I will have to go soon. We'll walk you to the bus.'

'No thanks, love. You go on.'

'It's going to be getting dark soon, Mum. You should

really be getting home. You know how you hate having to get off the bus in the dark.'

'That's all right, love. I'll be fine.'

I suspected that she was a bit tipsy. The niggling suspicion I'd had about her new-found friendship turned into full-blown disgust. I couldn't believe it. My mother, my own middle-aged mother, was on the pull. And, incredibly, she *had* pulled. And they were both so, so *old*. To my teenage brain it was beyond disgusting, but nothing I could say would persuade her to leave the pub with us and go home. Joan finally persuaded me to leave without her and let her sort herself out.

'She is a grown-up,' Jo reminded me gently.

'But how can she? That dirty old man. How can she do such a thing?' I protested. I had awful visions of the stories I'd heard of her hanging around the quayside waiting for fishermen when she was young, and to add to that, I had no confidence that she could look after herself – I'd seen her being bullied one too many times. I felt like an anxious mother leaving her daughter behind as we walked out of the pub.

Jo, I suspect, found it all rather funny, but she was careful not to let it show. She distracted me, promising me my first legal drink in a nightclub, and chatted as we walked across town about the good-looking boys we knew and whether some gorgeous new ones might turn up. I had a great night, one of those that go on right through until the next morning, but as I made my way unsteadily home to Nelson Street, I half expected to find Mum unconscious on the doorstep, or to be nabbed by the landlady before I could get up the stairs with a long, outraged rant about my mum and her fancy man turning up in the middle of the night. It didn't happen, but I still didn't forgive her for a long time afterwards. I did not approve.

At work, and in the evenings when we met up to go out together, Joan listened patiently to my many complaints about Jane – the frosty atmosphere, how she hardly talked to me. Finally she was able to say to me one day: 'My flatmate's moving out. You know how big the place is, you can have your own room instead of sharing with Jane – and we've even got the spare room. I know it's tiny, but it's OK for a couple of nights for mates. Or your mum. Why don't you move in with me?'

And so I did, early in the spring of 1975. It felt as if things were on the up again, and that this time I really was leaving behind the heartbreak of losing James and Trafalgar Square. I moved into the wonderful solitude of the front bedroom of Joan's flat on the top floor, sheer luxury after the shared room in Nelson Street.

Slowly, by degrees, James had begun to creep back into my life. He had called round a few times at Nelson Street when he'd been to visit his mum, and there had been a few nights when I'd smuggled him into the bedsit. We had made up, sort of, but it couldn't be a proper relationship when the two of us lived so far apart. When he asked me over to Bradford, I went. I still loved him, hurt though I was, and we got on as well as we ever had. They were quite strange weekends. They involved a lot of sitting around in his new mates' houses while everyone smoked spliffs. It wasn't quite my kind of thing, and I didn't care much for Bradford, which seemed so much more run-down than the area around Wakefield where Aunt Rene and Uncle Ted lived, but at least it meant I saw him.

James can't have thought much of Bradford either, because he moved again when his mum, keen to return to the south, managed to arrange a house swap with someone who wanted to move out of London. The flat she got was in Kensington, at the end of the long High Street, a short walk from its famous market and from buzzing Earl's Court. James decided to go with her.

I suppose he could have gone off without a word, but he came over instead to tell me all about it.

By this time I had a room of my own at Bellevue Road and no one on sentry duty on the ground floor, and he was able to come over and stay more often. My glamorous affair with the married sales rep had fizzled out – he'd gone back to the his pregnant wife. I'd always known it was just a bit of fun, and I wasn't missing him at all, especially now that James was easing his way back into my life. He certainly wanted me to know that he wasn't trying to get as far away as possible from me by moving to London, but I did a lot of flouncing about and sulking about him going off just at the point when we seemed to be getting close again.

'I don't know whether I'm coming or going with you, James. Every time I think we're getting somewhere, you disappear!' I complained. I was beginning to feel that enough was enough. But I also knew by now that I would always go back to him. Even though our relationship had had so many ups and downs, he had been a crazy kind of constant in my life for a while now. I felt we were soulmates.

'Mum needs a hand, I can't let her go alone,' he told me. 'And there's more work down there. But you could follow.'

This was a step forward, and once I'd decided I'd done enough sulking, I graciously conceded that it did seem like a lovely idea to go to London. It seemed even more wonderful over the next few months when I suddenly started getting long letters from James telling me how much he loved me, how much he wanted me to be with him, what a fool he'd been to let me go, and how he was sure that we were meant to be together. Why not? I thought. I'll take some holiday and go down and see him. I've never been to London before – how fantastic will that be for a holiday? And a free place to stay, too.

I think my catchphrase during that first weekend was 'Bloody hell' when my mouth wasn't doing an impression of the Blackwall Tunnel. When you grow up a long way from London, it's even more wonderful and amazing when you get there than the pictures you've seen on the news. It's a more fabulous, glamorous place than you ever imagined. I was completely bowled over by the crowds, the neon signs – as a seaside girl I'd seen a few of those, but never on this scale – and the aroma of every kind of food under the sun. In the 1970s, Scarborough had chip shops and that was about it – I'd simply never seen such a thing as the first pizza I had in London with James, and it tasted wonderful. My senses were overwhelmed by the heady spice of the place, walking around Earl's Court with all the other young people, particularly the Aussies and New Zealanders who all seemed to end up there when they were back-packing through London, seeing streets full of people at ten o'clock at night as if it was midday on the Scarborough sea front in high season, standing outside a kebab shop – another extraordinary new kind of food that fascinated me. I was head over heels in love that summer, and not just with James.

I went up and down on the train several times. It was great to see him again, of course, and getting together after a while apart meant we had a terrific time in bed when I first arrived. And then when we got up to go out, it just got better. I wasn't sure whether I was there to see James. I think he was just a great reason to come and see London. I loved it. It was a million miles away from my life back in Yorkshire.

Coming back home got more and more difficult. I began to board the train at King's Cross Station with a heavy heart. I felt as though London brought out in me the woman I was born to be. As the two-and-a-half-hour journey flew by, I always felt I was leaving my hopes and dreams behind, and I was never sure I would get back to retrieve them.

But I had Granddad to think of, stuck in his nursing home in Filey. I knew he hated it, but even so I was startled when he turned up in Bellevue Road one day having somehow found his way to the new flat. He announced, like a small boy with a spotted handkerchief slung over his shoulder on a stick, that he had run away.

I rang Silver Birches to tell them where he was.

'Well, I'm not sure we can have him back here,' the

prim, snotty voice on the end of the line informed me. I was speechless. I had expected her to sound at least a bit relieved to hear that he was safe and sound with me.

'What do you mean?'

'He attacked a member of staff. We can't have staff subjected to that kind of violence.'

'Granddad? He's in his seventies. He can hardly walk and he couldn't hit a dartboard.'

'That's all very well for you to say. We have to care for him day after day. If you'd like to ring back in a couple of hours or so, we'll be able to tell you whether we can have him back or not.'

'Don't bother!' I shouted, and slammed down the phone.

Jo agreed with me that Granddad should stay with us, that he couldn't go back to that revolting place. We moved him into the spare room, and without the faintest idea of what it was going to involve, I became his carer.

That put paid to my visits to London, but to begin with I went off to work each day much happier about him, knowing that he was safe in the flat, that he had the telly and a comfy chair, and that I'd left him some lunch so that he didn't have to do anything too difficult for himself while I was gone.

If he'd had all his faculties, I think it might have gone on like that for a long time. Maybe I would have found a place for just the two of us eventually, and been his flatmate for as long as he needed me. But I found out the hard way how difficult and painful it is to live with someone whose memories, and the personality shaped by them, is being permanently erased, cell by cell, with every day that passes. When he started to refuse the meals I'd cooked because he didn't know what they were – there were days when he couldn't recognize stew and dumplings, which we'd eaten at least twice a week all through my childhood – I thought he was being awkward and grumpy. When he refused to let either Jo or me choose what we watched on the telly, I thought he was being selfish. When he got angry with me for a trivial oversight, like offering him a jumper he didn't want to wear, I didn't recognize my wonderful Granddad.

We did have some good times during those few months, including a Christmas when Jo went home to her parents in Whitby, and I had Granddad and Mum with me in the flat. I cooked a turkey and we gave each other presents and watched the telly – very simple stuff, but very happy because the three of us were together and we could do what we wanted without having to tip-toe around Gran. Then, after the Queen's speech, *The Wizard of Oz* came on. Perfect, I thought. Something we can all enjoy. But as the hurricane blew Dorothy to Oz and the witch's feet stuck out from under the log cabin with the ruby slippers on them, Granddad threw a monumental wobbler. 'Stop it, stop it!' he shouted. 'That's a bad, horrible film. Get it off.' The images were scaring him to death and we had to switch the television off for the rest of the day.

By the early weeks of 1977, I knew I couldn't cope any more. I sat down one evening and cried after another tussle with him, thinking that I'd tried everything, I'd been patient, I'd put up with his tantrums. You're my Granddad and I love you, I thought, looking at him through the tears. But I don't know you any more.

It might have been different if I'd had a proper home of my own and plenty of time to give to him, but I couldn't afford to rent a place on my own, and I certainly couldn't afford not to work. Joan was simply wonderful with him, but I knew that I couldn't expect her to put up with his increasingly strange and aggressive behaviour.

I called Social Services and asked for help in finding Granddad a care home where people who knew what they were doing could keep him safe. I was adamant that I wouldn't let him leave Scarborough again, and we found him a place at the northern end of the town.

I cried as if I would never be able to stop the day I took him there and settled him into his room. I felt such a failure. I felt I had betrayed him, just like Gran had done. I had let him down in a way he would never have let me down.

'You are going to love this beautiful home and the gardens that you can sit in,' I coaxed cheerily. 'Look out there, Granddad! You're right next door to the Oriel cricket ground. You love cricket.' I tried desperately to raise a smile from him, but I wasn't going to get my way on this one. Granddad had become quite cold.

'I hate it here. Why am I here? I want to go back to Quarry Mount,' he declared obstinately. He was breaking my heart. Didn't he remember that Gran had chucked him out for ever?

'Granddad, please. I've hunted high and low to find you

the best place I possibly can. You're not too far away from me, and I promise I shall visit every week.'

The grandfather I adored stared straight through me as if I didn't exist. I walked away knowing that there was absolutely no reasoning with this man I no longer recognized, but I also knew I would always love him, and I resigned myself to spending whatever time we had together in making him as comfortable as I possibly could, even if I couldn't bring him the happiness I felt he deserved.

Within a few weeks of moving in, it seemed to me that the light had entirely gone from his eyes. Increasingly I had to force myself to go and visit him, because each time I arrived it took him longer and longer to recognize who I was.

I took refuge as best I could in taking on lots of overtime to pay for my resumed trips to James in London, which had been suspended while I had Granddad with me. Neal was pushing me hard at Arundale. He was building his business and wanted me to master any technology or skill that might give him a competitive edge, which meant there was plenty of overtime to be had. I very firmly put aside the sense that I was being pulled in several different directions at once – work, Mum, Granddad, London – and for the next year or so focused on the money and the escapism of spending it in London.

Going to Wakefield to see Granddad's relatives now felt humdrum to me, but stepping off the train at King's Cross was one great big hit of freedom and release. Sometimes James would be there to meet me and I would swoop down the grubby platform alongside the chuntering diesel engines and up on to the concourse to fly into his arms – like being in my very own movie. He had guided me through the mysteries of the Underground on my first few trips, getting off at Kensington High Street and walking through the subways that were always thrumming with wall-to-wall buskers in the 1970s, but it didn't take long for me to feel perfectly capable of getting around on my own and seeing the sights. James was working as an auxiliary in a hospital by then and he often had to work shifts. I'd head out with him in the morning as he set off to work and then leave him for the West End and the deli bars, the like of which we didn't have in the north. I didn't have a great deal of money to spend, but I was happy just walking along streets whose names were on the Monopoly board, captivated by the sheer variety of faces and clothes on people of every shade of skin from darkest Nigerian black through to palest Scandinavian, and the amazing jewellery that women walked around in during the day.

As I sat at the top of Piccadilly one afternoon waiting for James to join me after his shift, watching all the tourists go by and the pigeons landing on Eros – still stuck then on his little roundabout in the middle of the thundering, endless waltz of taxis and red buses – and marvelling at the neon signs at the bottom of Regent Street, a bloke wandered up to me. He must have been in his mid-thirties. He was quite smart-looking, but there was something a bit seedy about him too.

'Hello, darling,' he said.

I looked at him.

'Do you speak English?'

'Yes, thanks,' I told him, looking him right in the eye with what I hoped was a 'don't even think about trying anything on, pal' look on my face.

'You're a pretty girl.'

Silence.

'You looking for work? Good-looking girl like you, you could earn a hundred pounds a day round here. Nothing tacky – the classiest nightclub in the West End . . .

I smiled a little, got up and walked off, saying, 'No thanks. I'm waiting for my boyfriend.'

I hoped I looked dignified, but I was secretly thrilled to bits that I'd been asked if I wanted to work in Soho. I knew he probably meant a job in a strip club, as I'd already had a good look round Soho, just a few streets away across Lower Regent Street. I couldn't wait to tell Joan – what a laugh!

I got used to the wheelers and dealers, who seemed to be everywhere, always sidling up to you if they thought you were from out of town and might be an easy target for whatever it was they were trying to do a deal in. I was even offered drugs.

James and I did all the things I'd read about in magazines: we went to a jazz club in Kensington, watched plays in Holland Park, browsed among the antique stalls on Portobello Road and walked miles across London to see the clothes in Petticoat Lane in the East End. We had a favourite old-fashioned pub near the Bayswater Road, had picnics by the Serpentine and listened to the mad people who ranted away at Speakers' Corner. On those early visits James was always the attentive lover who needed me by his side and never wanted me to leave him. It was like the early days at Trafalgar Square in Scarborough – and we talked about our time together there as we wandered across Trafalgar Square in London, feeling that we were both a little more grown-up and a bit more careful of each other now.

Every now and then he'd press me. 'How are your mum and Granddad getting on in Scarborough, Flic? Can't you start to look for a job down here?'

How I wanted to tell James that everything was fine and that I would love to join him. But in reality I knew I couldn't.

'Things are just the same, James. I can't see myself getting away. But hey, let's just have fun. Let's just enjoy ourselves for now and take things as they come, yes?'

'Whatever you say, Flic. I just want you to know that I would love you to live down here with me.'

I went down to London to spend the Christmas before my twentieth birthday with James and his sister. Their mum was away, and his sister's boyfriend was staying over too. It was the most fantastic Christmas Day of my life. We went out the day before to buy our dinner on Soho's street market, and all the Christmas lights blazing on every shopping street were just wonderful. The others got back to the flat before me and when I arrived the turkey's legs and head were poking through the letterbox to greet me. On Christmas morning we started drinking far too early. We managed to cook dinner, but we couldn't seem to get round to eating it.

I did some outrageous stuff in London with James,

things we'd never have tried back home. It was the era of the squatting movement – young people occupied empty houses sometimes for political reasons and sometimes just because they wanted a free place to live. I did it a couple of times with James when I was down in London with him, sleeping on a floor in a flat in Earl's Court and another in Kensington. I took a week's holiday one summer on the strength of James's promise that we would be able to stay with a group of his friends in a squat right in the heart of Bayswater – free, of course. It was a lovely house, huge, with enormous windows looking over a tree-lined street.

We'd been there for a few days when the police arrived with an eviction order and raided the whole building. Squatting wasn't exactly illegal – it was a civil offence – but there was always the possibility that landlords would press charges for any damage done to the building if they got an eviction order, and then it became a criminal matter, and a criminal record wasn't something I wanted. James's friends had told me that the police weren't too fussy about who they arrested and charged. The last thing I wanted was to end up in court during my week's holiday. How would I explain that to Neal? So I was as keen as everyone else to get out of the building under my own steam, before the police could get hold of me. Panicking, James and I crammed ourselves into the little downstairs loo, hoping to escape unseen through the window. 'Quick! Help me up! I can hear them outside!' I hissed.

'Move your leg, will you? I'm never going to be able to fit through there!' he hissed back.

'This is absolutely ridiculous, James! I don't do things like this. What if we get caught?' I remonstrated.

'Will you just shut up and deal with it, Flic. Quick! And take those bloody silly heels off, will you.' I could hear the exasperation creeping into James's voice now. He hardly ever swore at me.

'Jump – now!' he shouted in military fashion.

'You know I don't like heights,' I protested. Too late. I felt myself being unceremoniously pushed out. We were spotted by one of the officers who was standing outside, waiting for something like this to happen, and he chased us down the alley and along a few streets before deciding that it wasn't worth the effort. I thought I had been wild back in Scarborough, but this was real adventure. I have to admit I was relieved to get back to James's mum's safe little maisonette.

Then James got really serious and asked me earnestly to move down to London to be with him. To give up my job for him – for the second time – but this time with a view to us building a life together, far away from all the difficulties of the past – mine, not his; we both knew that – where I could grow in a way I would never be able to in Scarborough. He had a very high opinion of my talents, and he said that someone with my get-up-and-go would do well, whatever I chose to turn my hand to. There would be so many more career opportunities for me to take advantage of in London.

'You'll find it even easier than me to get work, that's no problem,' he told me. 'And they'll think you're brilliant.

Compare the wages you'd earn here with what you get in Scarborough. You'd have the pick of the best jobs on offer.'

And I'm sure he was right. There was nothing wrong with my work ethic and I was good at what I did. That was why Neal had by now promoted me to chief cashier at Arundale. I was maturing and becoming more reliable, and really enjoying the responsibility. I had already been wandering up Kensington High Street looking in all the secretarial agency windows – there were scores of them, and literally hundreds of jobs going, all paying double what I was earning – and I'd been thinking, 'What if?'

I got as far as handing in my notice and telling Neal I was going to London. But while I was trying to convince myself that this was the right thing to do, I couldn't get it out of my head that I would be abandoning Mum and Granddad completely if I moved so far away. Granddad was safe, and hardly aware of his surroundings by now. I was clinging to a loyalty that he really no longer needed from me. Maybe I was using it as an excuse to avoid such a big step. But it was much harder to argue myself out of my fears for Mum. Really, what would she do without me? She was such a lost soul, and I couldn't bear to think of her left alone with Gran, with not one other person to turn to, and no temporary refuge when she needed a break.

I withdrew my notice. Unable to face James, I wrote him a letter to tell him that I wouldn't be coming. I felt a huge sense of relief, which I disguised by telling myself that I was staying to see out my responsibilities to my family, but I can't deny that I was also pleased that I wouldn't have to leave my friends behind. And if I was honest, I wasn't sure that I loved James enough any more. I wasn't missing him that much when I was away from him. It was as if the storm of our passion had blown over.

James was devastated, of course. He couldn't understand why I didn't want to come, and he went on and on trying to persuade me. He didn't succeed. In my own mind, my London dream had come to an end.

Then Granddad died.

It was March 1978, the year I had turned twenty-one. The manager of the care home rang me at work to tell me. I imagine she knew I wasn't officially his next of kin, but she must have known enough about us by then to judge that of the three of us, Gran, Mum and me, I was the one she could most easily speak to. I stood at my desk with the receiver in my hand and howled, a primeval wail that must have made skin crawl and goose pimples rise all through the building. It was the kind of noise you'd hear coming out of the guts of someone whose entire family had been wiped out, and, actually, that was how it felt. Granddad was the only adult I had ever been able to trust and depend upon. Mum and Gran didn't come close. I felt in that moment that I had been orphaned, that I would be alone in the world for the rest of my life.

It was made worse by guilt. Because I couldn't bear to see Granddad looking so vacant, as if his personality had moved out of his body and gone to live somewhere else, I had hardly been to see him at all in recent months. I salved my conscience by sending him postcards, though I doubt whether he had any idea of who they came from or what they were of – and I had a postcard in my handbag that I was planning to send him at the end of that week.

I had to be the one to tell Mum and Gran. Joan took me home to our flat that day, and the next morning I went to Quarry Mount instead of going to work. Mum was fifty-nine, a year off retirement, but she no longer worked full-time and she was there in the kitchen doing the pots. Gran was in her place on the sofa, as ever. I got Mum to come in to the living room and sit down.

I started by saying, 'I've got to tell you . . .'

Tears filled my eyes and began to spill down my cheeks, even though I was trying very hard to be calm and give them the news without being too emotional about it. I tried again.

'Granddad. He died yesterday.'

That was all I could manage. I hung my head and just let myself cry quietly, trying to get it over with so I could see how they were taking it.

Neither of them said anything. Mum just sat there, trying to be invisible, looking as if I'd hit her. Gran had apparently not reacted. Yet there was a change, one that I could feel rather than see. The news had hit her in some hidden soft part of her. She was somehow stiller, more silent. It was as if the fight had gone out of her in that moment, perhaps because she knew that there would now never be another chance to fight Albert. I had a sudden moment's insight into the part he had played in her personal drama, as both her punchbag and the shield from behind which she could lob insults at the outside world.

Even when she was a monster to him, he had protected her above anyone else.

Exposed by his death, it was if she was looking around and thinking, 'Oh. They can all see me. Maybe I'd better behave.' From that point on, she made more of an effort to behave normally when I went round, although to see her smiling and nodding at me from the sofa was so odd that it was almost worse than being ignored.

I was dazed with grief, but I knew that I would have to do everything that needed to be done for Granddad, and I didn't have a clue. There was no point asking Mum to help, and I couldn't bring myself to speak to Gran, his betrayer, about it. Staff at the care home came to my rescue and told me where to go and who to speak to. I went alone to the Town Hall to register his death, and then to the Co-op to ask for help with organizing his funeral. Doing it all on my own when I was barely twenty-one and distraught was almost more than I could cope with.

Bossy, opinionated, full-of-herself Flic was gone, and in her place was a dazed, bereaved child who was worried sick about how she was going to pay for the funeral. I think I gasped when the funeral director told me it was going to cost around £300. I was only earning about £25 a week, and although I was reasonably good about putting some away for rainy days and holidays, I certainly didn't have that kind of money saved. Granddad, of course, had left nothing. And nothing could have persuaded me to ask Gran if she could pay for it. Thankfully the man at the Co-op, most tactfully, explained about a death grant that would cover the cost.

It was just us three at the funeral. I had considered telling Gran she couldn't come – I felt so angry at her for casting him out – but as I was explaining to Mum what time the funeral was and how she would be taken there in a car that the Co-op would send, she said, 'Will you come and get us?'

The 'us' was automatic with her. Of course she couldn't imagine a funeral for Granddad that wouldn't include Gran. And as I looked at Gran over Mum's head, I realized that it wasn't about what I thought. It was about Granddad, and about sending him off properly. They had been young and in love once – he must have loved her to look after her for so long – and it was not my place to come between them if she wanted to do something to make amends for some of the terrible things she'd done.

'Will you come, Gran?'

She nodded.

'I'll come with the car. Can you make sure you're ready on time?'

Another nod. 'Oh yes, yes.'

It was a one-size-fits-all kind of funeral. As our service at the crematorium was ending, the next family group was arriving behind us. Just keep moving. Yes, just keep moving, I told myself, and it will all be OK. I got Mum and Gran home, made sure they had some sandwiches for lunch, and caught the bus back to my flat in Scarborough. Then I lay on my bed and wept and wept.

I was sitting in my summer house recently, looking through photographs, and I happened to pick up the strange photo

I'd taken of Gran's retreating figure and turn it over. There, in her turn-of-the-twentieth-century copybook hand, scrawled unsteadily in pencil, were the words 'Elsie Baines, widow'. How did that happen? When did she get a chance to write that? I was as astonished as I would have been if she'd actually walked into the room at that moment, and by that time she'd been dead twenty-five years.

Then I remembered that I often let Mum take my photo albums home to the prefab with her after she'd been staying with me because she so enjoyed looking through the many pictures I'd taken of my friends and my holidays over the years since I'd left home. She got such pleasure from it – she was like a little girl looking through a picture book. It had never occurred to me that Gran might look through them too. It is just possible that when Gran came to Joan's flat on Bellevue Road that day, she had some confused idea that she might find Granddad there. When she found the picture among my photo albums, what on earth did she make of it? If she did knock on my door that day, did she realize I'd deliberately ignored her? Probably.

Certainly she would have known that I had seen her and I'd made no attempt to speak to her. In spite of all the bad things she'd done to me and to Mum and Granddad, there was something unbearably sad about this thought, and I found myself on the brink of tears. An older, wiser me would have run out into the street that day to ask her what it was she wanted. Did she want to see the last real home that Granddad had ever had? Did she want to say sorry to him and perhaps even to me? That was probably too much to hope for, of course, but perhaps she did want to make some gesture towards seeking forgiveness for letting fear and suspicion squander the many possibilities of love and happiness that had been on offer to her.

This message she'd left told me that, like me, she had regrets about the choices she'd made. Elsie Baines, widow. Three words, and a world of loss and longing.

Chapter Ten

A FUNERAL AND A TRIAL

'I don't doubt that Swann thrashed his wife often, but I do not think he was habitually cruel to her,' was the strangely contradictory opinion of the Wombwell police superintendent, Mr Quest. 'The wonder is he had not killed her. He has frequently gone home after leaving work and found his wife drunk in the house and nothing prepared for him in the way of food.

'Glass blowers are a class of men who from the nature of their work imbibe very freely and the deceased man was no exception to the general description of them . . . he was a good workman, attended regularly at his work and got on very well with them.'

In other words, it was a sin punishable by violence from a man twice her size if Emily drank and failed in her marital duties, but it was fine for Bill to be as drunk as he chose and to keep his family short of money. The many convictions he had for being thoroughly obnoxious when in his cups were forgotten, and even his work colleagues had rewritten history now that he was dead and could no longer pick a fight with them. His bosses sent a fine wreath to the funeral, and six glass blowers acted as pall-bearers.

He had been someone who few people were pleased to see coming down the street towards them, but in death Bill Swann became the most popular man in town. The crowd that followed his coffin to its final resting place in the town cemetery was so enormous that it gave the fine Wednesday, 10 June 1903, the atmosphere of a Saturday, as if the whole town was on its way to Barnsley to watch a football match.

The earliest arrivals had gathered in the streets around the Square, jostling one another to get a good look at the fine hearse waiting with its black-plumed horses outside the Swann house. It had been paid for by a wealthy local 'well-wisher' who chose to remain anonymous. Without the scandal that surrounded his death, Bill would certainly have had a pauper's funeral. Those onlookers who couldn't squeeze into the Square lined up along Station Road, three and four deep all the way to the cemetery on the other side of the Barnsley Road where they knew the hearse would pass by. What they really wanted to see, of course, was the Wombwell Murderess of the headlines, the adulterous wife who had egged her lover on to rid her of her inconvenient husband. They were to be disappointed.

Charles, holding the hand of young Ernest, followed the coffin, as did his Hinchcliffe aunts and two of his three sisters, Annie and Frances. Their uncles, the three older Swann brothers, who had barely had anything to do with Bill or his family for years, followed with their wives. Meanwhile, although Emily was ready to go too, she was being kept back in the house with little Elsie, still only four years old. The child, not allowed to go to the window, sensed the great, silent gathering beyond the front door and watched carefully from a corner as two policemen came to stand in the kitchen with their helmets under their arms.

They spoke to her mother quietly but sternly, as if she had done something wrong.

'I must go – how can I not go?' Emily was saying, but she didn't sound certain about it. Her voice sounded broken, and she didn't look at the policemen. She kept her eyes on the floor as she spoke.

Emily was dressed in the best clothes she had and, in her little girl's opinion, looked wonderful. When one of the policemen said, 'They don't want to see you, Mrs Swann. You had better not go,' Elsie could not understand why anyone would not want to see her mother.

The other policeman added solemnly: 'It can only end badly if you do go. You cannot want to provoke any unseemly display, today of all days.'

Emily's solid little figure, usually so upright, suddenly flopped as if she was a stuffed stocking doll. She sat down heavily on the kitchen chair behind her, bending her face low towards her knees and moving one hand up to the side of her head as if to fend off a blow. She tugged at the black bonnet strings beneath her chin and pulled the widow's bonnet backwards off her head, defeated and exhausted.

The policemen didn't say another word. They looked at each other. One nodded, and the two of them walked out through the door into Alma Square, stooping to replace their headgear as they stepped over the threshold. From outside there was a swelling, rolling buzz of murmuring as the crowd realized that Emily would not be seen in public today. The officers were swallowed up by the bright daylight and then the kitchen door closed on the outside world, leaving mother and daughter alone together in the gloom of the scullery.

Nothing could excuse what had happened. No matter what the circumstances, no one deserves to be beaten to death in their own home. But the vilification of Emily and the total lack of compassion for her situation was astonishing. Emily had struggled for two decades to find food and a warm bed for a new baby every two years or so, and had suffered at the hands of a violent drunkard. Yet that wasn't at all how the public saw it at the time.

Emily was excluded from her husband's funeral for fear that her appearance would cause a riot, and Bill was accompanied to his grave by his many hundreds of new best friends.

There were more police outside keeping onlookers well away from the house windows, but Elsie would have been able to see the bare heads of the men from Aldham's, her father's factory. Six of them had taken Bill Swann's coffin from the kitchen table and carried it to the hearse, and they were now getting ready to walk ahead of it, leading the way to the High Street and Station Road.

As the hearse clattered slowly off across the cobbles, Elsie might just have been able to glimpse Uncle Alec, Uncle Tom and Uncle George, her father's brothers, all of whom had refused to come into the house to watch the coffin being closed. Even Elsie knew that a coffin should not be closed without all the family being there to see it. When they were all gone, taking the crowds with them, Emily would have had some quiet moments in which to tell Elsie that she would soon be going to live with her grandma Hannah, or perhaps with one of her married sisters, and that she must be a good girl and try to help whoever was looking after her. By this time Emily knew that once Bill was in his grave, it would not be long before the police came for her.

The police did come, but they took a little longer than she expected. They waited until they found Gallagher at his sister's house in Middlesbrough on 5 August, and took Emily into custody on the following day. She was taken to Leeds to be held at Armley Gaol, rather than Wakefield, because she faced a murder charge, and appeared briefly at the courts next to the Town Hall there with Gallagher before being committed to the Assizes at York, where there were sittings four times a year to hear the most serious cases.

The imposing Assizes building, which looks like a mini Buckingham Palace across the green from ancient Clifford's Tower, is still the area's crown court today. The court room where she and Gallagher were brought up from the cells to the dock on Monday 7 December 1903 is still there and remains much as it was then, a symphony of heavy mahogany and brass designed to impress on everyone in it that the business under way is very serious indeed. They sat side by side, although a good metre and a half apart, each with a prison warder of their own sex sitting behind them. They were ordered to stand, and both pleaded not guilty to the wilful murder of Bill Swann on 6 June 1903.

The court reporter noted that 'in the ladies' gallery [the public gallery separated men and women] were numerous friends of the prisoner Swann, some of her relations dressed in deep mourning, occupying prominent positions directly over the witness box'.

The first witness was Mary Ann Ward, Emily's friend who had lived opposite the Swanns in the next terrace, and the woman who had given John Gallagher a room when Bill had first kicked him out. Although Mary Ann had been hosting the beer-drinking party held in her kitchen on the Saturday afternoon that Bill died, it was Gallagher who had paid for the beer from his larger than usual pay packet. On the Friday he had worked his last shift at Mitchell Main colliery, and he had been paid off, the court heard, because he had decided to go to Bradford and get away from the difficult situation with the Swanns. Neighbours had already overheard more than one argument and bouts of fighting between the two men in the previous few weeks because although he'd moved out, Gallagher was still going in and out of the Swann's house to see Emily.

The drinking had begun just after the midday meal and had carried on until late afternoon. The party included Mary Ann's fourteen-year-old daughter Rose, her teenage son Edward, his friend Walter Wigglesworth, John Gallagher, Emily and 'some other people'.

Everyone who knew of the case assumed that there was something going on between Emily and Gallagher, but it was Mary Ann who sensationally gave the first public confirmation of it.

'Did she come to your house when the prisoner was your lodger?' asked the prosecution barrister.

'Yes, but I did not see anything, except that I once saw him with his arm round her. Nothing more. But she told me that he had been with her at night when her husband was from home at his work. Her husband worked shifts at the bottle factory and often had to work nights.'

Emily, sitting next to Gallagher in the dock in her black mourning dress and black bonnet, dipped her head to avoid the eyes that were turned on her as this was revealed to the judge, the twelve men of the jury, the court officials facing the dock and the public gallery. Her sisters in the gallery behind must also have studied their laps for a moment or two.

Mary Ann identified the moment when the fatal events of that afternoon began to unfold at Gallagher's request of fourteen-year-old Rose Ward that she run round to the pawn shop to redeem his best waistcoat and jacket. 'When she brought them back, Mrs Swann took them to her own house and Mr Gallagher followed her. Afterwards, about ten minutes later, he returned with the vest and jacket.'

Bill had chosen this moment to return after spending all day out drinking. They had only been in the house a few minutes, but Bill had lost his temper as soon as he saw Gallagher. Feeling that the man might calm down if he left, Gallagher had decided that discretion was the better part of valour and gone back to Mary Ann's. However, once he was out of the way, Bill had attacked.

'When he had had another drink, Mrs Swann came back with a shawl over her head,' said Mary Ann. 'She had a black eye. Gallagher said: "Who has done that?" and she replied: "Our Bill." Then he said: "I'll give the bugger something for himself," and went out. Mrs Swann had gone out before him.'

Mary Ann could not recall how long Gallagher had been gone, but recalled that when he came back, he had another glass of beer and announced: 'I have given the bugger something and I'll give him some more.'

She said she had been at the Swann's house two nights earlier when the two men were 'having a few words', and she had heard Bill order Gallagher out of the house. Gallagher had refused to go – 'I'll only go for a better man than you.' Mary Ann said that Mrs Swann then 'made an offensive remark to her husband'. Bill threw a pint pot at her and it hit Emily and broke, and part of it ricocheted on to Mary Ann. Bill then swore at Gallagher and yelled: 'If you want her, take her.'

She was asked if she could remember whether Gallagher had told her what he'd done to Bill Swann when he came back into her kitchen that Saturday afternoon.

'If I can remember, I think he said he had broken three or four ribs.'

This was a line that three other witnesses from the Square were to repeat during the trial, which is very curious as there had been no mention of this very specific detail in the evidence of witnesses at the inquest into Bill's death, even though events must have been very much fresher in the minds of the local people who gave evidence to the coroner. The first mention of Bill having had exactly four of his ribs broken in the attack was, indeed, made at the inquest, but only in the evidence of the surgeon who had carried out the post-mortem, who had found that the fourth, fifth, sixth and seventh ribs on the right-hand side of his rib cage were fractured. The cause of death, he said, had been a brain haemorrhage caused by a severe blow to the head. It makes me wonder if, during the five months leading to the trial, local gossip about Bill's death influenced the witnesses' memories, or if the police somehow suggested to them this is what happened.

The witnesses that followed Mary Ann were her fourteen-year-old daughter, her eighteen-year-old son, his seventeen-year-old friend Walter Wrigglesworth, Alfred Harper, described as 'a youth', which in the language of the time suggests that he was under the age of eighteen, and John Dunn, an eighteen-year-old miner. Apart from Mary Ann, there was no evidence at all from anyone who would at the time have been considered an adult – the legal age of majority was twenty-one – and yet it was on the testimony of these young people that the innocence of John Gallagher and Emily Swann was judged.

Mary Ann's evidence only proved that Gallagher had been drinking all afternoon, that Emily might have been drunk too, and that Bill Swann and Gallagher had argued before. She said that Gallagher had on at least one previous occasion given Bill two black eyes after he'd beaten up his wife, but this only tended to support Gallagher's assertion that he had never intended to kill; that he assumed Bill would survive the beating, as he had done other beatings.

It was what the young people claimed to have overheard Emily and Gallagher saying to each other that provided the prosecution with the evidence they said proved that the two of them had murder in mind as they crossed the street together after Bill hit Emily.

'I heard Gallagher say he had broken Bill's four ribs and would break four more,' Rose Ward told the court.

Her brother Edward repeated this word for word with the added embellishment of 'I heard Mrs Swann say "I hope he will kill the bastard" when the prisoners went out together from the kitchen.'

Alfred Harper, the youth, also said he'd heard Emily say she hoped Gallagher would kill her husband. Then, he said, as Gallagher left Mary Ann's kitchen, he heard him say: 'I'll finish him out [kill him] before I go to Bradford.'

This was the only moment at which it seemed to occur to anyone in the courtroom that the hearing of the witnesses had become conveniently acute.

'Do you swear that he said he would finish him out?' asked Gallagher's barrister.

'Yes, sir.'

'Have you ever said this before?'

'Yes, sir.'

'Was Mrs Ward there, or Mrs Swann?'

'Yes, they were in the house. I was on the doorstep.'

'You are aware that you are the only person who heard it?'

'Yes, sir, I am.'

Alfred Harper's critical evidence of Gallagher's intention to murder Bill Swann was not challenged further.

Most damning for Emily, however, was the evidence of John Dunn, who lived in the house immediately opposite the Swanns'. He had been at home, apparently looking out of his window towards the Swanns' house a good deal of the evening, and had seen Gallagher go into it twice between 6 p.m. and 7 p.m.

A surveyor had given evidence at the start of the trial stating that Dunn's house was just over fifty feet away – about fifteen metres. Yet Dunn said he had heard struggling inside the house opposite and that he heard Emily shout: 'Give it to him, Johnny.' This, if it was true, strongly suggested 'common purpose', the principle in English law that made it possible to accuse someone of murder even if they hadn't struck the fatal blow. Dunn followed this up with the even more sensational assertion that as Gallagher returned to make his second attack on Bill, he had heard him say: 'I will murder the fucking swine.'

Dunn topped even that showstopper with one more allegation that must have had the courtroom gasping; he insisted that Gallagher had left Bill Swann's house with Emily, and that the two of them had been holding hands and smiling. This seems an obvious lie. The prosecution hadn't been able to produce any other witness who was willing to say that they had seen the pair being so openly intimate, and even Mary Ann had insisted that she had only once seen Gallagher put his arm around her in the relative privacy of Mary Ann's kitchen. But Dunn was not challenged and the jury members were free to deduce that Emily was a woman without morals and without shame.

No one contested the prosecution witnesses' statements,

and no witnesses were called by the defence. Emily and Gallagher were never given a chance to speak for themselves and give their side of the story. All this was common in murder trials at the time, and their lawyers had advised them not to seek permission to go into the witness box in case they incriminated themselves – but it's hard to see what they could have said that would have been more incriminating than the evidence of their former neighbours.

I came across Emily's story again in *Dead Woman Walking*, written by criminologist Annette Balinger, who lectures at Keele University.* She summed up the attitudes towards Emily of all those who didn't know her:

> *For them there was only one truth about Emily Swann; she was a drunken, violent, foul-mouthed, unfaithful wife – a woman who was both out of control and uncontrollable, hence in dire need of discipline.*
>
> *Emily's experience as a battered wife and as a human being was almost totally silenced . . . official documentation showed Emily to be a drunken, violent prostitute, a sluttish housewife who had stepped beyond the boundary of acceptable female conduct and behaviour.*

Her lawyer, Mr Newell, made one last-ditch attempt to show that she was not an entirely bad woman, saying he was going to call fourteen-year-old Frances Swann to the

* *Dead Woman Walking: Executed women in England and Wales 1900–55*, Ashgate Publishing Ltd, October 2000.

witness stand to give evidence about what kind of mother she was. But the judge said, 'Had you better not?' instantly discouraging him. He added ominously, 'I don't know whether you know as much about her as I do,' referring to the list of Emily's convictions he had in front of him, and which he was hinting heavily would do her no good if the jury found out about them.

'The little girl says she has been a good mother, and so on,' said Mr Newell.

'Yes, but if you call a witness to prove she has a good character, it won't stop there. It cannot,' the judge pointed out, by which he meant that once evidence was brought to show her in a good light, the prosecution would have every right to reveal her criminal record. In the context of her adulterous relationship with John, the conviction for prostitution would go particularly badly against her.

Emily's lawyer backed down, and nothing else was said in mitigation about the relentless ill-treatment Emily had suffered at Bill's hands for twenty-two years.

Gallagher's lawyer suggested it had been a crime of passion, by which he meant that Gallagher was angry about what Bill had done to Emily and wanted to punish him for it. What he had done was manslaughter, not murder, because he didn't intend Bill Swann to die.

'He no more thought of taking Swann's life than he did on several occasions when he had been similarly protecting this woman,' said Mr Mitchell Innes, Gallagher's barrister. 'When Mrs Swann was hurt she went to Gallagher as her natural avenger and protector. He then and there, besotted with drink and inflamed by this misdirected love for this woman, went to the house and administered the chastisement which he intended. A struggle took place between the husband and wife and Gallagher then intervened because such a struggle was unfair.'

Although he insisted that Gallagher did not want to shift 'one ounce of blame' for what had happened on to Emily, and he told the jury that they were not a tribunal of morals sitting in judgement on the adultery committed by the pair, this line of defence can't have done Emily much good in the eyes of the jury.

Her own barrister, Mr Newell, declared: 'Her past, no doubt, has been extremely reprehensible.'

But he insisted that there was no evidence that she had struck a single blow, and even assertions that she had urged her fellow prisoner to kill her husband didn't take account of what he called 'the vernacular language of the place' where they lived: the words she used meant no more than that she wanted her husband thrashed.

'I ask you to believe that she was horrified beyond measure when she found out he had gone beyond anything she had ever dreamt of,' he concluded. And those were the only arguments offered in Emily's defence.

The trial had begun at 10 a.m. and was over by ten to three that afternoon. It took the jury forty minutes to come back with their guilty verdict. Jury foremen were allowed to tell the judge if their jury wanted a prisoner convicted of murder to be shown mercy, if they felt the circumstances merited it. This jury had been told nothing to suggest either Emily or Gallagher deserved mercy, and the foreman passed no comment.

As a matter of routine, but without any expectation that it would alter the judge's decision that they should both be hanged by the neck until they were dead, the trial papers and various reports were to be sent to the Home Office in London, where the Secretary of State had the power to recommend to the King the offering of a pardon or the replacement of the death penalty with penal servitude. This was Emily's last hope, and a slim one.

Far from turning their backs on her, three of her sisters and a number of the Hinchcliffe family's friends travelled all the way to York to sit through her trial, and took all her children, including little Elsie, to Leeds from Barnsley to see her one last time. It was said by the family that none of the people who had known the Swanns refused when they were asked to sign the petition appealing for clemency. These, however, were people with no power and no influence. Those who did have power and influence accepted the judge's view as he donned the black cap and sentenced them both to death.

'There can be no doubt that the verdict is the right one,' he said. 'You used language that, unless language is held to mean nothing in the north of England, meant that if you had occasion to assault the deceased, you would either of you have taken his life. You had occasion to assault him and you did take his life.'

Emily was asked whether she had anything to say before sentence was passed upon her. 'Yes,' she said, speaking clearly and without any sign of nerves or hysteria. 'I am innocent. I am not afraid of immediate death because I am innocent and will go to God.'

As she was taken down, she glanced towards the gallery and looked directly at her sisters. She smiled and kissed her hand, and blew the kiss to them before vanishing out of public view for the last time.

Chapter Eleven

MOTHERHOOD

I had a bad New Year's Eve on the last night of 1977, just as Granddad was going downhill, wondering what on earth it was all about. I was in the process of accepting that James was a faded dream. Granddad was my excuse, but all the other reasons for going to London seemed to have evaporated too. With Granddad in decline at the same time that my future with James was coming to nothing, it was as if someone had pulled the rug out from under my whole life. Nothing seemed that much fun any more, not even my flat-share with Joan and our happy-go-lucky social life. I was discovering that it's all very well spending most of your life wanting to be free, but when you get there, you find that you haven't got solid plans about what you'll do with it. Face to face with my future, it looked like a big blank empty nothing.

I sat miserably in the club, getting quite drunk, surrounded by people I knew, feeling uncharacteristically miserable. I could call on any of them for company when I felt like it – and if I wanted a boyfriend, it wasn't difficult to find a man who wanted to be with me – but I felt desperately lonely.

A few weeks later, in January, I organized my own twenty-first birthday party to try and cheer myself up, a big do at Scarborough's Granville Lodge Hotel where I'd had an evening job over the last couple of years on and off to earn extra cash for my trips to London. I invited all the friends I'd shared my late teenage years with. And that night I met Phil.

Phil was about five years older than me, and separating from his wife, who was someone I worked with. He had a small son who he seemed to be looking after much of the time. He had an indefinable air of competence about him. He seemed more in control of his life and his emotions than anyone I'd ever met before. He seemed, in a nutshell, to be grown-up and able to take charge. After having been forced to run my own life and to organize things for the adults who were supposed to be looking after me from such a young age, I found the prospect of a man who wouldn't want me to do this for him very attractive.

However, a new relationship was the last thing on my mind at that particular time with Granddad steadily fading and James and I drifting ever further apart but not quite finished. I met up with him a few times over the next few weeks, but then Granddad died in March, and for some months I could think of nothing else but getting myself and Mum through the whole sorry business of sorting out his funeral and dealing with the deep grief his death had thrust me into.

But when the dust settled, in early summer, I started to see Phil in a different way.

Perhaps it wasn't surprising, after an unhappy conclusion to his marriage, that Phil wasn't keen on getting involved again without some proof that I was serious too. He had another girlfriend in tow, and started to see me at the same time without making any excuses for the fact that she was still on the scene. I think she also knew about me, and all three of us trotted along in a fairly light-hearted way, imagining that we had that thing which had become quite fashionable at the time, a 'non-exclusive' relationship. Except, of course, that it was driving me quietly insane. I was growing to like him more and more, but I had never had to share before, never in my life, and I found I wasn't able to do it.

When I couldn't stand it any longer, I gave Phil an ultimatum – her or me – and I meant it. I was quite prepared to take myself off and be single again rather than live this awful half-life.

'I've had enough of sharing, Phil. You need to know that I like you a lot and I'd like to be with you, but if you feel the need to be with Karen as well, then I need to move on.'

I was braced for more disappointment, but Phil's reply took me by surprise: 'Fine,' he said. 'That's all I need to know. It's you and me from now on, and no one else for either of us. I just wanted to know whether you cared enough, or whether this was just a bit of fun for you. I'm ready for it if you are.'

I was quite shocked. It wasn't what I'd expected at all.

Throughout that summer, I saw Phil more and more

often. He was a carpenter and joiner, and always busy. When I had a day off while he was at work, I sunbathed and read by the pool at South Bay. I still wondered about James. I hadn't completely let go, though we'd stopped calling each other for the time being.

At the end of August, Phil asked me to move in with him and his son. They lived on the Eastfield estate between Scarborough and Filey, on the same road out of town as the prefab but a little further south – not too close to Mum and Gran for comfort. Many people I knew had moved to Eastfield when they started their families. It was reasonably easy to get a house there because it was where most of Scarborough's council houses had been built in the years after the Second World War – there was so little spare land in Scarborough itself. A mixture of houses and flats was added throughout the 1960s, and it had become one of the largest council estates in north Yorkshire. Unlike the notorious Edgehill estate a couple of miles away where my dad had lived, it was considered a pretty good place to be. The houses were unmistakeably council houses, but they were mostly well built and there was lots of open space around them for children to play in. As in any community of any size, there were a few people about the place who might not have made the best of neighbours, but the majority of Eastfielders were like me – working class, ready to do an honest job, wanting to earn enough to get by and have a good family life.

Phil had a nice three-bedroomed end-of-terrace house next to a little green space, and I thought it was ten times better than the prefab or the flats in the ancient divided-up houses I'd been renting in Scarborough. Because he was a joiner, a practical man who was good with his hands, it was beautifully fitted out and maintained – it had a lovely kitchen, nice cupboards and shelves, and was tastefully decorated. I told myself that moving in would be exactly right for me, and ignored a niggling doubt lurking in the gloomiest corner of my mind that would have told me that Phil, his son and his house were important to me mostly as a distraction from my fear of facing a future with no Granddad, and because I had no other goal in life. They offered some of the structure and meaning that I was beginning to crave. I told myself I was ready to set up family with Phil. I wanted to build a nest.

But before I made the decision, I had to take one last trip down to London to see whether it really was all over with James. It was one of the worst weekends of my life.

'Yeah, come on down, it's been ages,' said James when I called him. He sounded interested enough, but not exactly keen.

'Will you meet me off the train?'

'Yeah. I'll be there.'

He gave me a hug at the top of the King's Cross concourse and we walked hand in hand down to the Underground ticket barriers, but as we exchanged pleasantries – nice journey, yes, bit crowded, shame – I felt like I was having a conversation with a best friend's friend. I was trying hard to feel interested in him because I thought I ought to be, but it wasn't coming from the heart.

When he kissed me that night after we got back from an evening in the pub with his friends, nothing happened. It sometimes happens when you've spent all evening chatting and flirting with someone you think you fancy, and then the kiss comes, and . . . nothing. That was how it was with James that night, and the sense of let-down was terrible. I had loved him for six years, since I was fifteen.

A memory popped into my mind – I remembered telling him a couple of years ago how I'd walked past one of the flats in Scarborough where we'd spent some time together and how it had been badly burned out by a fire – through the blackened broken windows, I described how it was just a shell.

'That must be us,' he'd told me, grinning. 'That's our passion. The embers carry on smouldering until they burst back into flames again.' We had laughed at the time because it was absolutely true. But there were no sparks now.

We hardly had a word to say to each other the next day.

'Shall we go to our usual Sunday pub?' James asked as the morning dragged on and we couldn't pretend to read the papers a moment longer. 'They still do the fantastic chips.'

'Yes!' I said, faking enthusiasm. At least eating would fill in some of the stifling silence.

When afternoon came I was only too relieved to get on the train and get away from him. I never saw him or heard from him again, never wanted to, and a few weeks later, at the end of September 1978, I moved out of Joan's flat and into Phil's house. It was as if a huge cloud had been dispersed. I felt quite sure that I was doing the right thing.

It didn't take long before we decided to get married.

James's mum, who I still kept in touch with, had seen

that the last year had been all about me trying to find a way to get over James and get away from him rather than make it work, which was why she reacted the way she did when I called to tell her that I was going to marry Phil. 'That's very quick, Flic – it sounds to me like this might be on the rebound. Are you sure about it?'

'No, no – he's absolutely right for me,' I insisted.

I was dismayed. I hadn't expected her to question it, to be so honest, so direct. I had expected her to say something nice and encouraging, like 'How wonderful, I'm so glad you've found someone to be happy with.' Or even, 'James should have snapped you up when he had the chance.' I wanted her to back me up, to make me feel sure of my decision. Instead, like the good friend she was, she tried to make me consider the possibility that I was being a little too hasty.

'I want to be with Phil more than anything – he's everything I could wish for,' I assured her, probably protesting too much. 'He needs me, and I need him. I've found the man I really want to settle down with.'

But she was right to be worried. The thing that felt best about deciding to marry Phil was feeling released from James at last. It felt wonderful. It never occurred to me to consider what other options there were that might give me the same sense of breaking free – quite simple choices like moving to London under my own steam, for instance, or making a fresh start in a city not too far away, like York or Leeds, close enough to come back often and keep an eye on Mum. I thought I was properly independent, but to me 'freedom' only meant being free of what other people expected of me, not striking out on my own.

Choice was a muscle that I had never exercised. Of course I was under the illusion that I had been making choices ever since I'd discovered I could flick two fingers at Gran and live, but they were mostly negative choices about the things I was *not* going to do, and that included deciding to marry Phil. It meant I was not going to have to think about James a moment longer.

Phil and I got married the following summer, a few months after my twenty-second birthday. As I was being driven to the register office in Scarborough on my wedding day, I had a major panic. Why on earth was I doing this? Why was I tying myself to this man when we could have just carried on living together? I'd known him barely a year. I knew, too late, that I shouldn't be doing it. And then I had a 'tea towel' moment, like that story about Princess Diana's sisters telling her a few days before the royal wedding, 'It's too late, sis, your face is on the tea towels now.' I decided it would be too embarrassing to call it off because everything was organized and everyone was waiting for me to arrive. It would be all right. It would have to be.

When the official bit was over, Phil and I stood on the steps of the register office surrounded by our friends taking pictures. My mum was there, looking lovely. She was all the family I had, while Phil had a huge family turnout, many of whom came all the way from Somerset, where his mum's people were from. I had gone to town on Mum, making sure she had her hair done and that we found a really beautiful outfit for her. My flatmate Joan, who had been through so much with me, was my maid of honour, and her boyfriend, Dave, who knew Phil, was his best man.

Something made me look up into the distance to take in the surroundings, and there was Gran, looking across the stream of traffic that separated her from us. She was wearing the same old beige raincoat, but this time we locked eyes. She looked tight-lipped and smug, as if she was saying, 'I can see what you're up to.' Then she smiled very slightly. Was she giving me her blessing? I couldn't stretch myself to believing that – I was far more scared that she'd start shouting and making a scene. But she just turned away and walked off.

Mad as a coot, I thought. I wasn't as shocked at seeing her unexpectedly this time, but I didn't mention it to anyone. I thought it might upset Mum, and I wasn't going to have her spoil my day, never mind that I felt uncertain about the whole thing myself.

Secrets come out at weddings. During the reception, Joan let something slip. Suddenly I knew why Jane had become so difficult to live with in Nelson Street. Perhaps it was what had got in the way of how James and I felt about each other. I suppose Joan thought that now I was in love, getting married, completely over James, the secret she'd kept for so long couldn't do any harm.

She said, 'Remember when you moved in with me after Jane started being so weird?'

'Yes,' I said.

'She was like that because she'd fallen for James,' said

Joan. 'I was always a bit surprised that you didn't see it. Did you know?'

'No,' I said, appalled.

We looked at each other. Joan said: 'She slept with him while you were away one weekend, visiting your aunty in Wakefield. She told me.'

'*What!*' I yelled.

Joan, who was getting comfortably woozy after her second Whisky Mac, jumped as if I'd shot her. As she jumped, I jumped. I remembered just in time that I was at my wedding, that I was now married to someone who wasn't James, and that I really had to keep a lid on it. I wasn't supposed to care any more.

But I did.

I was heartbroken all over again, and the shock and sense of betrayal flavoured the rest of my wedding day with a disappointment and sense of anti-climax that I did my best to hide. There. It was done. I was married now. Although it didn't feel right yet, I knew I had to get on with it, and maybe it would feel right in time.

Phil and I did have a lot of good times, but it was a stormy relationship. As always, I gave as good as I got, and, if I'm honest, I often deliberately ramped up the emotional temperature to get a reaction from Phil, as I had done with Dave and sometimes with James too. Simply getting along with Phil in an even-tempered, everyday kind of way was too boring for me, and I couldn't seem to break out of my pattern of aggression and apologies. I was so accustomed to explosions and crises that I created them if they weren't readily available. And, boy, could I sulk, big time, when I didn't get what I wanted. I once refused to talk to him for a week because he said that hoovering was women's work.

There was more to it than that, of course. Phil was a very in-control and orderly person and he wanted things just so. He wanted the house tidy, regardless of whether his son had a friend round to play and they needed to make a mess, and he wanted meals at certain times. He liked a regularity about things that wasn't in any way abnormal, but which didn't match my approach to life. Although I've always been house-proud and organized, I've always enjoyed leaving enough room for life to surprise me. Phil's orderly mind was what had first attracted me to him, but it was also too reminiscent of Gran's obsessive approach to be wholly comfortable.

During our first few years together, I had a recurring nightmare where I was being pursued through a dark house by a character whose identity I couldn't fathom, moving from room to room trying to get away from it. No matter what I did, I felt that my legs just wouldn't do what I wanted them to do to get me away to safety. I was trapped. It seems strange that I started having this dream just as I was feeling at my most settled and happy. Maybe it was because I was so settled. Maybe my subconscious was looking for something to feel fearful about because I didn't have anything to fear.

I decided I wanted to have a baby, and Phil was keen too, as he didn't want his son to be an only child for too much longer. On the day I was told that my pregnancy test was positive, I called Phil to let him know straightaway and he was as happy as I was. He had a job as a joiner on the other side of Scarborough at a private school at the time, but they let him come home early and it seemed as if he was by my side in a matter of minutes, giving me the biggest hug.

I had a wonderful pregnancy and two years after the wedding our son Oliver was born. He captivated me with his dark, dark eyes the moment I looked into them. I was instantly besotted. I hadn't known that it was possible to love another human being so completely.

It didn't seem to matter that I'd had such a strange, unkind childhood myself; I knew instinctively what Oliver needed and I had no trouble giving it to him – all the cuddles, the gentleness, the attention – and I loved every second of being his mum. I made all his clothes, knitted all his jumpers, used terry towelling nappies long before it was a 'green' thing to do because I thought they were kinder to his skin than throw-aways. Phil's little boy was about six years old when Olly arrived, and he was thrilled to have a little brother. The boys were really attached to each other – and still are, even now – and as a family we went on holiday together, had days out, organized family parties at the weekend with Phil's relatives and my mum, did all the things that families do. Phil really loved Mum and was kind and careful with her, and she began to spend a lot of time with us. It was a delight to see how much she loved little Olly, her first grandson, how thrilled she was to be allowed to cuddle him, and when he began to toddle he made a beeline for her whenever she appeared.

Naturally, Mum came to stay with us every Christmas. These holidays are some of the happiest memories I have. I would look around the table as we got ready to eat our Christmas dinner, Phil and his boy on one side, Mum next to Olly on the other, and be amazed by how normal it all looked. We looked like a real family.

'Happy, Mum?' I would ask her.

'Yes thanks, Flic.'

She would beam at me and the boys and Phil, and quietly tuck into her meal. She pulled crackers, bent down meekly to let Phil's little boy put a paper crown on her head, and after dinner sat happily on the sofa with her wonky crown on and a glass of white wine in her hand, as content as any human being could be. Often she'd stay until New Year, and then I'd take her back to the prefab and to Gran.

I have no idea what Gran did at Christmas time. I didn't ask. Although she had mellowed a little since Granddad's death, she still treated Mum with contempt and nothing would have persuaded me to invite her to spend Christmas with us. She had always made it a grim, miserable time when I was a child, and I wasn't about to let her ruin the perfect family I'd created. I didn't think I would ever be able to forgive her for the stinking upsets she caused at Christmas, her refusal to allow decorations or a tree or any nice food, any more than I would ever be able to forgive her for stealing my childhood from me. No, Gran was not invited for Christmas. But I still went round there every couple of months to check on them both, and one afternoon I decided to take Oliver with me rather than leave him with his dad and brother.

Gran took very little notice of him. She sat glued into

her usual position on the sofa by the fire, staring at the telly, which was no more than I had expected, while Mum held Olly's fingers as he toddled about the place. We kept him well away from Gran. I was understandably astonished, therefore, that she wrote a letter to him on a piece of cheap lined writing paper and – I assume – got Mum to post it. It was oddly written, of course, but it referred to 'Olly, a wonderful little man.' I didn't know what to make of it. When I thanked her the next time I went to visit, she just looked at me, nodded and smiled.

A flash of normality, like this, a display of common grandmotherly pride, was puzzling, not least because it made me wonder why she couldn't be more normal more often.

It was hard to make any sense of Gran these days. A lot of her obsessions, especially the ones associated with painting, cleaning and cooking, had petered out. That probably made Mum's life more pleasant, but she wasn't capable of taking Gran's place in the kitchen, because she was worse than useless at cooking. When it came to housework, having never been trusted by Gran to do anything of that kind, Mum didn't even seem to be aware of the dirt around her. Each time I went round, almost always taking Olly now because I felt he'd officially been accepted by Gran, the house looked filthier and filthier. I began to worry that Olly might get seriously ill from touching the surfaces or the floor.

Gran had not mellowed so much that she would let the council come in and update or fix anything in the bungalow. For years they'd been offering her central heating, a new kitchen, a new bathroom, a boiler, insulation and new windows, but Gran had ignored all the letters and refused to speak to any council officer who came to the door. I managed to organize a home help through the council – Mum was sixty by this time and a pensioner like Gran – and they were generally allowed in to keep the kitchen in order and do a bit of vacuuming unless Gran was having a particularly bonkers day, but I often had to roll up my own sleeves to clear out the bedrooms or the kitchen and get them into decent order.

Olly was still quite small when I went into the kitchen one afternoon to wash up the cups we'd used, looked round the tiny space that hadn't changed in the slightest since I was Olly's age, and decided I had to put my foot down.

'Gran, I'm going to put some tiles round the sink and put new lino down. The old stuff is filthy and it's so old that it's impossible to clean.'

She switched her gaze from the telly and looked at me for a moment. Then she nodded, and turned back.

It wasn't that much of a surprise that she didn't challenge me. Lately it was as if she was slowly melting and becoming a bit more normal. I didn't feel the same hostility when I walked in; I felt as if she accepted that I was now in charge. Perhaps she was grateful for the practical help.

Anyway, that nod was good enough for me. It would have been better if she had let the council rip the whole lot out, but if she would let me do that little bit, there was at least a chance that she and Mum wouldn't get ill from the squalor. I don't know quite how the two of them rubbed along together. As time went by, and Gran cooked less and less, I saw more and more evidence of ready meals, which I assumed were Mum's idea of catering.

However much I softened towards Gran, though, I couldn't stomach the idea of having her in my own house. This wasn't the problem it might have been, since it was clear she didn't want to leave her chair, her fire or her telly on any account, so I left her to it. There was never any mention of Gran needing our help, at Christmas or any other time, and I didn't ask. It wasn't out of spite, it was just years of habit and a reluctance ever again to get pulled into her mad world. In any case, I was very busy with my own young family.

I had given up my job at Arundales after seven happy years there just before Oliver was born. Although he didn't say so, I knew that Neal, my boss, thought I was wasting my talents by turning myself into a housewife and mother. I had an inkling of this myself, but I really wanted a family to call my own, one that wasn't weird. A normal family wasn't just normal to me; it was the summit of all imaginable ambition. Motherhood certainly wasn't the worst route I could have chosen to take me away from my awful childhood. I took pictures of everything Oliver did and felt I was the luckiest mother alive.

I might still be that mum even now if it hadn't been for the increasingly stifling atmosphere of my marriage. It felt as if no allowances were made for the fact that I was tired because I was looking after two young, active children, or that they needed to have their things out in the living room to play with, the way all children do, even if it did make the place look a bit chaotic. I didn't see why it mattered if an ironing pile was left waiting to be tackled. There were times when it felt like living in a boot camp.

Phil would moan if tea wasn't quite as perfect as he thought it should be. One night he threw a fit because the poached eggs were hard. It struck me suddenly that the days of women having to have tea on the table for when their husbands came home belonged to my Gran's generation, not mine, so I threw a fit back. I literally threw his plate across the room, along with every other item in the crockery cupboard.

The next morning, when I went out into the garden to hang out some washing, my next-door neighbour was already at her washing line.

'Bloody hell, did you hear that couple up the close last night?' she said by way of conversation.

I looked over at her and felt more than a little uncomfortable, but she carried on, oblivious.

'We couldn't work out where it was coming from, but it seemed to be coming from up that end,' she said, pointing across the way to the blank ends of the houses across the little green from our block. 'They were going at it hammer and tongs for ages. It sounded like someone had gone berserk in a china shop.'

I looked at the gable ends of the houses and thought to myself that they obviously did a fantastic job of confusing the acoustics round here.

I waited until she'd gone out to the shops before I risked putting the thousand shards of crockery into the dustbin. I felt thoroughly ashamed of us both. Perhaps if I had grown up in a more normal family, Phil's pickiness wouldn't have bothered me so much. Perhaps I could have laughed it off, reasoned him into a better mood and more tolerance.

Oliver was soon old enough to go off to playschool for a couple of hours here and there, and then to pre-school every morning, and before I knew it, full-time primary school was on the horizon. The days when he wouldn't be at home with me any more were looming, and I didn't know what I'd do with myself. I became more and more restless, and the urge to cut loose was increasingly powerful. I wanted to earn my own money again instead of being given 'housekeeping' from Phil's wages – I felt like a charity case – but Phil wanted me at home. After a lot of rows and a lot of top-class Felicity sulking, I got myself a bar job at one of the local holiday camps.

'How are you going to look after me and the boys if you go back out to work?' Phil asked in exasperation. He just didn't seem to get it. He didn't understand my need for independence.

'I'll pay for childcare if you want me to, and my mum can help out. Don't you understand how important this is to me?' I pleaded, willing him to understand.

'It's not about childcare, and you know it. You should be here, not swanning around in some bar or other,' he stormed back.

I could feel his frustration at the situation, and I could hear the growing anger in his voice. I didn't want to cause yet another scene, but I knew I was going to go out to work, and that was that.

'Well, that's tough, Phil, because I'm going and there's

nothing you can do about it,' I shouted as I stormed out of the front door. I really didn't care about what I would have to face when I got back. If he was going to refuse to understand, then I would have my own way and bugger the consequences.

It was the perfect job: I had plenty of experience at this kind of work, I could go out at night after Phil got home. After virtually running the accounts department at Arundales, handling money and keeping the tills straight was no problem for me, and it wasn't long before they promoted me to duty manager on my shifts. But the best thing was that I was getting paid for doing a busy, buzzing people-job out in the thick of a social life again, even if the social life belonged, strictly speaking, to the customers. It was a guilt-free return to normal life a few evenings a week.

It was such great fun that on my days off I would sometimes ride up there on my bike with Olly in his child seat on the back and show him off to all the staff. He loved being fussed over and adored by everyone, and I started to feel really happy again for the first time in ages. Meanwhile my relationship with Phil worsened almost by the day. Even so, I wasn't prepared to give up this new-found freedom and go back to being a housewife.

And then Martin arrived, a student whose parents lived near Scarborough, and who had applied for temporary bar work during his university holidays.

He was tall, blond – a bit of a Dave-lookalike, to be honest – and great fun. He was also very intelligent. He'd done A levels, and unlike Phil could talk to me about books. Reading was a precious hobby to me. It went right back to those days in my secret den deep in the wilderness next to the prefab with my Enid Blyton books. Even though I'd been determined to pay as little attention as possible in English lessons during my school days, escaping into a book was then and still is one of my greatest pleasures.

I was almost eight years older than Martin, and a mum, and his boss, and I kept reminding myself of all of this as I flirted shamelessly with him and he flirted right back when we were on duty together, but the age difference didn't seem to matter at all.

'Come on, Martin, I want you to go down to the small bar and help me cash up,' I said one evening as a way of getting him on his own. We would have to step outside the Pavilion and walk round outside the building, away from prying eyes.

'Oh, very clever, Flic,' he smiled as we kissed, hidden from view. I had him held firmly against the fire-escape door. 'You didn't need me to help you cash up. You just wanted to get me alone.'

'Anything wrong with that?' I laughed as he gave me that penetrating blue-eyed look which made my insides skip somersaults. His hand skirted my thigh.

'Enough of that,' I teased, 'I only asked you to cash up with me, Martin.'

'A likely story,' he flashed back as he took control, kissing me until I conceded that he just might be right.

It all seemed like harmless fun.

Sade was the biggest new band around at this time, and I got a couple of tickets to see them at Harrogate Pavilion.

Phil and Mum had promised to look after the boys while I went away for the weekend with a friend and stayed in a bed and breakfast, because neither I nor my friend had a car so we couldn't get back until the next day, but when my friend had to pull out, I kept it quiet and asked Martin if he would like to join me for the weekend. In his very easy, laid-back way, he told me that he had no plans that he couldn't rearrange and he would love to come. I couldn't believe this easy way of existence, which seemed so middle-class somehow. He had such lovely ways, and I was captivated by him.

The Harrogate excursion was the real beginning of our relationship. I took my cue from him, and phoned Phil to say that we'd met some people at the concert who'd invited us to go to Newcastle for a couple of days. I played it down as much as I could and he was fine about it. I knew Mum was capable of sorting out the boys when he went to work. I phoned work and rearranged my shifts, and we went straight from Harrogate to Martin's place in Newcastle on the bus and spent the rest of the week there. I stayed in his student house and we cooked together for the first time and made love to Air Supply's 'Making Love Out of Nothing at All'. I told Phil what I'd done the moment I got back, and that's all I can say in my defence.

When Martin's holiday came to an end, he headed back to Newcastle for the start of a new term there. I carried on working at the bar throughout the week and looking after the boys, getting them to and from school.

Phil, to my utter surprise, tried to persuade me that we had something worth fighting for in our marriage, that he would try to change. I was completely taken aback because things were so far gone that I hadn't realized he'd even thought about us and how we were. He really wanted to give it another go, but I had fallen so completely for this very different kind of man that I could see no way back. At the same time, Phil insisted that whatever happened, he would not give up the house to me and the children.

There was little prospect of getting another council house any time soon, so we came to a rather strange arrangement which involved the boys staying exactly where they were, while Phil and I took turns at living there. I stayed there through the week while he stayed with a girl he'd met, and Phil took over at the weekend so that he could spend time with the boys. I sometimes stayed with friends in Scarborough, but I usually got on the train to Newcastle to be with Martin in his university digs. I saved my tips from the bar to fund these trips because it didn't feel right to take my fare out of the household budget.

'I'm coming back to Scarborough, Flic,' Martin said one afternoon in November.

'Why, has term ended?'

'No, I'm jacking it in. I hate uni. I'm only doing it because it's what my parents want, but I hate writing essays and reading books. Will you look for somewhere we can live together, a bedsit maybe?'

I was thrilled – far more thrilled than I should have been. I didn't make any attempt to persuade him to stay on and finish his course. I was too pleased about being with him, about being able to see him through the week as well as at weekends.

His parents were in the dark all the way through to the following summer when he should have been finishing his second year. Martin would get on the train for the north at the end of each official visit home when they took him to the station, and get off at the next stop and come back to Scarborough and me. When they finally found out – many months later – that he was no longer at university, they were furious. And they were more furious with me, I think, than with him. All that promise of a good education and the possibility of a fulfilling career given up for an older woman who had a young son, and who wasn't even divorced from her husband. I'm sure they felt that I was entirely to blame for the disastrous turn, as they saw it, that their son's life had taken.

Eventually we managed to get a house on the other side of the Eastfield estate, and we moved in and set up home with Oliver. My divorce finally came through, and in 1986 we got married. I adored him, I really did. I knew that with this man there would be no doubts, no mind games, and that he would be my friend as well as my lover. He had handled the messy split in such a calm way, was great with Olly and had such compassion and empathy.

Not long after we were married, as we travelled south for a belated honeymoon, we stopped off in London and went to see James's mum. She put us up for the night, and we spent a lovely evening chatting about all that had happened to me in the seven years since I'd married Phil and had Oliver. She was kind enough not to remind me what her opinion of my first marriage had been. James, she told me, had done some travelling and had met and married an Italian girl, and seemed very happy.

Where once I would have felt jealous, now I just looked at Martin and thought what a lucky woman I was to have found Mr Right after so many left turns. I left a picture of Oliver with her, and told her to let James know how happy I was for him. I wanted him to know that I'd found the right person too.

Chapter Twelve

PETITION, VISIT AND EXECUTION

At Armley Gaol, the prison chaplain took very seriously his job of doing all he could for the spiritual welfare of the prisoners, and for the condemned this meant helping them to confess to their crime so that they could meet their maker with repentance in their hearts. When Emily's papers went to the Home Office in London for review before her execution, he was invited to offer his opinion of the woman he had come to know since she had moved into the condemned cell.

Emily refused to be repentant and even Armley's chaplain, the Reverend Mansell, wasn't himself convinced that she should be. 'I have spent hours myself in trying to get her to make a confession of her guilt,' he wrote, adding doubtfully in brackets '(supposing she was guilty)'.

'She persistently denies having touched him with the poker and says that she did not wish for his death,' he went on. 'She had tried to break off her connection with

Gallagher, but he had great power over her because he was kind when her husband was cruel.

'While acknowledging other offences, the prisoner denies that she was an accessory to the murder except in so far as she contributed to it by her adultery. She has not altered her first statement that she is innocent and that it was Gallagher and Gallagher alone who beat the life out of him.

'Sister Sarah, one of the Lady Visitors, thinks it is possible Swann took no active part in the murder of her husband.'

Anyone, of course, would say they were innocent when the hangman's noose was dangling in front of them, and while there was even the remotest possibility of the authorities taking a merciful view of her case and commuting her sentence from death to life imprisonment with hard labour, there would be no point in admitting guilt.

It wasn't likely that either Emily or John Gallagher would be in a position to consider appealing against their sentence, but the trial papers and various reports had been sent to the Home Office, and they might have had a faint hope that the Secretary of State would recommend a royal pardon, or penal servitude in place of hanging.

The report of the authorities in the area where a convicted prisoner had lived at the time of their offence carried a great deal of influence in London. The Home Office relied on local knowledge to give a sense of the background to a case, the personalities involved, and the strength of local opinion. In Emily's case, this report was written by Police Superintendent Quest, the officer who had said publicly at Bill Swann's inquest that he would 'pay due attention to the point' when the foreman of the jury offered his opinion that Emily was as much to blame for her husband's death as Gallagher. When asked to prepare his background report on the case, Quest let all his chauvinistic prejudices run riot among the facts. He clearly knew nothing about Emily, her friends or her family. He mentioned none of Bill's sixteen years' worth of appearances in the local magistrates' courts, not even his serious assault on Emily. He dwelt in detail on those of Emily, declaring that her convictions proved 'she is a drunken immoral woman who was much more to blame than her husband was for their unhappy existence. Local feeling is against her and she has sunk so low in depravity that her family will have nothing to do with her.'

Not a word of this was true. There was plenty of evidence to show that her mother and sisters had been in constant touch with her in recent years despite the trouble she'd got herself into, and a reporter who had knocked on Hannah's door at the time of the trial wrote a report that was published in every national newspaper saying how eager her sisters and children were to defend her, and how convinced they were that she had never intended Bill Swann to die. At her trial, Elizabeth, Annie and Clara had sat in the front row of the public gallery, directly over the dock, as publicly supportive of her as it was possible to be.

None of this helped Emily's or Gallagher's cause. The Home Office was unswayed, and the sentence was confirmed.

Putting family before what any of the neighbours in

Havelock Street might have thought – although they seem to have been more than sympathetic – the Hinchcliffe family decided to set out on an expedition to Leeds to see Emily one last time before she was executed.

On Boxing Day, 1903, Elsie Swann stood meekly next to the black iron cooking range as her big sister Eleanor scrubbed her face and hands with green soap and cold water. The grate of the range was just about at eye level for a four-year-old. The fire hadn't been fed and stoked up that morning because the house would be empty all day. Her granny Hannah was spending the day with neighbours. Aunties, brothers and sisters were milling about in the back room of the cramped terraced house which did service as kitchen, bathroom, living room and dining room.

It was less than a week away from what would be Elsie's fifth birthday on the last day of the year. When this holiday was over she would at last be joining the big children on the morning walk to the Board School, a few streets away from her grandmother's house, where she had been living with Eleanor and her new husband Herbert ever since the summer.

Now she was being dressed in the best clothes the family could beg or borrow, stockings and skirts finished off with a crisp white pinafore that Eleanor had washed and blued and starched, and which she'd smoothed last night with the big flat iron that had to be heated up next to the open fire in the kitchen range. For the first time ever, she was being included in a family outing. She would travel on a train, and she would see a big city. Eight of them, all her brothers and sisters and three of her aunts, were going to Leeds to see her mother.

This was a trip that had to be made, there and back, in one day, and they left the house just before daybreak. Charles, thin and weary, swept his baby sister up in his arms and on to his shoulders as they began to tramp towards the railway station. There was not a soul in the street who did not know where they were going. Almost every household rose long before dawn anyway, most of them home to colliers who started their shifts at 5 a.m., and many eyes watched them quietly and discreetly from darkened windows and from behind half-drawn curtains; one or two good friends stepped out for a moment to offer a wordless farewell, a quick sympathetic touch on the arm and a kind glance. As one neighbour said to another after the group had been swallowed by the gloom, words were worse than useless because it was difficult to know what could be said on such an occasion.

There must have been a few tears shed that morning, particularly at the sight of the bright, excited little face of Elsie beaming down from over her brother's head. There was no way such a small child could possibly understand what a terrible journey this was. Elsie Swann would never see her mother again after this day was over.

Some hours later, as the group approached the massive soot-blackened walls of Armley Gaol, even Elsie's innocent enthusiasm for her day out faltered. Sitting high on the grimy hillside above the busy Leeds–Liverpool canal and the railway, built from huge blocks of the local Millstone Grit in the form of a mock medieval fortress, it was quite deliberately designed to make the unruly masses below and all the many passers-by think twice about stepping out of line. The Swann children and their aunts, already walking as if they had lead in their boots, certainly felt the oppression of it as they approached the long ramp that led upwards from Canal Road to the imposing gatehouse with its thirty-foot-high wooden doors flanked by mock Norman castle towers complete with crenellations.

These doors were mostly for effect, they discovered. They were asked their business by the guards on duty at the small sentry post at the foot of the ramp, and then directed to a small side door that took them straight into the lobby outside the visitors' office. There the sombre group was inspected through the bars by two warders who had the authority to fill out visiting applications and issue tickets if the governor was willing to admit them. With much jangling of keys and clanging of gates, the group was allowed in; and, as the gates were locked behind them, they stood before the counter where their ages, names and relationship to the prisoner they were visiting would be recorded.

Before the officer acting as clerk would do this, however, he stared at them with astonishment, shocked to see that they had such a small child with them. One of the aunts was holding Elsie in her arms.

'This is no place for a little one like that,' said the man, clearly appalled. 'It's not right. You can't bring that mite into this place. What good can it do, to her or to her mother? Her mother can't want the poor child to remember her in this place.'

Charles and his aunts were dumbstruck. Ernest, it

seemed, was considered well able to cope with this traumatic interview, even though he was hardly taller than his little sister and not much more than a year older. Weary as they were after all they had suffered during the last six months, the family's only thought had been to fulfil Emily's last wishes, which she had set out in the final letter she was allowed to send her family, written on Christmas Eve and delivered to her elderly mother Hannah on Christmas Day. 'I want you to ask my sisters to visit me next, and bring my little Elsie with them,' was Emily's heartfelt plea.

It simply hadn't occurred to the family that Elsie's age would be a problem. They had no way of knowing how visits to a condemned prisoner were conducted. They certainly hadn't realized, for instance, that even during this final interview it would be forbidden for Emily's children to touch her in any way. They would have to stand at her cell door and speak to her through the barred inspection hatch, and at all times there would be prison warders on either side of the door to make sure that there was no physical contact with the prisoner. This was because it was not unknown for a condemned prisoner to try to cheat the hangman by taking their own life if they could somehow get their hands on a reliable poison or a sharp knife.

Once the death sentence had been passed, the prisoner was not allowed one moment alone, as Emily had discovered. For the last fortnight she had been attended day and night by at least two women warders, even in the few hours when she could manage to sleep, and the only cutlery she was allowed was a spoon. If her food needed cutting, one of the warders did it for her while the other watched vigilantly to make sure she didn't try to snatch the knife. This wasn't just about the criminal justice system not wanting to be cheated of its prey. Self-murder, however understandable it might be in someone who had been sentenced to death by hanging, was seen as just as much a criminal and moral offence as the murder of another. Since most of the condemned were convicted murderers, it was felt the last thing they needed was a second dreadful sin on their consciences when they met their maker. In Emily's case, to make sure she was despatched to her maker without any further stain on her immortal soul, she also had to be despatched to her maker without having the opportunity to hold her children one last time.

Emily Swann's sisters and children, very much overawed by their surroundings and by the stern men in uniform around them, and feeling all the shame of the reason why they were there, were not in a state of mind to protest about a mother being denied not only a last touch of her youngest child, but even a last glimpse of her. Their dilemma was only about which one of them would have to stay with Elsie while the others made the only visit that would be possible before Emily's execution in two days' time.

'The child can stay here so that you may all go to see the prisoner,' said the clerk, speaking more gently than he had before. 'She will be quite safe. We will have her in here with me, by the fire in the back office.'

His colleague went to the half-glazed door in the corner of the reception office and unlocked it, allowing Eleanor to lead the little girl through. She settled Elsie on a little stool by the hearth and ordered her to be good until the family returned. Normally Elsie would have had something to say about all of this, but she was rendered utterly speechless by where she was and what was going on. She said nothing about her mother, nothing about where the others were going, nothing about being left behind. Mute, she watched through the office hatch as they all trooped off to some secret, terrible place hidden deep inside this dreadful building.

Tears began to stream down her face and the clerk, turning to see how she was getting on, frowned and slipped a hand into the small pocket on the front of his uniform waistcoat. He stood up and pulled out a shiny silver sixpence and showed it to her.

'Have you ever held a sixpenny piece, young lady?' he asked her, smiling a little.

She looked at him and at the coin. After a long pause, she shook her head slightly.

'Then hold this one now for me,' he said, stooping and holding it towards her. 'Keep tight hold and keep it safe for me until your big sister comes back.'

Elsie took it, and stared hard at the face of the clerk. He unbent himself and resumed his position at his desk in front of the hatch in the wall. She put the coin carefully in the palm of her hand and looked at the face of the new king on the one side, and of the British crown framed in leaves on the other. It was a beautiful thing, and, never having been trusted with more than a copper penny close up, she was transfixed by it. She did not forget the others, but her tears dried and she sat patiently, guarding the man's sixpence with all possible care, uncurling her hand now and again to check it was still there, knowing that he would want his sixpence back and that the sixpence was therefore her guarantee that her brothers and sisters would return.

It had been a long shot, but Emily's family had thought it worth a try when their solicitor had suggested a petition, first to the Home Office to try to make the Secretary of State see that Emily was much more sinned against than sinning, and then a shorter version to the king to ask him to exercise his right to offer a royal pardon. They were touched, when they asked neighbours in Barnsley and Wombwell how they would feel about signing it too, to prove that she was not universally regarded as a dreadful wife and mother, that they were able to collect around seventy names. It was solid proof that the mob that had jeered Emily as she left the inquest was just that, a mob, and that the people who really knew her felt that public opinion had been far too one-sided. The words, of course, must have been crafted by the solicitor, but it is possible to hear the authentic voice of people who genuinely loved and admired her behind the formal phrases. It was described as being primarily drawn up by her children, who declared:

'Emily Swann was always a good mother to us, notwithstanding the drunken habits of our late father William Swann who, by his drunken habits destroyed our home life and rendered us unhappy, causing our mother to go out to work in order to keep the home together, although our father earned good wages which he spent in drink and debauchery.

'And had it not been for his drunken habits and

continued ill-treatment of our mother, we do not think that our mother would now have been in the painful position of a woman condemned to death.

'We would further point out for your consideration that there was no evidence before the court that our mother ever struck our father, she being at the time under the influence of drink and also suffering acutely from a brutal assault just committed on her by our father. Consequently she had not the power to resist to the extent she might, had she been sober.'

The plea ends with their declaration that they 'desire to say nothing against' Gallagher either. There is not one good word for Bill Swann in the petition from any of the signatories. The neighbours who put their names alongside those of Eleanor, Charles, Anne, Frances and Ernest had no quarrel with this either. The petition wasn't a plea for the authorities to take pity on a sinner, but a last-ditch attempt to give Emily a fair hearing. There can be no doubt about where the loyalties of family and friends lay, despite Superintendent Quest's perverse view of the situation. His, however, was the view that prevailed. The note on the papers scrawled by a Home Office bureaucrat's hand reads simply 'No extenuating circumstances'.

Curiously, Emily recalled the date of her wedding anniversary as she sat in the condemned cell, and on 19 December had asked the women warders watching over her day and night for 'a little currant cake' to mark the event. They sent to the prison kitchen and found some for her in the staff stores, but they must have thought her request odd, if not downright hypocritical.

It's possible that she hoped this might create a favourable impression if news of it reached London. Yet it also seems likely that Emily genuinely did want to mark her wedding anniversary; she must have loved Bill Swann once, and, after all, he was the father of her eleven children. She was obviously a woman capable of great passion and warmth, and she could not have been happy contemplating the sordid way in which Bill's life had ended, whatever he had become and whether he deserved his fate or not.

She mentioned the anniversary on Christmas Eve in the last letter she wrote to her mother:

> *I write a few lines to you, hoping that you are all trying to bear up. I know it is a very hard trouble to you all.*
>
> *Dear Mother, it is 22 years on Saturday since I was married. It was a very unfortunate day for me, my married life has been a very hard one and a very unhappy one. Dear Mother, I feel it very hard leaving my children and my sisters. May God bless you all.*
>
> *I have sinned but I have suffered. No one knows but God and myself what I have suffered. I have asked God to help me and I feel that he will help me if I only put my trust in him, and I know that I shall have to answer for my own sins.*
>
> *Dear Mother and sisters, I know it won't be a merry Christmas for you. I hope you will spend it in prayer, and may God be with you all.*

Then she broke free of the formula that the prison visitors expected of her. They were writing at her dictation, but the letter reads very much as if they were also suggesting and inserting the platitudes that seemed appropriate to them in the circumstances. Suddenly, there was in the next sentence a flash of the old Emily, the one who refused to take her punishment meekly, whatever it cost her, and she would have her say:

> *Do not mind, dear Mother, what people say about me. If they had their sins written on their foreheads it would perhaps take a big Salvation Army bonnet to cover them. I feel that God has forgiven me my sins but we are all sinners and I cannot help but feel they sinned greatly against me. I have suffered that much that I feel that it will be a happy release for me. I have children to meet, and I have children to leave. I know my sisters will be kind to my children.*

She thanks her sisters' husbands for their kindness to her and her children, and ends with a heartbreaking plea to her elderly mother to 'love my children while you live for my sake'.

Hannah had opened her door to a reporter just before Christmas in December 1903, shortly after the date of Emily's execution had been fixed. She was to hang at Armley Gaol on 29 December and there was not likely to be any last-minute reprieve.

'Eh, mister, I've had a hard life,' Hannah said wearily to the young man from the *Barnsley Chronicle*, sitting by the range in Havelock Street with Annie next to her. 'Of all the trouble I have had, this has been the hardest. I have never felt such a feeling in all my born days as I do over this. I could have buried every one [of my children] and not been put about as I have been over this. And I am sure my daughter has not had it shown her here,' she added, keen to make it clear that hers was not a family where the kind of behaviour that had gone on in Emily's house was considered normal.

Emily herself said much the same thing in a slightly different way a few days later. 'If I am a bad woman, it is what other people have made me,' she protested bitterly on the Sunday morning she was told by Captain Haynes, the acting governor at Armley, that the Home Secretary had 'declined to intervene in the matter' of her death sentence, and she would be executed with Gallagher within the next forty-eight hours.

'John promised me at the Town Hall he would see I was all right,' she wailed, losing her self-possession briefly, and referring to a snatched conversation she'd had with him when they had first appeared together at the law courts in Leeds Town Hall to be committed to the York Assizes.

'He could have saved me, and he has not done all that he could for me. He promised he would. How could he leave me to this, me and my children? What will happen to them?'

During the last twenty-four hours of her life, however, Emily's hysteria passed away. The newspapers said that she had finally confessed to her involvement in her husband's murder on the night before her execution. Then, as now, this was probably all in the imagination of the journalists, because it was what the public expected to hear. There is no mention of any such confession in the chaplain's notes. According to the chaplain, Emily maintained, as she always had, that she had never struck Bill herself, that she had tried to stop Jack Gallagher when he seemed to lose control and started kicking Bill when he was down, and that she had never wanted to see her husband die.

The chaplain's papers record only that on the night before her execution, Emily told him she had now accepted her fate and was determined to face it with 'all the dignity and strength that God might be willing to give her'.

'She knows that she has sinned, and that she is content to answer for her sins to God,' wrote the Chaplain. 'She is certain that God will know the truth and will judge her accordingly, and will know that although her actions played a significant part in the dreadful circumstances of her husband's death, He will know her heart and will therefore know that she did not wish her husband dead.'

She said that she forgave with all her heart those who had given false witness about her at her trial because they too had had hard lives, and she hoped God would not judge them too harshly when their time came. She mentioned Dunn and the young Alfred Harper by name, the two witnesses who had given the most sensational evidence at her trial, claiming she had urged on Gallagher's attack and held his hand in the street after the deed was done.

The morning of Emily's execution dawned. Her warders later revealed that Emily had needed a glass of brandy to revive her after a moment of faintness, but otherwise she faced her death with remarkable self-possession.

Her great spirit and fire had kept her marriage to Bill Swann lively – if that was the right word – when his behaviour would have sent many another woman into a defeated decline, and what remained of her spirit had attracted a man twelve years younger, even though she'd had eleven children. This strength of spirit came to her aid now, on the bleak, damp December morning when she was taken to the scaffold yard behind Armley Gaol's high walls.

She was supposed to be hooded before she was taken out into the yard and led up the scaffold steps, but this was overlooked, so she was able to see that John Gallagher had been brought out before her and had already been prepared. He was standing by his noose. Hers hung next to it. The warders hastily hooded her and walked her up to the trapdoor next to John, relieved that she had stayed silent and hadn't called out to her lover.

There were a number of indignities she had to submit to to ensure that she died as efficiently as possible. Her hands had to be tied behind her back with a leather belt to make sure that she didn't struggle and try to save herself by catching hold of the rope, and for the same reason, once she was standing in front of the noose, her legs had to be belted together so that she couldn't get her feet caught in the edges of the trapdoor. Prisoners commonly panicked when these jobs were being done by the hangman, but Emily remained calm. And she had the last word.

As was customary among hangmen, the one at Armley that day, John Ellis, carefully recorded every aspect of this unusual double execution. He wrote: 'We were putting the rope around Gallagher's neck when [Emily Swann] suddenly cried out: "Good morning, John!"

'Gallagher started violently under our hands. He had no idea up to that moment that Emily Swann was standing beside him. He answered, "Good morning, love!" By this time the other rope was around her neck, but again she spoke: "Goodbye. God bless you."'

This tender, compassionate and dignified exchange between the two lovers shows clearly how both of them were determined to go bravely to their deaths, in full command of themselves. Ellis commented on how unusual it was, in his experience, for anyone facing the noose to be able to speak at all, even if they had got that far without hysterically falling apart at the dread of what was about to be done to them. 'This, I had to confess, was an astonishing scene, a dialogue between two people, one of them a woman, standing with pinioned arms and legs, faces blotted out by shapeless white bags, and with ropes fixed around their necks. Then one quick pull of the lever and their conversation was still for ever.'

In the manner of her death, at least, Emily had made sure there was nothing more that could hurt her family. She had spent a lot of time worrying about the disgrace she had brought on the Hinchcliffes and on her own children as she talked to her warders, the charity visitors and the chaplain, and it obviously weighed on her mind that her mother particularly must be finding the thought of the death her daughter had to face almost unbearable. She told the chaplain that it was very important to her that Hannah shouldn't have to hear any distressing reports of her having struggled or panicked or cried when she was taken to be hanged.

Facing her execution without fuss was a very small scrap of comfort indeed to offer Hannah, but it was the last thing Emily had any control over. She had lost sight of her own strength in the last two or three years of her life, but in her final moments she was once more her resilient mother's daughter.

Chapter Thirteen

PEOPLE LIKE ME

The first year after Martin and I got together was very stressful. Before we got our own house, we had to live in a cramped bedsit, and I moved between that and Phil's house.

I wasn't able to keep such a close eye on Mum and Gran during that time, but just before our first son Nicky was born in 1987, when things were settling down, I started to take notice of what was going on at the prefab again, and it struck me that neither of them were eating very much. There weren't as many ready-meal containers around as there should have been. I spoke to Mum about it, and she said that she kept forgetting to eat and that Gran wasn't interested in food any more. I couldn't quite understand what she meant – how could Mum not be worried about this.

'I give her food, but she doesn't touch it,' Mum said. 'So I don't give her any more, because she doesn't want it.'

'People have to eat, Mum, otherwise they die,' I said, a bit exasperated that she hadn't mentioned this to me.

Mum looked baffled, dimly aware that I was telling her off in some way. 'She's got crisps. She eats her sweets.'

It didn't sound very healthy, and I sensed that Gran was probably only just eating enough to stay alive. I had the distinct feeling that she'd had enough. Whether she missed Granddad's endless tolerance of her, or the challenge of having him to fight with, or just the idea that he was out there somewhere ready to be fought with, I don't know. It was obvious that Mum's presence didn't fill the gap.

One morning soon afterwards when I turned up at Quarry Mount, I felt physically shocked. Gran was sitting on her throne of power as usual, but she looked tiny, defenceless, a fragile shadow of her former self. As I walked into the front room, she smiled in a kindly way. She still had beautiful soft skin, very few wrinkles and pretty pink cheeks. All of the old anger and hatred and gone from her eyes, and in its place I felt I could see a strong, quiet desire in her to end her life. I felt very strongly that she wanted to go to Granddad. That she felt it was all over for her.

'Gran. Why have you stopped eating? Mum said you haven't eaten for days. Not even your favourite Walker's cheese and onion crisps.' I wasn't used to speaking to her like this, but the emotional carer in me had kicked in.

'I've had enough. I'll not eat again.' She gave me her fierce determined look.

'You'll die, Gran. You can't survive without food.' I was upset by her response despite all the hurt and hatred that had flown between us over the years.

Gran turned away and started making her old hissing sound. But now it had no power. It sounded like a firework that had lost its ability to take off. Grounded, just like her, sitting alone in her splendid isolation with her back turned to me.

As I walked back out through the house, I stopped in the kitchen where Mum was making herself a cup of tea. 'Please don't worry, Mum. I'll sort it all out.' This was going to be very hard for me. I was only in my early twenties, and I was approaching my third funeral. Death seemed to be all around me.

I called the doctor and he rushed Gran into hospital, where she was administered TLC. She was there for two weeks. I went to see her a few times, if only so that I could take Mum to visit. But actually we'd called some kind of truce between us when she had accepted Olly and written him that strange little letter five years earlier, and I found that I was sorry that she probably wouldn't live to see her second grandchild. Gran had given up, and I now saw what it meant when people said that someone had turned their head to the wall. I couldn't help but admire her strength of character. She wanted to die and she made it happen.

Then the hospital warned us to be ready for the end. On her last day, Mum and I went in and sat beside her, but she lay in bed showing almost no interest in what was going on around her. Often she was asleep, and if she was awake, her eyes were fixed on some point far beyond the end of her bed. I could tell she just wasn't interested in being alive any more, or in fighting back. God knows, I thought, she's done quite enough fighting.

The hospital called me in the middle of the night to tell me she had died.

I went round to Mum's. 'Oh,' was all she said when I told her. She looked lost, and her expression and the way she glanced down at her hands reminded me strongly of the day I'd left the bungalow, while she watched and wondered what would become of her. What would become of her now, I thought?

The death notice I put in the paper was going to be just Gran's name, her age and her date of death. I was pretty sure there was no one out there to miss her. But when I wrote these bare facts on to the standard death announcement form at the local newspaper office, they looked lonely, a bit too stark. I wondered what else I could honestly add. I could hardly write the usual 'much-loved mother and grandmother' without being a complete hypocrite. I stared out of the window and watched some of the people passing the newspaper office, running their own errands, perhaps on holiday, and I hoped that not one of them had lives as full of bitterness as Gran's had been.

I looked down at the form again, and added, 'Now you will be happy, Gran.' That was just right.

I felt no grief at her passing, and I was still as angry as ever about the way she had treated me, but at a time when everything was going so well in my own life I was willing to believe that she had been released from the grip of some unknown misery that she wasn't fully responsible for. I felt released too, and the biggest relief was that at last I could get Mum out of the prefab. I went to the council to get it sorted out and discovered that they were desperate to renovate it and would put Mum on the priority list. They found her a new one-bedroom flat in a little block designed for the single and the elderly just across the road from the back of our house. It was much easier for me to keep an eye on her there, and she would be able to see more of Olly and the new baby. She might even be able to babysit for us occasionally. And I would never have to go back to the prefab again.

Life resumed its normal pace, Nicky arrived, and within a year his brother Joe was born. These were amazing days, so full of love and happiness. Martin was very understanding of my moods.

'What's going on, Flic?' he would ask when I was sulking.

'Nothing,' I'd snap back, refusing to stop cooking or cleaning, or sorting out children or clothes or shopping.

'Flic, I can tell something *is* wrong, but I can't put it right if you don't tell me what it is.'

'I'm fine. Give it a rest. There's nothing wrong. I'm just tired.' Or busy, or thinking about something, or fed up of being questioned.

At this point, he was supposed to say something like, 'Suit yourself, then, I'm going to the pub,' or, 'You're impossible to live with,' so that I could have a proper row and get my anger out. Aggressive silence was a trick I had used to powerful effect throughout my teens and early twenties, first to wind up Gran in a way that she found difficult to attack, and then to punish my various friends and boyfriends when they didn't deliver what I expected of them, reasonable demands or not.

It just didn't wash with Martin.

Instead Martin would say something like, 'Look, I've

hurt you, and I'm sorry. I didn't mean to hurt you. If you tell me what I've done, I'll try to put it right. But now, Flic, you're hurting me. Why do you want to hurt me?'

He was a man who could cry when he felt like crying, and it worked on me. I'm a sucker for a cause, and if anyone is sad around me, I have to sort it out. He also, quite simply, loved me and was kind. This also meant that much of the time we were so happy together that I just didn't want to sulk at him. It wasn't necessary.

When the kids were very small and going out wasn't an option, we would put the boys to bed and make a huge performance of our Saturday night meal together, searching out recipes and devising our own amazing dishes. Martin was a great cook. Saturday night was also when we had our 'talks'. I was usually relaxed after lovely food and wine, and he would take the opportunity to gently pull me up over some unkindness or thoughtlessness I'd inflicted on him or the boys with my too-sharp tongue. These discussions could well end up with both of us in tears, but at least problems would be discussed and sorted out, in a very different manner from anything I'd ever known.

The downside of this was that it was emotionally draining for both of us. Martin was a vital part of my journey back to becoming as whole as was possible, but I knew that there were times when I was too tired to make the effort and I'd revert to my unemotional, no-nonsense approach of 'let's just get the job done, because the past can't be changed and it's a waste of time thinking about it.'

But on the whole he gave me a lot of stability. He was very articulate, and he had a way of communicating so clearly that I never had any doubt about where I stood with him. When things got difficult, he handled it head-on instead of grabbing his jacket and heading out for a drink with his mates, as my other boyfriends had. He was a calm man, and much of the time he made me feel calm, and he made it possible for me to enjoy being calm. He was also demonstrative, perfectly honest most of the time about how he felt, and he had no difficulty putting his feelings into words.

He was good at spotting when I was at the end of my tether too. Our first son Nicky was, from the start, a mischievous little monkey who loved to wind up his little brother Joe, who was so close to him in age. Mum found it particularly hard to cope with Nicky when he was in full teasing flow and could never step back from it, particularly if Nicky answered her back when she told him to leave Joe alone.

'You're a mean little boy,' she'd sometimes shout at him, and there were occasions when I was so cross about the way she spoke to Nicky that I would tell her to put her coat on because I was going to take her home.

'Mother, you've let me down again,' I'd say, all the old hurt rushing back.

'He shouldn't speak to Joe like that,' she'd retort.

'Don't you understand? They're brothers, they're very close in age. They're bound to fight.'

She would scowl and spit back, 'I wouldn't have got away with that with your Gran.'

'That's probably the problem!' I'd say, angry now. 'You couldn't deal with her, and you can't deal with Nicky. He needs your love, not your scorn. You couldn't show it to me either. Could you?'

'Don't speak to me like that, Felicity. You'll miss me when I'm gone. When I'm not here.'

'Oh, Mother! Not that old cliché again.' She'd thrown this back at me so often over the years that it had lost all meaning.

It had to be said, however, that even I found Nicky a handful. Olly and Joe were two of a kind – laid-back, quiet, willing to please and be pleased – and Nicky was a one-off – sparky and argumentative. His favourite question was 'why?' He was a lot like me, in fact.

If it was the weekend and Martin was at home, he would pile us all into the little car we'd managed to buy, and stop at the shop to get a picnic of cheese, bread, pickles and cooked meat and take us off to Dalby Forest on the edge of the North Yorks Moors. He'd tell me to bring whatever book I was reading, or a pen and some paper. The kids played on rope bridges and swings while we drank some of the wine he'd packed, and he would play rounders and cricket with them while I lay quietly on a blanket in the sun, among the peace of the trees, reading or having a go at writing some poetry.

Martin worked tirelessly to entertain the boys and give me space and time to think things through. He was always patient. My experience had been that men didn't do these kinds of things and didn't even notice that they needed doing. I found it quite strange at first, and I wasn't sure if it was manly to behave this way. But I loved it. Most of my boyfriends had never had a lot to say, but Martin and I could talk for hours without running out of ideas to discuss. This, then, was the romantic love I had fantasized about but never believed would come my way.

Martin found a job at the steel works on the edge of the Eastfield estate. It involved a lot of night work, but the pay was OK. He was certainly capable of doing more intellectually demanding work, but he said he would much rather have a job that had fixed hours and was over and done with when he clocked off than try to work his way up a corporate ladder within a profession, staying late, working at weekends, worrying about a career.

These were tiring years for both of us, with two young children so close in age, and there was continuing disapproval from his parents, which was hard. We saw them as a family, usually at their house, not ours, and they were lovely to the boys – they took all three to their hearts, including Olly. But they never changed their minds about me.

When the younger two were getting close to school age at the turn of the 1990s and the promise of release from the world of toddlers was on the horizon, I began to wonder about going back to work. Or, more than that, whether I could think about getting some qualifications. Having a husband who read books, who was interested in serious subjects such as politics and current affairs, and who treated me as his intellectual equal had helped me think of myself as someone who might even be able to pass an exam. With Martin right behind me, I was encouraged to take that brave step back into education, and at the age of thirty-three I started a GCSE in Child Psychology at the local adult education college. It was a small class consisting mostly of young women in the strange but rather lovely setting of a former convent in the heart of old Scarborough town, near the castle. We could hear the seagulls shrieking outside during lessons as they wheeled above the cliffs a few hundred yards away, and we were told that the top floor, where we were, was haunted by a nun. I fell more easily into the whole business of going 'back to school' than I had expected, even down to my old preference for hiding at the back with a new-found best friend, another mum called Chris. This time round, however, I shut up and listened. I have always loved stationery – pens, notebooks, pencil sharpeners – so I had a great excuse to go out and get some squeaky new ring binders and A4 pads. For the first time in my life I did all my homework, writing and rewriting essays late into the night after the boys were in bed, trying to get them as perfect as possible.

Going back to school gave me a bit of perspective on the fifteen-year-old Flic who thought she was so cool, who was more interested in the fact that she shared her nickname with the choreographer of Pan's People, the dancers on *Top of the Pops*, than she was in the opportunities she was missing when she chose to stare at the boys' school next door rather than look at the board and listen to the lesson. 'What a waste that was,' I thought. 'Learning is fun. Maybe I'm not stupid.'

No more Gran, no more prefab. Love in my life and an amazing new world of education opening up before me. Mum safe, my own family secure. The hardest years were behind us, and the future was bright. Anything seemed possible . . .

For weeks I had refused to open the bills that came through the letterbox because I couldn't pay any of them. One of the drawers in the living room was stuffed full of unopened official envelopes, a lot of them bearing the words 'final demand' in red. Martin and I had separated.

Without either of us really noticing it, his world had become the wrong way round to ours. I was an early riser – I had to be with three children, two of them still young and awake at six in the morning – while he was often working on night shifts. It got to the point where he didn't want to stay up for a couple of hours to see the kids before they went off to school. I knew that he had come to hate his job at the steel works with a passion, but I reckoned he had the gumption and the ability to look for another if it got so bad that he really couldn't stand it. As I saw it, this was just what had to be done while the boys were young. I was doing a job I didn't much care for too, working as a part-time cashier at a local garage so that I could also be there for the children. I had passed my GCSE in Child Psychology, but I was now focused on making sure we had enough money for the family, so I hadn't taken my studies any further. Meanwhile, it seemed to me that Martin was increasingly opting out of our family. There were a lot of arguments.

'For God's sake, let's just get on with it,' I often snapped when he started on one of his 'what does it all mean?' musings, wondering how we might have gone wrong in the past and how we might do it better in the future when I was tired and just wanted to get the thing over with, whatever it was – the hoovering or making the boys go back to bed when they kept getting out and being naughty. I know I hurt him a great deal when I brushed him aside like this, and the way I did it hurt me too, as I felt myself falling back into old patterns. I knew that we had laid out a tough path for ourselves, having two babies so soon after we'd got together, but it had been our choice, and my attitude was that we should get on with it with a minimum of bleating. It was Martin, of course, who insisted that we needed to get things sorted out between us.

'Look,' he said firmly, taking no notice of my suggestion that this could be best left for another time. 'It's always "some other time", and I want to come clean with you about something, tell you what's on my mind, what's going on. Then we can start again.'

Come clean? He had my attention now.

'I want us to work, Flic, but I need to tell you something that will hurt you.'

I was worried now. Before he even uttered the words of betrayal, I knew. I could see it in his eyes.

'You know those works' nights out for the lads that I help organize? I've had a few one-night stands. Not affairs, just one-offs – in the park or behind the nightclub. They meant nothing. I know that now. I only want you.'

I reeled with disbelief. 'How could you?' I gasped. 'I thought we were so solid. I thought we had it all worked out.'

I was dumbstruck. I had to get out of there. I couldn't

bear to see the pain in his eyes, knowing he knew that I knew it was over.

This betrayal by someone who I believed would never treat me the way others had was more than I could handle. Never for a moment had it crossed my mind not to trust him. I felt overwhelmed by his treachery, and my faith in him evaporated and never returned. I felt I could have understood if he had been having a proper affair, a real relationship with another woman, but casual sex? I had believed that whatever our other problems, our love life was still pretty good, and I couldn't understand where the temptation was. I took it very personally, convinced that I wasn't enough for him and never could be.

I resented it so much that the old, unforgiving part of me, a part I had believed Martin would never be able to trigger, reared up, and wouldn't allow me to pardon him for doing this to us. I loved the man so much, but I couldn't accept that he meant it when he said he still loved me.

I went to work at the garage that day with a fierce physical pain in my heart. By the time I got there, the pain had gone and I felt numb all over. My own body had been snatched from me and plonked down at the till without me in it. My mind and my emotions were somewhere else. In between customers, I took a notebook out of my bag and, rather like a war correspondent reporting on events at the front from a distant hotel room, tried to write a poem that might express how profoundly shattered I was. It wasn't great literature, but it began to unlock me from the shock. Then the bitterness set in.

The next year was hell. Yet again, I was stuck in a house

and a marriage with someone I couldn't bear to be with any more. It was a financial fact of life that we couldn't afford to set up separate homes, so we lived separate lives in the same house. The only good thing that could be said about this period was that both Martin and I made every possible effort with the boys, and did all we could to be a loving mum and dad without bringing them into the battle that was going on between us. However, they must have felt the sadness and disappointment that hung in the atmosphere – children are so astute when it comes to reading all those non-verbal signals, particularly between the two people closest to them. I now realize my Gran's whole life was proof of that.

I didn't know any more what Martin was doing in his social life and I no longer asked. He started to come home early, long before the pubs shut.

'I can't enjoy those kinds of nights out any more. I want to be with you, Flic,' he'd say pleadingly.

I didn't even look at him when he said things like this. I could only think about what he'd been doing when he had stayed out until closing time and beyond.

'It's too late,' I would say, bringing the shutters down hard on his fingers.

I had my own nights out, and I did meet someone with whom I had a brief and sweet friendship. Tim came from the south of England. He came to Scarborough regularly for a few months that year because he was doing some work on the North Sea coast with the water board. Seeing him was about the relief of spending time with someone who couldn't hurt me, because we weren't going to be involved with each other in an intense way. He was a good friend to me and spent a lot of time listening as I raked over the ashes of another broken marriage.

In the early summer – it was 1992 – Martin said, 'We should try again.'

He was standing under an archway of roses and holding my hands a little too tightly because he sensed, rightly, that I would walk away if he didn't. We were at The Cayley Arms in Brompton, a village on the edge of the moors on the road to Pickering that had long been one of my favourite places.

Wordsworth was married in the church there, and it has the most picturesque churchyard with a beck flowing just yards away from its ancient wall. After Gran's death, when Mum and I couldn't think what to do with her ashes, since at that time we knew of no family to reunite her with, no roots to return her to – I had come up with the idea of scattering her ashes here, in the most peaceful spot I knew. We'd considered finding a place along the coast, but all her life her nature had been more restless and stormy than the North Sea itself, and I couldn't see that she needed more of that in death. What I wished for her was peace of mind to equal the tranquillity of the little beck gliding past Brompton Church. Pouring her ashes into the soft peaty water was like releasing a dog that had been chained up for years.

This was the place where Martin hoped to find the glue that might mend our broken marriage. We had spent many happy afternoons here when we'd first met, and more in the woods nearby with the children when they were small. He was hoping, I know, to remind me of how it had been before the pressures of a young family had got in the way, and he was determined to persuade me that it would be possible to bring that relationship back to life.

'It's gone wrong, and it shouldn't have gone wrong,' he said. 'I know it's my fault, and I'll do everything I can to put it right. I am truly sorry – you know I mean it. Whatever it takes, I'm going to win you back.'

He'd already tried once to woo me back. He'd arranged for Mum to have the boys and had picked me up from work at the garage late one night and taken me to Peasholm Park in the heart of old Scarborough for a midnight picnic. Its moonlit boating lake and Victorian walks in the heart of the North Bay valley were like another country compared with the daily drudge of life on the Eastfield estate, where we had been through months of distrust and unhappiness in the wake of his confession. He wanted to remind us both that something else that had gone amiss in our marriage was failing to appreciate the wonderful possibilities on our own doorstep. We lived by the sea, after all, in a seaside resort, and one surrounded by beautiful countryside. But the moonlight failed to work any magic on me, and the rose-covered arch failed too. For the sake of the boys, however, I knew I had to give it a try. I explained this to Tim who was about to leave Scarborough and go back home to the south anyway. We parted on good terms, and I did the best I could to put my marriage back on track.

Yet by the end of that summer, I was sitting in the car in a quiet spot at the top end of Osgodby, out towards the cliff tops from our estate, with my first-born, Oliver, explaining to him why he was about to see his mum and his second dad separate. He was eleven years old and he loved Martin, who was as much a dad to him as he was to Nicky and Joe. I hated having to do this to him a second time.

I apologized for having got it so very wrong twice over. Then I silently made a vow to all the boys that this would stop, this rollercoaster of me not being able to make a solid and lasting relationship, and promised I wouldn't drag them into another unless I could be absolutely certain it would last.

That was one resolution. The second was to break free of the past in quite a different way. I know exactly when the decision was made. The boys were at school – Joe had just gone into Year One – all the housework was done, and it was about 11.30 in the morning. I wasn't due at the garage for an hour or so, and I had the television on. Richard and Judy were wittering away in the background while I made a cup of tea. They were talking about a new scheme to give adults who had missed out on education the first time round a second chance to find out what they were capable of. I examined the screen more carefully and saw a woman of about my age sitting on the sofa between Richard and Judy, talking about her degree. Now, take a look at yourself, I thought; anyone who looked through this window at this moment would see a single mum, three children, two different fathers, watching daytime TV. They would see a no-hoper. When, I asked myself, am I going to get a grip on my life and make something different happen? The answer came right back. Now. I'm going to be that woman on Richard and Judy's sofa with a degree. I'm going to use my brain, for a change. I will be the one to bring home the bacon for my children. I wrote down the number on the screen and reached for the phone.

If I needed further motivation, it was given to me shortly after I enrolled on Scarborough's Access Course.

After Martin had moved out, I could just about keep us going day to day, but debts had started to build up – gas bills, petrol, school gear – that no amount of maintenance from him was ever going to clear. Even when we'd been together we'd only just got by.

I made a decision that I was going to break even, at least on day-to-day living expenses, and build up no more debt. The thrill of getting to the end of that first week with twenty pence left over and the boys fed was amazing. My courage began to rise by the day, and finally the moment came when I dared to look at the drawer full of unopened bills that weren't going to vanish, and knew that I was strong enough to open it.

On this particular morning, after making my sixteenth cup of coffee, I decided I couldn't possibly put off calling the council about my community charge debt any longer. I was seeing stories on the news every week about bailiffs being sent round to people who hadn't paid it, and I was beginning to dread every knock on the door. I had to swallow my pride – and I had a lot of it; always had, probably always will – and ring the council to negotiate some kind of payment plan to clear my arrears.

I looked at the phone, wondering why I was so afraid, given all the argumentative bolshiness I had inherited from Gran. The problem was that, like Mum, I also hated confrontation. A row is one thing. A shouting match, trading recriminations, throwing a tantrum – Gran had taught me how to do all that to perfection. But discussing a problem, facing up to it, weighing up each side of the story, the kind of thing Martin did so well, was a way of dealing with others that had always frightened me to death. I couldn't tell the difference between being open to another point of view and being defeated and humiliated. I was frightened because I didn't believe I could express myself well enough to put my point of view forward in a way that would be listened to. Making that phone call to the council to ask for help with my bill was very hard indeed, but I picked up the receiver and began.

As the conversation progressed, it was clear to me that my worst fears were being realized. The woman just didn't want to listen to what I had to say. She was short, snappy and dismissive and made it quite clear that she didn't believe I had any genuine difficulties. She might as well have said it out loud. She thought I was an irresponsible malingerer.

'The thing is,' I said, swallowing another big hard chunk of pride, 'my husband has gone, and I am alone with three young boys of school age. The youngest is six and the only income I have is from my part-time job. I am going back to college to get better qualifications to improve my job prospects. In the meantime I do want to pay my community charge, but I need to agree some kind of regular payment plan with you so that I can pay it off bit by bit.'

That was quite reasonable, very calm. Absolutely clear, I thought.

She sighed heavily, well aware, I'm sure, that I could hear every breath she took. If anything, the more detail I gave her about my situation, the more irritated she got. Holding on hard to my temper, I told her that the way she was talking to me wasn't helpful. I was asking for help, I was being very polite, and I didn't feel I had done anything to deserve being spoken to this way.

'Well,' she snapped back, her voice loaded with contempt. 'The fact is that I have been trained to deal with people like you.'

'What do you mean "people like you"?' I bit back. 'You have no right to make assumptions about me. I expect to hear from your department with a payment plan by the end of the week, or there will be trouble.' And I slammed the receiver down. I stood and looked at the phone. I realized I was shaking. Two steps forward and one back, I thought to myself.

I sat down. Why was every single step so bloody hard? Was I really one of 'those people'?

I looked out of my living-room window, across the street, up the road, into the estate where I'd been living for about a dozen years by now. Actually, when I thought about it, I didn't know any of 'those' kinds of people. Eastfield had a reputation, I knew, but it was a reputation that existed only in the minds of people who didn't know anything about it. Everyone I knew here lived decent lives, had jobs, loved their children, kept their heads above water. None of them were rich, but they worked bloody hard and minded their own business.

My weariness and depression lifted, to be replaced with

the fury that I was finally learning to put to constructive use. It was blind, bigoted prejudice, the lot of it. How dare they judge us just because we were hard pushed. I wasn't going to let them bully me into the gutter. My family was going to rise up and survive.

Chapter Fourteen

AFTER THE EXECUTION: BRADFORD

Elsie's fifth birthday must have been the saddest birthday that any little girl ever had to endure. 'I hope my daughter Eleanor will not forget that it's Elsie's fifth birthday the last day of this year. I hope she will not forget to give her a Christmas doll,' Emily had written in her final letter to the family.

She had been dead two days when Elsie got her doll, handed to her by a big sister whose eyes were full of tears and who could not utter the words 'happy birthday', and who hugged and held her too hard and too long for Elsie to feel that the embrace was really meant for her. For a brief moment she felt as if she was the big sister and Eleanor was the baby who needed petting.

She was back now with Eleanor and her husband Herbert Crossland in Granny Hannah's house in Havelock Street. There were comings and goings throughout the day and people came to her to pat her on the head and tell her what a big girl she was, but no one mentioned her mother in her hearing or offered to explain where her mother was. Elsie was wise enough not to ask.

Shards of the truth began to come at her, however, very soon after she started school that January in Barnsley. All these strange children, none of whom had ever been her playmates before, seemed to know who she was, and they talked about her mother being dead, and about her 'swinging with her fancy man'. Some children told her that they were not allowed to play with her because their mothers had told them to keep away from her. She was never able to put her finger on the moment when her knowledge of the world reached a point when it all made sense, or when someone told her in a straightforward way what exactly it was that her mother had done and exactly how she had died. One thing was certain – this was too shameful a subject for Elsie's own brothers and sisters ever to talk openly about. The older ones, who remembered their father more vividly than she did, and who had suffered more at his fists, were unhappy about their mother's fate, but this wasn't something they could discuss without breaking the great taboo about talking ill of the dead.

Left to piece the story together mostly on her own, the year of her father's death and of her mother's execution became a lumpy, grotesque patchwork of cruel playground gossip and whispered snatches of conversation between the older members of the family, stitched here and there to the explosive, disjointed series of flash-bulb moments which passed for her own memories of that time – her father's coffin, the great black prison in Leeds, the prison officer's silver sixpence.

Her mother had been a whore. She had been a whole load of other terrible words too, and altogether no better than she should be. Elsie dimly recalled John Gallagher, whose name she heard from time to time, because he had brought food home and had sometimes given her a farthing to buy a barley-sugar twist.

By the time her sixth birthday came round, the cheerful innocence which had brought tears to the eyes of the neighbours as she passed down the street on that Boxing Day morning was gone. Elsie had been transformed into a sullen and troublesome child who kept her own counsel, talking little and smiling rarely outside the house, wheedling and demanding when she was with her sisters, and sometimes spiteful to their small children. Hardly older than the growing band of nieces and nephews that her sisters were producing, she must have been deeply envious of them. They had parents and they belonged. She had been passed from sister to granny to sister for as long as she could recall, even when her mother was alive, and she didn't belong anywhere.

'Our Elsie', the baby of the family, lived up to her name, still throwing tantrums when she didn't get her own way when she was a young woman, always wanting attention, jealous of anyone who got noticed more than she did. Difficult and demanding, unable to control her temper, and nowhere near humble enough – that was the picture painted of her to me by the elderly members of my Granddad's family, who could recall their parents talking about her.

'Mum said she was the kind of person who always

imagined insults where none was intended,' my Aunty Rene told me. 'She was considered really very difficult to be around. Not much fun at all.'

Certainly she didn't seem to have had any strong links with her siblings, even though some of them must have looked after her in the years after Emily's execution.

Eleanor had long since become a Hinchcliffe – refusing to put her father's name on her marriage certificate at her wedding in 1902 (even though he was still alive) – and was married to a Barnsley man, so her future was settled and she was the only one of the Swann children to remain near their birthplace. The rest, possibly without Elsie, went off to make a fresh start in Bradford. Annie, who had married Bradford mill overlooker Harry Middleton in mid-1903 while her mother was awaiting trial, was already looking after Frances, who was coming up to her fourteenth birthday and was working as a wool comber, and she now took in Ernest who was almost seven. Charles had found lodgings and work in Bradford not far away from the Middletons and was a carter. It wasn't the most prestigious or well paid of jobs, but it was a start.

Their grandmother Hannah finally died in Havelock Street in 1905, aged eighty-five. Eleanor and Herbert could have stayed there and taken over the tenancy, but they already had one baby and there was another on the way, so they decided to move closer to Herbert's family just outside Barnsley at Gilroyd, a few minutes away from the pit where Herbert worked as a surface labourer rather than a collier. Annie Hinchcliffe, Hannah's unmarried daughter, found herself a smaller house where she could live alone on the pension that was granted to her by the Oaks Disaster Relief Fund. Although I couldn't discover when she died, I did find her still in Barnsley in 1915, retired from the linen mill and apparently comfortable in her one-bedroomed terraced house along the Dodworth Road, near Eleanor. I like to think of her as a devoted great-aunt to Eleanor's children, thoroughly enjoying her hard-earned retirement.

In Bradford, Annie Middleton's family grew rapidly. By the time the 1911 census was compiled, she had four children and Frances, twenty, was still living with her, still working as a comber and presumably helping her sister with the little ones. The bond between the two sisters seems to have been a close one, because they were still living within a couple of streets of each other ten years later, after Frances had met and married her husband, dyer's labourer Orlando Walshaw.

Only a few more streets away in 1911 were Charles and his wife Florence. Charles was doing well. By the time he married Florence in 1905, he had hoisted himself a step or two up the ladder and was working as a wool packer. He was to rise further over the next decade, eventually getting himself trained up as a maintenance electrician on the wool-combing machines, a skilled job that wasn't easy to get into unless you had family connections. Charles must have been both clever and persistent and, I would guess, the kind of likeable chap people wanted to help. Whether his fellow mill workers knew about his parents' story I have no way of knowing, but I think it's fair to assume that having escaped from his father's profession, he prospered on his own terms and was his own man.

He and Florence had only one child, a daughter they named Doris, and she wasn't born until quite late in their marriage. On the 1911 census, six years after their wedding, they have Ernest with them, aged fourteen, and he is working as a box minder, another woollen mill job that was traditionally done by women and teenagers, both boys and girls. Sadly he turned out to have been born at just the wrong time, along with almost a million other young British men of his generation. He was seventeen when Lord Kitchener launched his campaign to persuade young men to join the army and fight Germany in 1914, and he volunteered for the West Yorkshire Infantry. He joined them in early 1915 and two years later was killed in action in France on the Western Front. He hadn't married.

That leaves Elsie, the only child of Bill and Emily that I can't find in the 1911 records. She must have been somewhere, of course, and people were unlikely to miss filling in their census forms in those times because they were collected by hand, partly to make certain they were returned, but also to make sure that illiterate householders had help filling them in. A twelve-year-old must have been recorded somewhere on census night – Elsie can hardly have been sleeping rough when her five brothers and sisters all had homes. What I can be sure of is that she was not in the homes of any of her siblings that night. Not in Barnsley and not in Bradford. Nor was she with any of her married Hinchcliffe aunts. She was nowhere I could find, not even in local orphanages.

As I trawled through birth and death records, it struck me that there was no Emily or William in the next generation, and I can quite see why those names would have been seen as inauspicious; there is, however, an Anne and a Frances, an Ernest, a Clara who was presumably named after one of Hannah's daughters, and a Charles. Nowhere is there another Elsie.

My grandmother doesn't appear again in the records until 22 November 1919, when she walks down the aisle of St Stephen's Church, West Bowling, Bradford, with Albert Baines. She is a comber, and he, unusually, is a motor mechanic from Wakefield who has just come out of the army after active service as an ambulance driver and mechanic, having survived almost the full duration of the war.

I have only about half a dozen family photographs that are older than me, and two of them are of Granddad in his uniform, puttees wound around his trouser legs, standing in front of his ambulance with the medical team he worked alongside. He is a cheeky-looking and rather handsome young man, cheery and with kind eyes. He is quite different from the stern colliers, glass-blowers and woollen mill hands that Elsie had grown up amongst.

The family of Albert's mother, Emma, had no tradition of working in the heavy industries of Yorkshire. They were in service working as maids, cooks, gardeners and stable hands, and, as my Aunty Rene put it, because they worked alongside the well bred, their manners were a cut above those of other working-class people. I am guessing that my granddad was drawn to motor mechanics as a trade when it was in its infancy because he grew up in close proximity to rich families who were buying newfangled motor cars, and saw carriage drivers transforming themselves into chauffeurs. He joined the Territorial Army early in 1914 when he was still sixteen, and perfected his mechanic's skills on the military vehicles that were beginning to replace horses. He had been born in the same year as Ernest Swann, but his decision to go into the Army early probably increased his odds of survival significantly. Even though driving an ambulance was still quite a dangerous job, particularly when the lines were under heavy artillery bombardment, it was obviously a lot safer than going over the top with a rifle.

How he met Gran I don't know, because this was the kind of thing that no one in the bungalow ever talked about when I was a child, and there's nothing in the records to explain what Granddad was doing in Bradford just a few months after he had been released from his Army service early in 1919.

It is odd that when Frances had married her Orlando Walshaw in 1912, her big brother Charles Henry had been one of the official witnesses. Yet the job of witness for Elsie's side of the family when she married Albert seven years later was fulfilled by her brother-in-law, Orlando Walshaw, even though Charles was living about five minutes away. I suppose Charles might have been at work, or perhaps ill. There could be any number of reasons why he couldn't be Elsie's witness, but my suspicion is that she had managed to fall out with him and possibly with other members of the family. Frances was married from her sister Annie's house, and yet Elsie was married from a houseful of casual lodgers, none of whom seemed to be related to each other by blood or marriage. Charles and Florence were the obvious candidates to have taken on Elsie since they had no children of their own, and there was less than two years between her and Ernest, yet they took Ernest and not her. Was she just too difficult to have around?

When I visited my Aunt Rene recently, just after my mother's death, I asked her about Gran.

'Aunt Rene, why did my Granddad marry my Gran? Did he truly love her? Because I know that she was pregnant with my mother.' I had looked at the dates on the wedding certificate and my mum's birth certificate. Their wedding was at the end of November, and Mum was born just seven months later, in June 1920.

'Your Gran was the belle of the ball, love. Quite mad. Always volatile. But he adored her and never stopped. When Albert brought your grandmother home to the village near Wakefield where his mother Emma lived, she was not impressed,' Aunty Rene told me. 'Mum always said that Emma warned her son to stay away from her.

'She was a very beautiful young woman, really striking to look at, but her manner didn't match her looks.' The family story always went that Emma told her son quite bluntly: 'She's the belle of the ball, I'll give you that – but she'll be trouble, son, mark my words.'

'My Mum said she often heard that Elsie had had all the young men chasing after her, and Albert was smitten,' Rene went on. 'She could turn the eye of any handsome young man at the Alhambra when they went dancing. He couldn't be persuaded to give her up.'

'But what about later on in life when she became ill?' I asked, quite taken aback.

Aunt Rene looked surprised. 'What do you mean taken ill? She was always like that. Your Granddad used to come back with some sorry tales of her antics. But when my mother asked him why he didn't leave, he told her that he wanted to protect her and would always love her.'

I know that in the first months of their marriage, Albert took Elsie away from Bradford and her family and brought her back to his mother's village of Haigh, a few miles out of Wakefield, because that's where their baby Marjorie, my mother, was born. There, of course, if Elsie needed help with her new baby, she would have been able to call on the knowledge of her mother-in-law and at least two of Albert's sisters who were also living there at the time with their young families. Albert must have thought it was the perfect arrangement, and as he had skills that were increasingly in demand in the 1920s he would have been able to get work almost anywhere.

Everyone in Albert's family knew the story of Elsie's parents, that much is clear. For Albert's mother Emma, the case of the Wombwell murder was within living memory, and Haigh was no more than eleven miles from Elsie's home town. But there was another reason why the story of the Swanns might have stuck in Emma's memory. Granddad had always told me that he hadn't known his dad – perhaps he was trying to make me feel there was something to be said for my own strange situation – because he had gone on a trip to Scarborough one day, when Granddad was two years old, and had never come back.

When I dug out the records for Emma and her husband Arthur, I discovered something very odd. On census night in 1901, Arthur was not in Scarborough. He was in Wakefield Prison serving a three-year sentence with hard labour for seriously assaulting his wife. This rocked me back on my heels. It so closely mirrored the circumstances of Emily Swann and her relationship with Bill, and his conviction for his aggravated assault on her. The difference was that while the Wombwell magistrates decided to let Bill Swann off with a fine, the magistrates in Wakefield took a very different view. I couldn't find any official records about either case, so it's impossible to compare the two properly, but the charges were identical. I find it hard to believe that the circumstances were so very different that this could explain sentences as far apart as a fine and three years in prison. It makes me wonder how different Emily's story would have been if she had been better protected by the magistrates in her town.

There was a grain of truth in the story about Arthur going off to Scarborough and never coming back. It just wasn't the whole truth. But it wasn't a surprise because I knew a lot now about how families conceal and deny their secrets. It seems that Arthur attempted to return to his wife and family briefly after serving his sentence, but was told to get out of the village and never come back. He did indeed get to Scarborough, because he died there in 1903, the same year as Bill, Emily and John Gallagher, at the age of thirty-six, as a resident of the Scarborough Union Workhouse, a pauper with tuberculosis. Although Emma told her children very little about it, and certainly nothing about the prison sentence reached my mother and Rene's generation, she must have known it all. She must have known that Arthur was dead, because she remarried, and she couldn't have done that without proof that she was a widow rather than a deserted wife.

Emma knew a lot about troubled marriages and troublesome spouses, then, and could have been the ideal mother-in-law for Elsie, as she would have understood a good deal of what she had been through. Instead, all the evidence suggests that they loathed each other. I base my belief that this was Elsie's fault, not on my own prejudices against her, but on the way my gentle mother talked so fondly of Grandma Emma and her little house by the railway track. She used to go there for holidays when she was a child, she said, and she loved her grandma and her step-grandfather who was, by all accounts, a lovely man. The happiest times of her childhood were spent in Haigh with the extended Baines clan.

'Grandma Emma was *so* kind,' Mum used to say wistfully, as if it was quite out of the ordinary for a woman to be gentle with her own flesh and blood.

Albert was the only one of the children who moved any distance away. All the rest remained clustered around Emma, and her children, grandchildren and great-grandchildren created a warm, supportive clan that is still closely linked to this day.

'They used to come back, you know, Albert and Marjorie, to visit – but Elsie never came,' said Aunty Rene. 'My mum said that after they moved away, when Marjorie was no more than a year or two old, Albert's family never set eyes on her again. Albert would come and Mum said he always brought stories of rows and violence and things being smashed. I got the impression that she threw things at him and maybe even hit him. The whole family talked of 'Albert's tales of woe'. I also got the impression that one of the reasons why Emma and Elsie fell out so badly was because Emma didn't like the way she was treating the baby, and Elsie hated being criticized about anything.'

It's easy to imagine that someone like Emma, who had been so clear-sighted about the kind of wife Elsie would make and who didn't hesitate to tell her son what she thought, wouldn't have held back tactfully if she thought a child was in harm's way. She hadn't put up with her first husband's violence, after all, so why would she stand by and let a child be mistreated? I felt a real pang about this, thinking about my mother's childhood.

'I wish they'd stayed around here, Aunty Rene,' I sighed. 'Mum would have had some kind of life and wouldn't have been bullied as badly as she was if she'd had family around to look out for her.'

'And then we wouldn't have had you,' Rene pointed out. 'Life takes its course, and we have to do the best we can with what's on offer.'

Albert, ever the peacemaker, ever hopeful, always looking for the compromise, decided something had to be done. For the protection of his mother and the families of his brothers and sisters and also, it has to be said, for Elsie's protection, he decided that he had to get her right away from her past, right away from west Yorkshire.

This insight into his desire to protect Elsie came to light

when I was looking through the few papers he'd left me, which were slotted into a scrapbook with the words 'Look after this for me, Flic' written on the front. I had looked through them from time to time over the years. Now a piece of what looked like old-fashioned sugar paper fell out while I was leafing through it. On it, in his characteristic clumsy block printing – I don't think he flourished at school – he had written a few words. 'A little peace and quiet to calm her mind is what she needs,' was his opinion. He was of a generation when most men would have had her locked up, but he was obviously his mother's son rather than his father's.

One of the stories Granddad never told was why he chose to go to Scarborough, of all places. Once I'd found out about his father, I wondered whether that had anything to do with his choice. However, it's just as likely that with even quite wealthy families doing away with their servants after the end of the First World War because they couldn't afford them, it wasn't as easy to get a job in service as it had been during his childhood, and Albert decided he was likely to have better employment prospects in an area where there was plenty of demand for the newly flourishing tourist trade.

Sometimes Granddad and Mum would take me up to Cloughton on the north side of Scarborough for day trips in the holidays and show me Mum's first school, a classic brick Victorian schoolroom, and the tiny window over what had once been a garage and workshop on the main road.

'That was our bedroom window,' Granddad said. I longed for a bedroom like that. Growing up in a bungalow made the idea of stairs and an upstairs bedroom unspeakably glamorous.

I've no idea how Granddad found the job at Cloughton garage, but since it came with accommodation, it must have been just what he was looking for. Almost opposite the school, at the top of a little hill overlooking a lane running down towards the coast, was an Edwardian villa called Cober House. This was another object of interest.

'Your Gran used to work there, at the grand house, as a cook,' Granddad would tell me. To my eyes it looked like a mansion, and for a long time I was under the impression that Gran had been in service like the rest of Granddad's family. I knew nothing of Bradford or the woollen mills, only this house and Gran's amazing stew and dumplings. However, I found out that shortly before the three of them moved to Cloughton, this house was bought by a member of the philanthropic Rowntree family to create a college and conference centre to improve the training of teachers, social workers and charitable volunteers, so the job Gran got here must have been the equivalent of working in a canteen rather than in a wealthy family's kitchen, but I feel sure that it must have been here rather than in the poorly paid mill workers' communities of Bradford that she was able to make the most of her natural talent for cookery.

What happened then? Well, I know that at some point in the late 1920s and into the 1930s Granddad was working as a charabanc driver. I have a picture of him at the wheel of one of these amazing vehicles, effectively an open-topped stretch limo with room for about thirty people, outside the old Floral Hall in Scarborough, a hugely popular entertainment venue for holidaymakers from the 1920s onwards. He looks very relaxed and happy, and I know that he would have loved the job, chatting to strangers, helping them have a good time, putting them at ease. Charabanc rides out into the countryside around Scarborough were a big holiday treat for the tourists, the equivalent perhaps of helicopter rides around the bay now. An afternoon's drive up the coast to a beauty spot and back cost about five shillings – 25p – at a time when a mill worker's wages were about £1 a week.

I also know that the family moved out of Cloughton and into Scarborough, and that Mum went to the senior school in the centre of town.

'A very gentle girl,' said a fellow pupil I managed to track down, as she recalled the teenage Marjorie Baines. 'But – if you don't mind me saying so – she was a bit absent, as though her mind was always on other things. It was quite hard to feel as if you really knew her.'

I was beginning to have much the same feeling about all three of them. It was a strange thing, but the closer I got to the year of my own birth, 1957, the fainter the historical trail became. For obvious reasons, I hadn't expected this. The nineteenth century had been so much easier to fathom, with Hannah and Emily standing right in the spotlight, but Elsie and my mother had slipped through the first half of the twentieth century in the way that shadows appear and disappear as clouds cross the sun. Although I found some descendants of the Swann siblings, none knew of their existence, and there were only glimpses of them from the Baines side of the family, and these never included any sightings of Elsie, even when Albert's family came to Scarborough to visit him.

The first thirty-seven years of my mother's life seemed to have passed without anyone outside the family knowing what was going on, with the exception of one momentous period for which I could find no formal records and no oral family history. All I have are the wispy recollections that Mum sometimes shared with me when I was a child.

When the Second World War began, Albert, Elsie and Marjorie left Scarborough and, curiously, mother and daughter went back to Bradford. There's no record of them living with or near any of Elsie's family, and both women went to work at English Electrics on Leeds Road, on the other side of the town centre to the Horton and Lidget Green areas where the Swanns had settled. My mum never mentioned any cousins – yet certainly her Aunt Annie had a big brood – but she did talk happily about visits to the Alhambra Theatre to see music hall-style shows with Gran and – astonishingly – about going dancing with her too.

There was no detail about these shows and dances. Mum would simply say things like, 'We used to go to the Alhambra. It was lovely, all the people and the lights, and I wore a lovely dress that Mum had made for me.' Or, 'I went dancing with your gran, and I had my best frock on. It was such fun.'

The look in her eyes, sparkly and delighted, filled in the gaps for me. I got the impression that this had been a time when Marjorie – and perhaps Elsie too – had been let off the leash. Whatever other difficulties Mum had, she did at least get this brief experience of being young and going out and having fun. Elsie, perhaps under cover of the role of chaperone for her young daughter, seems to have had a last fling too, perhaps making up for all the fun she'd missed out on in her own teens and early twenties. Granddad had disappeared completely off the scene, as far as I can tell. He would have been in his early forties, and I suppose it's possible that he was called up to do war duty as a driver again, but there doesn't seem to be any official record of this. It's a mystery. Had he and Elsie actually separated, perhaps? There was, said Rene, some suggestion in his own family that this might have been the case.

'But separation or divorce wasn't something that was discussed in front of children in my day, and I don't think my parents would have let us know if something like that had been going on,' said Rene.

What I do know is that the family reconvened as a threesome back in Scarborough when the war was over, and then had immense difficulty finding somewhere to settle because of the way Gran was until they finally ended up at the prefab in 1959 when I was two.

There were a lot of gaps and more than a few mysteries in this period of my family history. But there were a few certainties that I'd not been aware of before. The most important of these, for me, was that if Gran had been mentally ill, then it wasn't something that had somehow come on in later life. Like her mother and her grandmother, she had always been tough and difficult to shift from anything she'd set her mind on, but she clearly didn't have their charm or vitality to make her easy company – not with her husband's family at least, and it seemed not even with her own.

As I was talking to Rene about Mum and Gran, and we were talking about another of Emma's daughters who had run a newsagent's, a childhood memory returned of Gran hissing at the sight of a silver coin. I wondered whether all her life the flash of a silver coin could trigger an unwelcome remembrance of the grand day out to Leeds when she was four which had turned into something so much more sinister. I know that all her life she hated official buildings, hospitals, town halls, council offices, old-fashioned doctors' surgeries and all those other places where the institutional tang of carbolic soap on damp stone still hung in the air. That visit to Armley Gaol, of course, was the great watershed of her life. On one side was the supreme happiness of her first train ride to the big city and of being trusted for the first time to hold a silver sixpence in her hand. On the other was all the pain of being orphaned and of the abuse that had rained down on her ever afterwards because of the manner in which she had lost her parents.

It shaped her profoundly. I think she was always stuck there, halfway between the innocence and the terrible things that they said her mother had done, and not even marriage or motherhood was able to offer her a reliable escape route. I could now see her as an emotionally fragile woman rather than just an evil, spiteful one, plagued by the fear that other people were talking about her behind her back and that no one liked or respected her, whether it was her dismayed mother-in-law or our neighbours around the prefab.

She was right on both counts, of course – they did talk about her and they didn't respect her. The tragedy was that, actually, this had nothing to do with what her mother had done and how she had died. Elsie had only herself to blame. If she could have brought herself to put her fears aside and behave, no one who mattered would have held her history against her, certainly not Emma Baines.

As it was, everyone who had the misfortune to come into contact with her during her long life paid very dearly indeed for the fact that Elsie Swann's first silver sixpence had belonged to a prison warder.

Chapter Fifteen

EDUCATION

As the teacher stood in front of the whiteboard, droning his way through this afternoon session, I wondered, not for the first time in my life, how I was going to stay awake through the lesson.

It was always just after lunch. We were on the canteen side of the George Pindar School where the Eastfield Estate kids whiled away the years between eleven and sixteen, and the oily, cabbagey smells of school dinners drifted through the ill-fitting windows of our drab cream-coloured Portakabin, adding queasiness to boredom.

Not far away there was the McCain's frozen chip and pizza factory adding a tang of overcooked tomato to the mix. That was a smell that really did make me feel sick because I had applied for a job there in my teens when it first opened. Word went round that there was a staff draw every week for a £20 cash prize. I had come within an ace of handing in my notice at my proper job at the car sales showroom before I came to my senses and realized that the chances of winning it were so remote that I was more likely to be killed by a freak accident in the potato chipper.

Almost two decades later, here I was again within sniffing distance of the loathed tomato mush, but this time with a notepad and pencil, trying to get myself an education through the Access Course I'd heard about on the Richard and Judy show. This was a temporary classroom that the Yorkshire Coast College had rented from the school on our estate, making it as easy as possible for a few of us to have another go at aiming for something a little more lasting and satisfying – and hopefully rather more of a dead cert – than a weekly £20 lottery. If I could see it through, it was going to give me a full qualification that would be the equivalent of the GCSEs and A levels that I hadn't taken.

The Portakabin's gas heater hissed gently in the background, not doing quite enough to banish the icy chill of the east winds coming in off the North Sea a few miles away and whipping round its uninsulated walls, but at least preventing us from freezing to death. I had thought it would be exciting, getting an education at last at the age of thirty-four, but there were moments when I wondered why I wasn't doing something useful like trying to get a few shifts at the garage. Especially in these deadly afternoon sessions.

Then the sociology lecturer said something that actually made me sit up. Cycle of deprivation. Actually, it wasn't that. It was what he said after that.

'The only way out of the cycle of deprivation is education,' he said.

He pushed his plastic-rimmed octagonal specs back up to the top of his nose. He was, to my eyes, a typical sociology teacher. Not that I'd seen any others, but he just fitted the stereotype nicely. Baggy cord trousers, too big in every direction, and a baggy, scruffy shirt not quite properly tucked in. Badly cut hair a bit too long and a comb-over not covering the bald patch on the top of his head. He was altogether too laid back for me. I wanted him to get on with it, put on a bit of pizzazz.

'It's a theory that explains the persistence of poverty and other forms of socio-economic disadvantage down the generations,' droned the teacher. 'Families that are poor and have had little success with education raise children who expect to be poor and have little education.

'No education leads to no skills, leads to a low-paid job or no job, leads to the dole queue. And round we go again. Until you break the cycle and get an education.'

He had me at the phrase 'and round we go again'.

I felt dizzy and the cabin's fluorescent light seemed to glow just a little bit brighter, giving everything in it a migraine-ish aura. My stomach flipped over with a nausea that had nothing to do with school dinners or the pizza factory. It was shock. He was speaking to me. This theory was about me and my life. It described Gran, and Mum, and then me. It described perfectly my ill-informed decision to leave school at fifteen without taking a single exam, the terrible choices I'd made again and again in life and love, the damage I'd done not just to myself but also to my three sons.

At that very moment, what I had amounted to was a second failed marriage, no job and very bleak prospects for the future. At that moment, though I didn't know all the facts yet, I saw how trauma and deprivation had been passed down through my family for generations. Whatever cards my gran had been dealt, my mum had inherited. What my mum had, she'd passed on to me. And what I had, my children would have.

'The only way out of the cycle of deprivation is education,' the teacher repeated. He had my full attention. I knew that he was absolutely right.

I had made a start, at least. About a year after my marriage to Martin had ended, I'd met Michael. He was a single parent too, with kids about the same age as my boys. If I'd met him a few years earlier I think we'd have probably thrown our lots in together: moved in, got married, tried to make our children get along. But this time I was taking things more slowly. It was a small gesture, but I needed to be able to stand on my own two feet. I would break this cycle if I had to do it with my bare hands.

Almost five years later, in the summer of 1999, I stood in my hall looking at an envelope that had just dropped on to the mat. It was off-white, creamy, and made of paper thick enough to give the envelope a certain plumpness. I knew it would not bend or crease when I picked it up and it definitely would not have a plastic window in its front, or have a bill inside. When I turned it over I was not disappointed. My name and address were typed on the front, and the value of the postage was franked neatly on to it in red ink in the top right-hand corner. My university logo was next to that.

For a few moments I considered not opening it, because

once I'd opened it I would know, and I would never again have the choice of not knowing. Then I told myself I was mad. I glanced up the stairs. There was not a sound from the teenage boys upstairs who were deep in another of their summer holiday sleeping marathons. I could hear my own heart, and it was pumping so hard with adrenaline that my hands were shaking. I dug my fingers under the flap and ripped it open.

'Let it be a 2:1. Let it be a 2:1,' I said under my breath, pulling out the sheet inside and holding it closed, steadying myself to understand whatever it said when I finally opened it up.

'Yes! Yes! Yes!'

I was shouting at the top of my voice and I practically pogoed like the teenage wannabe punk I had once been from the hall into the living room. I jumped around in there, screeching and waving my sheet of paper. I stopped jumping and went over to the CD player, clattering through the piles of discs looking for some suitable music to screech and jump around to. I had 'Simply the Best' in my hand when a herd of stampeding elephants hurtled down the stairs and flung themselves into the room.

'Mum!' shouted Nicky. 'What's wrong?' Joe, then ten, stood behind him wearing only pyjama bottoms and an expression on his face that suggested he'd been forced out of his bed at 4 a.m. by armed robbers.

'We –' I screeched, waving my sheet of paper and bouncing up and down again ' – are *winners*!'

I thrust the piece of paper at Nicky and turned round again to get Tina Turner spinning.

'I suppose she's passed, then?' said Joe, anxiety vanishing and a note of grumpiness creeping in at the thought of the lovely sleep that had been so rudely interrupted.

'Yup,' said twelve-year-old Nicky in his best middle-aged voice. 'Nice one, Mum. Now can you turn that racket down, please, and try to think about those of us who are trying to get some sleep round here?'

My 2:1 meant that I had no trouble getting the place I wanted on the postgraduate teacher training course. Within the year, the girl who couldn't see the point of education when she left school without a single exam certificate was standing at the top end of the hall with the other teachers at Eastfield's secondary school, where my oldest son had done his GCSEs and my other two were pupils. I looked out over the heads of the eight hundred children who were trooping into assembly and saw several versions of my fifteen-year-old self looking back at me.

On the wall at home, I had A-level certificates from my Access Course and a framed bachelor's degree. I'd had my own graduation ceremony in a friend's garden with Michael, my boys and Mum. I was going to be teaching English, Religious Education and PHSE – Personal Health and Social Education – something that, with my background, I was particularly passionate about. It was all a long way from my part-time job at the garage, or running the cashier's office at Arundales.

Yet teaching was not something that I took to like a duck to water. Looking out across the sea of young faces looking back at me, some bored, some still bearing traces of childish innocence, some openly insolent, some mildly interested, I was sometimes petrified. There were days during my teaching practice, and for some time after I qualified and got a full-time job at Eastfield's secondary school, when I wondered why on earth I was scaring myself to death like this. And although I loved talking – as my head often pointed out to me – for quite a long time I didn't find it easy to do it standing in front of a class. But in spite of this, I knew that I'd finally found my vocation.

To my surprise, I discovered that some of the students weren't that interested in doing what I told them.

'Don't make the same mistakes that I made, Kayleigh,' I urged as I tried every trick in the book to make this petulant sixteen-year-old hand her Shakespeare coursework in on time.

'Why should I care?' she snapped back. 'I hate this school, and I can't see the point in learning about someone who died years ago. I don't even understand his language. Why does he speak like that?' I had to smile. How many children had started out with that attitude? 'I can't wait to get out of Pindar and Scarborough.'

'Oh yes! And where do you think you'll be without an education, young lady?' I asked. I cared passionately that students such as Kayleigh and many others that were to pass through my hands made something of their lives.

'I'm going to Bradford to live with my sister. I'll get a job on the market. No one cares here.'

She was right. I knew enough of her life to know she probably did need to get away. I had to accept her argument, knowing in my heart that we can all turn around our lives when and if we choose to.

I recalled my teenage self, mocking the teacher and the lesson, telling all and sundry that I'd done 'it' last night, enjoying the attention, the shock of some of my classmates and the admiration of others. And I reminded myself that that fourteen-year-old girl had been pretending a level of sophistication that she didn't even particularly want. All she really wanted was to be normal, and to feel loved and worthwhile. I don't blame the teachers who gave up on me, but I do think they could have fought a little bit harder to try to bring me back. I am a born fighter, and I decided that this was the insight that I could bring to my teaching every day and turn into something positive.

'I had a really hard time at home when I was younger, Miss Davis,' a boy said to me one afternoon as we talked about why he wasn't getting his homework done. All his teachers were saying that he was a bright boy who was capable of good things, but it was all going to go to pot unless he could get some consistency into his work.

'I know. And I know what that's like,' I told him. I saw a flicker of 'whatever' pass through his eyes – like this old woman knows anything about my life . . .

'But you can't spend the rest of your life saying "I'm just a poor, weak victim," I pushed on. 'Well, you can, but do you want to? The choice is yours. You can choose to be a victim, or choose not to be. Lots of people have had hard lives. It's what you decide to do next that matters – are you going to run your own life, or are you going to let your life run you? Here's the thing – do you really want to wait until you're thirty-five before you get to do the job you really want to do, like I did?'

That line stops them in their tracks every time. I feel privileged to be in a position to deliver it.

For a newly qualified teacher, I rose very swiftly through the ranks. Raising children and running a home means you develop terrific organizational skills, and I also had the years of office management at Arundales behind me. It's not all bad being the oldie on the block. I was propelled to the position of Assistant Head Teacher with a place on the school's leadership team within five years of finishing my teacher training.

I wish I could say that from then on it was all *Educating Rita* and happily ever after, but real life isn't like that.

I was now earning the kind of wage I thought only other people earned, and for a while I tried to be someone else. I made the huge mistake of moving us out of the comfortable terraced ex-council home on the estate where my boys had put down their roots, and into a five-bedroom Victorian villa in the centre of old Scarborough which I bought with a huge mortgage. I was stretching my organizational skills to the limit to squeeze fourteen hours' worth of work a day into a life that didn't have that kind of time to spare, what with Mum getting older and more frail, the attention my children needed, and just the everyday business of carving out a work–life balance for the sake of our sanity.

'Look at these fabulous houses – you can all have a bedroom of your own,' I had raved to the boys, waving estate agents' lists at them once I'd decided to move, so carried away with amazement that I could buy a house like this that I failed to notice the boys' complete lack of enthusiasm for the idea. More space, yes. In a place they didn't know and where they weren't known, no. Regardless, I steamed ahead with my decision that we needed a house that matched my new professional status.

'How can I put this?' asked a fellow student on the leadership course my head teacher had sent me on at about this time. 'Flic gets things done. But no one else gets a chance to do anything. She assumes that she is the only one who knows how to do what needs to be done . . .'

I was very hurt by this but in my heart I knew it was true. In the feedback and self-assessment sessions of the course, I discovered that the self-reliance I'd learned too early, and which I had always been so very proud of, was not always going to get me top Brownie points. For the first time in my life I was doing the kind of job that only really worked when you operated as part of a team, leading from the front but also falling back sometimes to give others a chance to shine, and to give yourself a bit of a breather. In a childhood controlled by divide-and-rule Gran, teamwork was a skill I had never had a chance to master.

I had begun to face this problem when I had first arrived at the school. There had been an assumption that because I was an older newcomer, I'd be more comfortable with hulking great Year Elevens, sixteen years old and full of attitude, than the younger graduates might be. I had to work out for myself that these students had been there a lot longer than I had, and I would have to build real relationships with them before they were going to start listening to me. Walking in and being bossy just wasn't going to work. It wouldn't have done with me at that age.

'Controlling' is a word that I think some of my colleagues would have used about me. So it was as if Life wanted to teach me, yet again, that no one can control every aspect of their existence when, one evening after work, I decided on impulse to turn left instead of right, towards the Eastfield estate. I'll pop in on Mum, I thought. She was still living in the little flat across the road from the back of our old house.

'My God, Mum! What's the matter?' I said, dropping my bag and keys on the floor and half running to her side when I turned into the living room and saw her bent double in her favourite armchair with her head between her knees. Gently I lifted up the top half of her body, trying to get her back into a normal sitting position.

'It hurts,' she said, looking right into my eyes and willing me to do something about it for her. 'I can't lift my head. What's happening to me?'

The tests showed that she had not only lung cancer, but secondary cancers that had spread throughout her body. She was eighty-seven, and I had already been trying to prepare her for the prospect of moving into a sheltered housing scheme of some kind within the next year or so, but now, finding her a care home where she could be properly nursed if she needed it became a priority. We were lucky enough to find a place at the old people's home right next door to the school, which made it as easy as it could possibly be to juggle my increasingly demanding job and time with attending to Mum.

At about the same time – because problems never arrive on their own – I was forced to admit that I couldn't really afford the swanky Victorian villa. I could just about pay the mortgage, but I hadn't taken into account the most basic expenses, such as the heating bill for such a big house, or the endless maintenance costs. We'd been there for two and a half years while I pretended it was working, and I was overstretched and running into debt.

The house had also robbed us of something more important than solvency. What I had thought would be a wonderful family home had instead become a house-share. The boys were old enough to be independent – they were nineteen, twenty and twenty-six – but even when they weren't on the other side of Scarborough spending time with their friends back on the estate, they were shut up in separate, distant parts of the house. Communication between us had all but broken down.

'Who are you?' joked one of my sons one morning when we met on the stairs after a particularly gruelling run of late nights at school for me. I'd hardly noticed that he'd not been back for a week, because it was just too much effort to come back from an evening out with his mates to this place, which wasn't home to him anyway.

I sold up in the nick of time before the building society could come in and repossess it. We regrouped. The boys were all spreading their wings anyway, and there was nothing I could do to reverse that now, but I bought a very small cottage in a village outside Scarborough which had enough room for them to use it as a refuge if they needed it.

Mum – or rather, how I felt about Mum – was, of course, a problem that didn't have a solution. I was going to lose her, and no amount of regrouping was going to change that.

When her cancer was diagnosed at the end of 2007, we expected at first that she might go into decline quite quickly. But as she had the physical hardiness typical of my family, it didn't happen. She was happy in the home and loved some of the care workers, particularly a young man called Simon – she'd always enjoyed male company, and even though she was approaching ninety, that hadn't changed – and she rather perked up. That gave me quite a lot of time to work out how I felt about the prospect of her death.

I wanted to understand more about our family before she was lost to me, but I realized I wouldn't be able to get any answers out of her now, not that I had had much success before. Her memory had gone to pot: she didn't recognize Quarry Mount and had no recollection of Gran by this time, though she could still remember her beloved grandmother, Emma. When I took her round Scarborough for a birthday trip on her eighty-ninth birthday and we went past my dad's house, she couldn't even remember who he was.

Inside I still carried traces of anger and puzzlement over Gran's treatment of me and now my response to those feelings, dormant for so long and certainly during the twenty years since Gran had died, was to embark on the research that uncovered our turbulent family history.

By the time Mum was in the last stages of her illness, I had unearthed many of the answers I had been yearning for. The events of Hannah's and Emily's lives didn't excuse

Elsie's behaviour, but knowing what had happened to them and to her did help explain it. When I saw how the reverberations of a great tragedy had profoundly affected three, four, even five generations of my family, it only made me more committed to my profession and my work with young people. I wanted to help them make choices that could free them from echoes of pasts that weren't their own. I knew I didn't have all the answers, but I was willing to live with that, even though I still didn't know why Mum hadn't got me away from Gran.

On the first Sunday of the summer holidays in 2010, I rang the care home manager to tell him that we would be along in about an hour to pick Mum up. We'd had a wonderful Sunday with her a few weeks ago, celebrating her ninetieth birthday by bringing her out to my cottage, taking a trip to the pub and making sure she got several glasses of her favourite white wine, which she loved. Now that I was through the horrors of an Ofsted inspection at the end of the summer term and the boys were around, two of them home from college for the holidays, we wanted to do it again while she was still strong enough to come out for the afternoon.

'I'm afraid you won't be able to do that, Miss Davis,' said the manager. 'We've had to put your mother to bed, and I don't think she's going to be able to get up again.'

Within minutes I had the boys on standby, ready to be picked up as I drove fast into Scarborough to get to Mum. As we walked in and saw her tiny head on the pillow, we all knew that something had changed and she was slipping away. Her white cloudy hair and pale face looked almost transparent, as if she was literally fading from view.

All of us choked, and Nicky turned right round and left the room, walking down to the end of the corridor to collect himself. He joined us a few minutes later and then the four of us sat there for a couple of hours, talking to her. Each of the boys told her what they'd been up to at work and at college, and I apologized for having been so preoccupied with the Ofsted inspection that I hadn't been to see her enough in the last six or seven weeks.

'Thanks for waiting, Mum,' I told her. 'Thanks for hanging on until the holidays started so that I could be with you again. You waited very patiently. You've always been so patient. Thanks.'

I took the boys off to make sure they got fed, and when I came back in the evening, just with Nicky this time, I asked her to make sure she looked out for us and watched over us all from wherever it was that she was going. She smiled and seemed to know what I was talking about. I'm quite sure of that.

We left at about 11 p.m. that evening. 'Mum,' said Nicky, just as I turned to leave the room.

'What?'

'She waved. I turned round to check on her and she waved, just a little one.'

That it should be Nicky who got her last wave, the grandson with whom she'd had the most tumultuous relationship when he was little, seemed exactly right.

She died at 4 o'clock the next morning. I thought I was

ready for it. I had spent two years getting ready for it. I wasn't ready at all.

Towards the end of the summer I rang my Aunty Rene and asked whether I could drive over to Wakefield to see her.

'It would be lovely to see you,' she said. 'Please come.'

We sat in her comfortable living room, drinking tea from the nice gilt-edged cups that I recalled so clearly from my visits to her during my teenage years. I told her how peacefully Mum had died, and how nice the funeral had been, and how good it was to have the boys with me this time as I worked my way through all the necessary paperwork. I had done it twice before, for Granddad and then Gran, entirely alone.

'Yes, you've had a lot to deal with, Flic,' Auntie Rene said.

'Can I ask – do you mind – why do you think my mum wasn't able to get away from Gran? Do you know?' It was the one question that, through all of this, had never been answered.

Rene looked quite puzzled. 'Well . . .' she began, and tailed off. She sat there looking closely at me, searching my face for something.

She tried again. 'Your mum – she wasn't – well, she was never quite all there, was she?'

'What do you mean?'

'It's strange – I would have thought you'd known. Didn't you notice? Didn't your Granddad ever talk to you about any of this?'

'Not that I can recall. Notice what?'

Rene took a deep breath in, breathed out, and began again. 'My sisters and I, we always knew that Marjorie wasn't quite like us. She was a little bit older than me, nearer my older sister's age, so she wasn't my particular playmate when she came to visit, but Mum would tell all of us to be nice to her, to be careful with her, because she was a bit – well, backward.

'And she was lovely, so gentle, always smiling, but she didn't have the same understanding of things that we did and that all the other children we knew did. We had to look after her when we were out playing together because she didn't really understand what was going on or how to talk to people.'

The air went still around me. I was too shocked to react immediately but a few days later, when I got back home, I cried for her. I had got to the age of fifty-three without realizing this, and yet in all that time my mother had never been very far away from the centre of my life. For the last twenty years she had been the mainstay of my boys' lives too, filling in for me when I was studying or working long hours, babysitting for me when I needed a break. She could do this job because all that was required of her was to be there and to care for them, to love them and be nice to them, moment to moment, just as she had cared for me during trips to the park or on Sundays going to Dad's flat. Anything more complicated was beyond her.

This simple, obvious truth about my mother had escaped me. She hadn't taken me away from Gran because she couldn't. She wouldn't have known where to begin. Even when she'd had her own flat after Gran had died, it was me who'd found it for her, me who'd made sure the bills were paid, me who'd sorted out her spending money and often done her shopping. I'd got cleaners in because she seemed incapable of keeping up with the housework, and I'd scrubbed and hoovered her home myself. So the list went on. I now saw with blinding clarity why she had found it easy to get on with laid-back, gentle Olly and Joe, and so difficult at times to cope with live-wire Nicky, into everything and always asking questions. Above all, I finally understood why she had sat on the bed on the day that I packed to leave the bungalow, asking tearfully, 'What will happen to me if you go?', as if she was the child and I was the parent, and I was abandoning her. That must have been exactly how she saw it.

No wonder Rene was puzzled at me. The fact is, though, that few of us weigh up our parents in the same way that we weigh up everyone else. They occupy a special place that makes it very difficult for us to judge and assess them; they simply are, and although we are programmed to break free of them when the right time comes, I think we are also programmed not to question too closely why they are the way they are. In our heads they must be perfect. Our survival depends on it. Having this image shattered, I suddenly felt frightened, even now it was all over, thinking of how vulnerable Mum must have been all her life, how unequal in the battle with her own mother.

In looking for answers, I realized that although I now understood so much more, I had so many more questions too, all of them unanswerable. Who had there been to protect Mum from Gran when Granddad was out driving his charabanc at all hours? Had she also lain in her bed in the dark hoping that someone would rescue her? Worst of all, had she actually been born with limited understanding, had she been damaged during a difficult birth, or had Gran's violence inflicted that damage on her vulnerable brain when she was very young? Had Gran suffered from undiagnosed post-natal depression; was that reason for her violent behaviour? There was no way forward from questions like these. There were memories locked in Mum's head, and, indeed, in Elsie's and Emily's, that I could only guess at. I would never know. So they had to be left where they were, untidy as it was. Life is not tidy. But it does go on.

Epilogue

GETTING IT RIGHT

Thinking back to that strange summer when Mum was slipping away from me and I was coming to terms with my family's past, one moment stands out clearly.

I decided to visit Barnby Furnace, the small hamlet where my great-great-grandparents Hannah and John started their married life nearly a hundred years ago. In their time it would have been a hive of industry – clanging and heat and dirt and dust all competing with the beautiful Yorkshire countryside. Now it is a place of calm. Lying at the bottom of a soft green lane lined with berry-laden hedgerows, the only sound that disturbs the air is a distant hum from the M1 as it charges through the Pennine foot-hills towards Leeds, and even that is muffled by long lines of mature trees and the rushing of the lively little beck alongside the single track road. It is a beautiful spot.

What would Hannah and John have made of it – young newlyweds with their lives ahead of them, and a revolution going on that they must have thought could only change things for the better?

As I stood on the old Waggonway embankment studying

my old Ordnance Survey map, I realized that the cottages the workers had lived in – the place where my great-grandmother Emily Swann had been born – were long gone. Not a stick or stone was left to show where they had once stood in a long row. I could see how my ancestors had worked, how they had lived, even, but it seemed as if the people they were, their thoughts, hopes and fears, had all been blown away like coal dust.

Yet these were the people that I had come to find. For me, this was the place where it all began; the last place that my family had actually seemed happy and prosperous. Once they moved to Barnsley, the Oaks Colliery disaster cast a dark shadow over four generations of my family, from which I was only just beginning to emerge. When that mine exploded it tore a gaping hole. Charles and Henry were an unthinkable loss, one that poisoned not only the rest of Hannah's and John's lives, but those of their other children too.

Retracing their steps, I expected to feel a sense of recognition in these places. Instead, as I looked at the scars of industry that are still traced on the landscape around their Havelock Street home, I realized that it was not just my family that had been affected. That day there had been hundreds of disasters, and probably thousands of lives torn apart. Who knows how their stories turned out?

If Emily Swann had been given a chance to break free of her abusive marriage, I like to think she would have taken it. If she had been given one last chance to see her youngest daughter Elsie, perhaps in some tiny way Gran's pain would have been lessened. But the legacy she left behind her proved to be one of bitterness. Much of what happened to my gran after her mother's death remains a mystery, but it can't have been pleasant. Misery breeds misery, and too often abuse breeds abuse.

Still, all of us have choices. During my childhood, my gran never made the choice to be anything but cruel to me. She wasn't well, and it would have been incredibly difficult for her to rise above it, but there were options nonetheless. The problems start when you think there aren't any.

As I looked into our ancestry, I thought I would discover tragedy upon tragedy raining down on each family member. Instead, what I found was generations oppressed by circumstance; children convinced that they couldn't do any better than their parents, and adults convinced they couldn't change their lives from one day to the next. When I was a teenager, I would have thought that this was weakness. Now I know that it is a tragedy in itself.

This book is for Granddad, and for my mum. It's for Emily and Hannah, though I never knew them. But in this way it is for Gran, too.

The reading I chose for Mum's funeral was the wonderful letter from Ecclesiastes about the nature of love. I'd gone to Bradford to find the church where Gran and Granddad had married, and the Bible on the lectern had been open at this passage. 'To every thing there is a season . . . a time to weep, and a time to laugh. A time to mourn, and a time to dance . . . a time to love and a time to hate; a time of war and a time of peace.'

I liked the idea of it helping to put things straight again, reminding us all of what really mattered in life instead of lingering over the mess that Elsie and Albert had made of much of their daughter's life and of my childhood and of their own marriage. It was as if Gran and Granddad had led me to the church to find that reading and understand that the time had come to stop crying and to move on.

As I threw my handful of dust on to Mum's coffin, I felt like I was saying goodbye to all of them – Hannah, Emily, Elsie, Marjorie. 'I've done the best I can for you all,' I told them. 'I have tried to put things right, and now let's lay it all to rest.'

And what of me? For a long time it looked like I would fall into the same pattern as the rest of my family. I spent my whole childhood plotting escape, yet when it came I didn't know how to deal with it. I was too trapped by my past to be free. But after decades of struggle, I feel I'm finally coming to terms with myself. If this story has taught me anything, it is that while the past needs to be known and understood, it also needs to be put in its place.

I will always be marked by the past. It is a part of me, in the same way that the Waggonway will always be a part of Barnby Furnace. But through experience, through education, and through love, I am different from how I could have been.

I have three wonderful sons, and a job I love. We can make our own history now.

Acknowledgements

This book was born from a personal quest to find the answers to questions that had weighed heavy on my mind for many years. That quest is now committed to paper for my sons, who needed to know the story of their ancestors and how the past has shaped our family's future. First and foremost, my love to my family, who have been my rock, always there with opinions wrapped in truth. A huge debt of gratitude to Ingrid Connell from Pan Macmillan and my agent, Jonathan Conway. I would also like to thank Cheryl Stonehouse, who helped me write my story and spent many hours talking me through the darkness and back into the light. Thanks also to Claudia Joseph for researching the missing pieces of my family tree. For their tender loving care of my mother, I would also like to thank Simon and the team at Braeburn House who cared for her as she bravely battled against the cancer that took her life only months before this book was published. Finally to friends across my world of education – it has been a pleasure walking the path with you.

Picture Acknowledgements

The author and publisher would also like to thank the following for their kind permission to reproduce pictures in this book:

Page 1 – top: © Illustrated London News Ltd/Mary Evans Picture Library; bottom: Reprinted courtesy of the Mary Evans Picture Library.

Page 2 – all four photos: Reprinted courtesy of the British Library (originally from the *Wombwell Guardian*).

Page 3 – top: Reprinted courtesy of the West Yorkshire Archives Service, Wakefield/NHS.

Page 8 – bottom: © Richard Wood Photography.